Antarctica

A Novel

Books by Durwood White

Antarctica

Sum of all Ages

Amphibia Island

Arabella

Echoes of Civil War

New Day Rising

Nibiru

Search for Phoenix

Pilot Error

Decline and fall of the American Republic

Beyond the Sun

Lost Treasure of Kurnah

The Black Satchel

The Gold Medallion

The Cure

Anthrax Conspiracy

Antarctica

By Durwood White

Acknowledgement

Dr. Stephen Quayle has written a fascinating exposé using photos and released documents plus many other sources, including the German Federal Achieves and the American Congressional Library describing events surrounding the long surmised escape of Adolph Hitler from the *Führerbunker* sometime before it was destroyed in 1947. In writing this novel, I have borrowed heavily from his subject by permission from Quayle's publisher, End Time Thunder Publishers; the publication, *EMPIRE Beneath The Ice.* © 2016.

Oblivion

Joseph Stalin sat behind his oak desk fingering his busy eyebrows, musing at the wrinkled pages of a report laid open before his tired eyes. The message seeped into his devilish mind as he strummed his stubby fingers on the desk, the staccato sound tickling his mental tension. He leaned back in his creaky chair and consoled the mounting anger as he remembered that his Soviet intelligence officer was due this morning with a verbal report.

The written report on his desk was political dynamite; the identity of the blackened bodies of Adolph Hitler and Eva Braun was an open question! The Russian dictator pushed back from his desk, gazed at the falling snow outside the window. A shaft of sunlit suddenly burned through the overcast and lit the bare twigs eerily scratching the windowpane from a fragile breeze. His barrel chest swelled with a sigh. He leaned forward, fingered a Havana cigar in a mahogany box, crossing a leg. Yellow teeth bit off the tip, thick lips spat the smelly speck on the floor. He swiped the head

of a match across the sandpaper sole of his black boot. A sulfur spark! A flashing flame lit the tip of twisted tobacco. He raised his massive head, puffed a few rings and watched the swirling smoke curl to the ceiling as it vanished in a silent wisp.

A light rap echoed from the door. His personal secretary cracked it open and announced that his intelligence officer was in the lobby.

He nodded. "Send him in," he scowled.

A man stepped into the dark office. He was a young officer of twenty-eight or thirty, a mole on his cleft chin. His face was wind-weathered and his eyes a deep brown. He stood lanky in his drab wool uniform. Ivan Hindenburg stood straight and stoic before the dictator, beads of sweat crawling down his sideburns.

Stalin laid his cigar in an ashtray; grey smoke twirled to the ceiling and vanished in a puff. "Relax Hindenburg—let's have your report," he growled.

The nervous officer spread his gangly legs; his hands clasped behind his back, and licked his tongue over chapped lips. "The physician says a cook in the bunker kitchen reports something funny about *Der Führer's* death— "Never mind that conjecture—was it *Der Führer* in that grave?"

Hindenburg squirmed in his tiresome stance. "Personally, sir I don't think it is his body."

The dictator's eyes narrowed, bushy eyebrows masked the festering rage in his red-streaked sclera. "I

want that physician in my office by 2:00 this afternoon—understand," he barked in measured do-or-die phrases.

Ivan's polished boots clicked at the heels. "At once, sir!" he saluted.

He spun about-face and stormed out of the office before he urinated in his trousers. Hindenburg walked directly out the front door into the dark, cold night, passing an open fire in the fireplace of the lobby. The cackle and crackle of the fire dissipated in the cinder-grey sky haze of falling snow. The chilling air felt safer than the dark room he'd just left, not wanting to stay another minute in the Supreme Soviet headquarters. Stories had spread through the ranks that Stalin had killed his ambassador to America last night.

Although the West would claim that Hitler had shot himself in his bunker. Stalin had a different belief. Hitler might have escaped Berlin before the Russians entered the city. He reasoned that Hitler had hidden away with the other Russian Scientists which the US had spirited away during Operation Paperclip, but that was not true.

However no one in the West really believed that Hitler was dead. Even Stalin was uncertain and ordered the NKVD (the KGB) to investigate the possibility of Hitler's survival. The Russians had confiscated documents from Hitler's headquarters and even had captured Hitler's personal valet and his SS adjutant.

They were in the best position to get at the truth. And Stalin would see that they did.

World War II cost more than 36 million lives, was the most destructive and widespread war in history. Germany lost nearly 6 million lives, the U.S.S.R. about 17 million. Poland 5.8 million, Yugoslavia 1.6 million, Japan 2 million, Italy 450,000, Rumania 460,000, France 570,000, Hungary 430,000, the USA 400,000, Britain 400,000, the Netherland 210,000, and multiples of millions were left homeless. Nazi Germany had attempted race extermination in a holocaust of 6 million Jews.

Upon the death of President Roosevelt, Truman asked Stalin point blank at the Potsdam Conference on August 1945, whether Hitler was dead. Stalin reportedly said simply, “No.”

Deep in the streets of Connecticut a newly formed newsletter dubbed the *Space Review* was established to report on the rash of UFO’s spotted over the world since the same newsletter had published reports of the Roswell incident in 1947. The government rushed to cover-up the story because this small publication was at the forefront of factual reports; deniable plausibility was at risk.

One dreary day in 1953, three men in black appeared at the *Space Review* office and shut down the operation. The editor subsequently wrote a book on the

sordid events. His book was not taken seriously based on his statements that flying saucers were sited flying out of a base in the Antarctica at twice the speed of sound. The pages reported that at Patterson Air force base a number of German scientists were placed there to work on missile projects. Subsequent stories emerged that seemed to suggest the Nazis had indeed achieved anti-gravity technology! In fact, a former SS officer came forward with a claim that he had been involved with building a city under-the-ice at Antarctica! He gave some convincing details of submarines shuttling construction materiel and thousands of workers to the site during the period from 1938 to 1939 and even into 1941 until the war broke out.

President Truman summoned the celebrated Rear-Admiral Richard E. Byrd to the White House. If the information in his mind got to the press, it would destroy any chance to stop the Nazis from building a Fourth Reich in the Antarctic. Washington had basically recovered following the war and people were trying to forget Pearl Harbor and the death of President Roosevelt. Truman was a different leader than Roosevelt. If he couldn't fix it, neither could anyone else.

The Oval Office was active on a bright sunny day in 1947, and President Harry S. Truman offered Admiral Byrd a cup of coffee.

"Sit please, Admiral—I have a few questions."

The celebrated rear-Admiral settled in his seat sipping his coffee. He was completely calm, a man with the nerves of steel with many hours of Navy operations under his belt. Byrd had traveled to both the North and South Poles.

Truman sat his cup on the desk and leaned back in his chair, both hands clasped, with index fingers under his chin. "Admiral, I know you have been unhappy by not commanding a ship in the war," he said and paused. "However, if you accept my offer this morning you will be more famous than you are today."

"How is that, Mr. President?"

"What if I told you that a host of Nazis including Hitler, most of the SS officers, escaped the war and have constructed a base in the Antarctica where we can't get at them?"

Byrd discovered at that moment that Washington could not keep secrets. He nervously balanced the coffee cup on his knee. "There are reports from South America describing some new type of aircraft," he injected for openers.

"That's why I need your expertise."

He nodded undecidedly "I'm impressed at the German ingenuity and their development of several new jet aircraft," he said offhandedly.

"These aircraft are not typical jets, Admiral."

A raised eyebrow tightened his leather-like skin. "How so, Mr. President?" he said surfing for details.

"There are credible reports that the SS has developed not one, but at least three functional flying saucers!"

Byrd gulped, sipped his coffee nervously, his feet trembling, his mind perplexed.

Truman leaned forward, his elbows on the desk surveying the stern face of Byrd. "America needs your assistance, Admiral."

He breathed deeply. "Whatever I can do, Mr. President." Truman unlocked the center drawer of his desk, seized a document, and slid it in Byrd's direction.

"This is a copy of my executive order and my notations on this mission. I'm placing you in charge of a task force to Antarctica. I'm told there is a city constructed under the ice and the only entrance is by submarine," he said.

Byrd took the file, his eyes glued to the title: Top Secret, Operation Highjump, yet the President's statement "under the ice" flashed through his mind with the stark realization that the Third Reich was alive and well.

Byrd's mission had been released to the press as a scientific expedition investigating a coal deposit, yet it had no drilling scientists aboard or obvious equipment that gave this impression. It was the largest task force to ever go to the Antarctica. There were over 5,000 sailors and naval infantryman, thirteen ships and twenty-six P-51 aircraft implemented by the US Navy's Task Force 68. Task Group 68.4 was commanded by Admiral Byrd, the Flagship aircraft carrier USS Philippine Sea (CV-57).

The USA had a beachhead in Antarctica known as "Little America," established by Admiral Byrd in 1929. Built on the Ross Ice Shelf south of the Bay of Whales, this base was used for three expeditions during 1933-1935, 1939-1941, and 1946-1948. Byrd and the task force returned to "Little America" in 1947, again making it his base of operations. After resupplying that base, engineers plowed an airstrip onto the icy surface as a landing surface for DC-3 cargo planes including a base for expedition seaplanes. The DC-3s were equipped with rocket-assist motors so they could take off from the aircraft carrier. The use of these aircraft made it impossible to scout oil deposits, neither was the Byrd flotilla an expedition for oil or coal deposits, nor was the aircraft carrier sufficient for such exploration.

History unveils that the Truman/Byrd Expedition to Antarctica was doomed from its inception, including the disappearance of Rear-Admiral Byrd.

1

Robert Caruso and his bride sat in matching lawn chairs on the sandy beaches of Bermuda on the fourth day of a much needed vacation. He had just received a telegram from the President of the USA and pondered the message. Jenny Lynn touched his firm arm and smiled.

"When are you leaving, Robby?"

He stared out beyond the white-capped waves at the sharp line of the distant horizon. If he accepted the President's offer Jenny Lynn would be living here on this island for a while, and that was some satisfaction. He dropped his gaze and faced his lovely wife.

"Tonight, Bruce is flying in this afternoon, and we will leave after dinner."

She leaned from her chair and kissed him on his tanned cheek. "I thought as much," she pondered. "You have never denied President Darcy's wishes."

He patted her hand and reset his gaze on the horizon, his mind refocusing on the telegraph message. The President was dealing with a subject that the government had been denying since 1947. It was an interesting assignment and he was anxious for more details.

Jenny Lynn stood and took her towel from her chair. "Thought I'd fix some lemonade—want some?"

"Sure," he said taking her hand. He gazed into her blue eyes, his thoughts rushing back five years when he first met her in the Jacksonville, Florida, University Hospital as an ER nurse. "Thanks honey."

She touched his broad shoulder. "Don't worry, Robby. You will figure it out—you always do," she smiled as she turned. Her flip-flops trudged through the sand to their little rented beach house.

As she reached the sidewalk she paused, turned and looked back at her husband, shielding her eyes from the blazing sun with her open hand. The President had appointed Robby as the assistant to the director of Homeland Security after he had captured the terrorist leader Phoenix. She couldn't imagine what mystery would unfold when he returned from Washington. But

she trusted him—he was her life. Her mind suddenly shifted to Robby's best friend, Bruce Allison. She logged a thought in her mind that she'd suggest to Bruce. She left her flip-flops on the porch and went inside.

Standing in the kitchen stirring a pitcher of lemonade, she suddenly dropped the wooden spoon when she heard the ring of the front doorbell. She hurriedly wiped her hands in the blue apron tied around her wasp waist, and rushed off to the front door. As she strode through the hallway she saw Robby's best friend through the triangular glass in the door. She gripped the doorknob and swung it open exposing the wide toothy smile of Bruce Allison.

"Hi beautiful," Bruce exclaimed as she threw her arms around his neck.

"Dear Bruce, it has been too long," she whispered, stretching back arms length, "how is Consuela?

"She is as independent as ever."

They settled back in a more relaxed position walking toward the kitchen, and Jenny Lynn touched his hand.

"You will take care of Robby, won't you?"

"You bet I will—if I can keep up with him," he smiled.

"He's sitting out on the beach. I'll pour two glasses of lemonade. You can take it with you."

She took a plastic bucket from the freezer and filled the glasses with ice, and then poured the lemonade.

Bruce took the two glasses, started for the door, but paused. He watched the worried countenance of the former ER nurse whom he'd come to respect.

"Don't worry, Jenny Lynn. I'm hoping that after this assignment Robby will retire to his desk job in Washington."

She flashed an embarrassing smile. "I wouldn't take that bet."

He smiled gripping the two glasses, looked once more into her depressed face. "I'll ask Consuela to visit you while we are away," he said, hopeful the suggestion would restore her joy.

"That's sweet, Bruce."

He nodded, and left the kitchen, negotiating the concrete steps. Finally he set his eyes on the lawn chair down by the shore. He and Robby had met in college back before the earth's crust hardened, it seemed. They became immediate lifelong friends. He had been at his side on many projects ranging from Alaska to the Middle East, from the placid Pacific to the turbulent Atlantic, from Hawaii to the Philippines. Always it was an unforgettable venture, often dangerous, more often covert, but Robby was a genius at them both. And somehow he wasn't even concerned about the details of this caper. He stepped up to the chair, his shoes mired in sand as a wave crashed on the shore, the water rushing to within a foot of Robby's bare feet, tiny crabs

racing back into the sea. He sat the two glasses on the empty lawn chair.

"Penny for your thoughts."

The tall man immediately stood and they shook hands. Bruce smiled sheepishly, and then they embraced in a manly hug. His strong arms wrapped around him, and Bruce felt secure. Finally he pushed back and gripped the glass, condensation wetting his hand.

"Jenny Lynn sent you this," he said extending the cold glass of lemonade.

Robby took the glass, and cast his hazel eyes on the intelligent face of his lifelong friend. "Thanks for coming, Bruce. I won't have much to say about this project until I meet the President," he said, as he sat.

Bruce looked at him over the glass of lemonade as if he'd read his mind. "I can understand," he replied, removing the cool edge of the glass from his parched lips. "What's your best guess?"

He gazed out at the horizon. "You remember Roswell?"

"Doesn't everyone?"

"Well, I think the President has information that the UFO's are real."

Bruce's left eye cocked but he said nothing.

Robby reached back into the open files stored in the shadows of his mind. "I can tell you that a flying saucer crashed right out there a hundred miles from the shore."

Bruce swilled the lemonade digesting the comments from a man whom he'd never denied that his words were truthful. "What's this scuttlebutt about demons piloting these UFOs?" Bruce asked just as a way to discuss this overworked subject.

"It's an open question. There are theories of interspatial openings in the atmosphere where they enter and exit from another dimension."

"Dimension?"

Robby caught the confusion in Bruce's reply. "Einstein proved that outer space is a dimension; in fact, you and I operate in two or three dimensions. Einstein's theory points to ten dimensions," he clarified.

"You don't mean these UFO's come from another planet?" he chided.

"According to the President's viewpoint, these UFO exist right here on earth, nothing alien about them."

Bruce bobbed his head. "As the assistant to the director of Homeland Security you should be able to search your files," he suggested.

Robby smiled. "I think the President has already accumulated every file available from World War II to the Roswell event."

"World War II," he repeated. "I think you are referring to the Nazis experimentation with anti-gravity."

"There is more than a hint of truth here," Robby confirmed.

Bruce dropped the conversation. "When do we depart?"

"After we eat dinner—you can go with me, I assume?"

He broke out in a manly laugh. "Robby, have I ever missed one of your projects for the President. Of course I'm going. Jenny Lynn insists that I take care of you!"

2

Walter Nichols, special assistant to Chief of Staff, Andrew Evans, sat in the office of the commander of intelligence at the Pentagon. Alexander Burton, a career diplomat from Massachusetts, had hundreds of counterparts throughout the Foreign Service, of which all could have been cut with the same cookie cutter. He wore the familiar black suit with a bow tie, a manicured mustache; the sideburns trimmed to perfection, highly polished shoes, and smoked Havana cigars. His Empire-style desk was barren of all clutter; the only objects sitting on the glass-top surface was his folded hands.

"I'm awfully sorry, Mr. Nichols, but I find nothing in the records department mentioning the disappearance of Admiral Byrd," he said with special reading glasses perched on his bubble nose.

"Do you have your dates correct?" Nichols wondered.

"I think so. Byrd was tapped by President Truman in about June of 1945 for a mission to Antarctica."

"That's correct," he affirmed.

"Do you want to pursue the matter?" asked Burton in an official tone.

Nichols clasped his hands thoughtfully. "It Might be worth a check with the Foreign Office in London to clear the political miasma—the British had an expedition into Antarctica. This is Andrew Evans requests, and he speaks for the President."

Burton shrugged apathetically. "Even a historical event a half century ago would hardly have a significant bearing on the present."

"That's a little vague, Burton. Still, I promised Evans that I'd see what I could find. Shall I make a formal request in writing," he charged with the brunt of his political clout.

Burton straightened his back. "Not necessary. I'll make some phone calls to an old school chum who heads up the library of the Foreign Service in London. He owes me a favor. Listen, Nichols I should have an answer by

this time tomorrow, but don't be disappointed if he fails to turn up anything."

Nichols grew tired of his apologies. "I won't—but the President will," he barked. "On the other hand, you never can tell what might be buried in the Foreign Service Archives," he chided.

A black limousine pulled away from the curb of Reagan Airport in a sleeting snow, Dr. Caruso and Bruce Allison seated in the backseat. It carefully merged into the traffic that seemed to crawl bumper-to-bumper north toward the Potomac. The traffic was unusually heavy this afternoon, must be the convention in town, Caruso remembered. The sleet had transformed into a mist by the time Pennsylvania Avenue appeared, and the limousine turned northwest toward the 1600 address of the White House. It slowed for the guard, bending his head toward the backseat. He tipped his hat at the Homeland Security Assistant, and waved them through. The limousine pulled into the back where the driver normally parked.

Bruce took the luggage which the driver had sat on the cub in an inch of snow, and followed Robby through the door. The doorman recognized Robby having frequently taken him to the airport, and tipped his hat.

"Your vacation went well, Dr. Caruso?"

"Just fine, Willy—how have you been?"

"My rheumatism is flaring up, sir."

"This weather makes my knuckles ache, Willy."

He smiled and doffed his hat. "Good to have you back, sir."

Bruce informed Robby that he'd go down and get a bite to eat while he met with the President. Robby agreed and said that he would meet him back at the restaurant downstairs. As Bruce left, Robby coursed his way to the Oval Office.

Andrew Evans, the chief of Staff, saw Robby coming and met him at the door.

"Good to have you back, Dr. Caruso. The President is anticipating your visit. Cindy will assist you—I must attend to a few pressing matters."

Robert smiled. "Thank you, Andrew. It's good to be back."

Andrew was a graduate from Dartmouth who met Winston Darcy when he was director of the CIA. When he was tapped by his party to run for President, Andrew directed his campaign. He protected the President with a vengeance; no one got in to see him unless he personally approved the appointment. If you didn't follow his rules you went on the Washington "black list."

Robby slowly strolled up to the desk where the President's secretary sat, and her head popped up from her computer.

"Good morning Dr. Caruso. The President is waiting," Cindy said, her pixy face beaming, and buzzed a button under the edge of her desk with one hand and with the other hand pressed a button on her intercom.

"Mr. President Dr. Caruso is here."

"Thank you, Cindy—send him in," a tiny voice squawked from the intercom.

President Winston Darcy sat back from his desk and closed his eyes for a moment allowing his mind to wander from the pressures of the day before he met the man he admired. Darcy was a medium sized man in statue, with brown hair streaked with white and thinning: his features, once cheerful and crinkling, were now set and solemn. He reopened his eyes, as a sudden winter sleet rapped on the glass of the floor-to-ceiling windows behind him. Outside on Pennsylvania Avenue, the traffic crawled at a sloth-like pace as the pavement transformed to ice. A convention of partisans protesting his immigration plan was in the city.

Robby cracked open the Oval Office door and heard the President rustle from his chair behind his desk. Although every President could alter the design and decor of this office, tradition dictated the correct position of the U.S. and presidential flags located on each side of the central window. President Winston Darcy had requested two Areca palms placed beside each flag.

"Come in Robby. Thank you for being so prompt," Darcy greeted standing beside his desk stretching out his hand.

Robby shook hands. "Mr. President, it's my pleasure," he responded, and took a seat in the chair, the chair the President pointed with his index finger. Darcy took a seat in his favorite chair by the sofa. Winston Darcy was in his second term, having appointed Dr. Robert Caruso the assistant to the director of Homeland Security last year.

"I'm sure you didn't get much detail from my telegram and for that specific reason I wanted to meet with you," he said, as his thumb and index finger gripped his bottom lip.

Robby said nothing remembering when the President gripped his bottom lip, he was thinking.

Finally, the President threw a leg over his knee and leaned back in his chair. He fixed a keen stare at the man who had never failed an assignment. "What I am about to tell you must not reach the press," he said, and paused as if choosing his next words. "When World War II closed there was never a reliable answer to the identity of the burned bodies supposedly those of Hitler and Eva Braun."

Robby crossed a leg, quizzing his mind. "I understand that Stalin confirmed the body was Hitler."

"That announcement was for the public. Stalin told Truman that it was one of Hitler's doubles."

Robby sat stunned the air in the room suddenly stale. "Then did Hitler escape?"

"That's the real question. Israel has the best information having tracked the SS Germans after the Nuremberg trials. There were confirmed reports of Hitler's presence in Argentina," he added, "the dates are confusing; Hitler could have been rushed off to Argentina during the confusion of the Berlin invasion."

Robby shook the cobwebs of jetlag from his mind. "So how do I fit in here—what is my mission, Mr. President?"

The Chief Executive seemed to ignore the question for the moment, more details for his appointee rising to the tip of his tongue. "President Truman sent Admiral Byrd in command of a rather large task force to Antarctica. Before he died, Roosevelt had already gathered a mountain of information with eyewitness reports confirming that the Nazis had built a city under the ice," he said with hesitation, and leaned back in his leather chair giving Robby chance to digest his intriguing words.

Robby gave the President a favorable grin. "I've heard scuttlebutt about this task force. But there were no reports on what or who they tangled with," he said, his countenance suddenly a myriad of expressions as he replayed the President's words, *a city under the ice.* Incredible, he thought.

The President solemnly nodded his head. "You have just answered your question, Robby. That's your mission—you get me information on that city under the

ice, and then you will know what or who Byrd tangled with?"

Robby uncrossed his legs, embarrassingly grinning at the President. "My information says the task force beached at Little America."

"That's correct, but that base is gone, floated away as three chunks of ice back in 1960."

Robby chose his words carefully. "Sir, what really happened to Admiral Byrd—I have no record on him in my files."

The President gripped his bottom lip with thumb and index finger, the signal that he was thinking. "It seems Admiral Byrd was not as tight-lipped as Truman had expected."

"You don't mean he was eliminated?"

The question seemed to hang in the air for long seconds, and the President's chest swelled, his lungs full of air. "Andrew has been looking into that question of Byrd's disappearance for two months and no information yet."

Robby shook his head. "Does Andrew have information on what attacked that task force?"

The President punched a button on the intercom. "Cindy, ask Andrew to come in, please."

"Yes, Mr. President," the electronic box squawked.

"I'll let Andrew answer that question, Robby," he said, retrieving his hand from the intercom.

Walter Nichols, special assistant to Evans, puffed on his brier-wood pipe, peering over his Franklin spectacles. He had an appointment with Evans and had arrived just as Evans returned to his office. Evans managed a smile despite the sickly sweet fumes that hung in the office like smog. Evans had installed a special fan in his office only last week for removing Nichols' tobacco smoke. He flipped a switch, the fumes evacuated as if he'd somehow removed an inversion layer.

"Still raining out?" Evans asked.

"Mostly drizzle," Nichols replied.

Evans realized Nichols was under pressure. He was the covert operative until Dr. Caruso came onboard. Now his face was a forest of wrinkles. His wife had left him when he began to heavily drink. "What did Burton have to say?"

"Not much. He's looking into some personal contacts."

"You know the President wants that information," he refuted.

"That's what I told Burton, but he said not to expect much."

"Keep me informed," Andrew said. "There's a pot of coffee in the kitchenette—help youself." He grabbed his briefcase and hustled off toward the Oval Office.

While they waited on Andrew, the President and Robby had had a long conversation on the subject of Admiral

Byrd. Andrew had been unable to uncover much. It was as if Byrd had vanished into thin air. The opening door to the Oval Office shattered the silence. Robby sat gazing through the nine-pane trio window behind the President's desk, the branches of the trees bare of their wintry leaves. Andrew stepped in and closed the door behind his entrance, a briefcase in his left hand, his right hand outstretched.

"Dr. Caruso, I trust your conversation with the President went well," he smiled as they shook hands. His thoughts stopped dead center on the four years that he had known this man. It was true that he and Caruso had crossed swords on a few issues. But he had learned to trust him implicitly; he had the mind of an elephant, the eyes of a fox, and was the most honest man he had met in politics.

The President's chair squeaked as he leaned back. "Andrew, brief Robby on Operation Highjump."

The squeak of the chair, not the President's comment snapped Andrew's thoughts of Nichols back to reality, as he sat in a seat opposite Dr. Caruso. He faced the President, and opened his briefcase on his knees. He took out a Secret file that had been declassified. The folder was marked "Operation Highjump." He fanned a few pages, and then looked up into the hazel green eyes of Dr. Caruso.

"You may find these facts hard to believe, Dr. Caruso" he began.

Robby rustled in his seat. "If the public only knew what goes on behind their backs, they'd burn Washington," he replied in an affirmative tone.

The President threw back his head suddenly laughing. "Well, Robby as a member of that Washington bunch, you have a chance to drain the swamp," he continued.

Andrew shielded his grin. "Admiral Byrd has added his personal notes. He says they were attacked" . . . Andrew looked directly into Caruso eyes . . . "by three flying saucers on the order of 20 meters in diameter—"

Robby's stern face interrupted, glancing at the President's unyielding face, then back to the Chief of Staff.

"I've never known you to kid me, Andrew. What else is in that file?"

He dryly swallowed. "The saucers were jet propelled by some sort of nearly silent force, and armed with a death ray. They shot down three P-51s and sunk a cruiser, according to Byrd."

The air seemed to evacuate the room in a sudden eerie silence, as Andrew handed the file to Dr. Caruso. Robby carefully read the recent copy of reprinted pages and redacted lines. The information went directly into his photographic mind. Finally he closed the file, handed it back to Andrew, and gazed into the President's solemn face.

"With all due respect, Mr. President, what tangible evidence do we have that these UFOs are factual?"

The President glanced at Andrew and smiled.

Andrew grinned. "Robby, Area 51 is tangible evidence."

The President nodded. "What if I told you thirteen of our American astronauts have seen the things?"'

Robby thought a moment and then shrugged. "How am I to doubt the most credible men in position to know the facts?"

The President slowly bobbed his head, his keen eyes looking at a man he trusted with his life, a man of great tenacity. Robby had never dodged a project, and this may the foremost, he mused. He leaned back into the softness of the specially modified leather chair.

"I'm sending you to the Antarctica, Robby. Admiral McHenny will be your contact at the Pentagon." He gripped a file on his desk and extended it to Robby. "I want you to take this file and study it before we discuss your involvement. Direct your questions to McHenny. Andrew will make an appointment."

"Yes, Mr. President." As Dr. Caruso stood and walked toward the door, Andrew touched his arm. "Could I speak with you just for a moment outside?"

That was a tall order, befriending the man you had replaced. "Certainly, Andrew," he replied and reached down and gripped the handle of Andrews briefcase realizing that he had forgotten it.

Andrew closed the door behind his exit and pulled Caruso aside. He stood for a moment gathering his thoughts. "You remember Walter Nichols?"

Caruso nodded, handing him the briefcase. "The man I seem to have replaced," he said, rather remorsefully.

"Nichols is going through a difficult life change. His wife has left him and he has been drinking rather heavily."

"Wasn't Nichols involved in covert activity before I came?"

"Damn good man, I'm told."

"What is it you want me to do, Andrew?"

He sighed deeply. "What you do the best. I've never found a man who made friends so easily. It rubs off you like water off a duck's back."

"Okay, Andrew. I'll do my best."

Evans stood embarrassed and it showed. "Robby, I owe you much, and I don't see how I can ever repay you," he said bowing his head, a rare occasion of confession.

"You take good care of President Darcy, Andrew. You are the best at that job."

Two weeks went by hurriedly so Robby thought, but he had taken the time to check in with the President for debriefing and returned the file that he'd absorbed over a pot of coffee last night. He spent a weekend with

Jenny Lynn before Bruce picked him up at his Bermuda home for his appointment with Admiral McHenny at the Pentagon.

Bruce was indifferent; he was deeply concerned about Robby scurrying off to the Antarctica. He and this man had been through hell and back on countless missions for President Darcy. He'd taken a cursory glance at the file before he returned it, and this would be the most historic and probably the most dangerous mission—a fitting opportunity for Robby's retirement, he thought. But Robby thrived on danger, and he wasn't about to let him go alone. He logged a message in the deep caches of his mind: The note to send Consuela to stay with Jenny Lynn.

Consuela sat on the front porch beside Jenny Lynn, having flown to the island that morning from Houston. The welcome warmth of the breeze blowing in from the Atlantic was somehow different from the moist air from the Gulf of Mexico where she and Bruce lived in her family château. She had first met Jenny Lynn in the Houston Galleria when Bruce had introduced them. Though not the first time she had met Bruce, it was during the romantic hour in that meeting as they danced that she sealed her love for him. She sat her half-empty glass of lemonade on a glass-top table staged between her and Jenny Lynn.

Consuela bowed her pixy head, her index finger rubbing the lip of her lemonade glass. "As always, Bruce was tight-lipped about this new project," she ventured.

Jenny Lynn touched her naturally tan-skin hand. "Women never know the finer details about their husband's business. That's why we serve by waiting," she smiled, gazing at the distant horizon as if she were sitting beside her husband and not her best friend.

"How true," Consuela replied, swilling a swallow of lemonade, the ice cubes rattled as she removed the glass from her lips.

The two words prompted a harbored scene in Jenny Lynn's memory—the day Robby said, "I do," when they were married and Bruce stood in as best man. So why was her heart so restless at this parting?

Why?

He was going to bottom of the earth, Antarctica—that's why.

Oh, it was so comforting to have Consuela with her in these tormenting hours. She stood, took the lightly-tanned hands of this beautiful Mexican woman and pulled her into her arms.

Dear, dear Consuela, I am so pleased to have you with me if only for a week."

Tears beaded in Consuela's dark brown eyes. "The feeling is mutual, sweet Jenny Lynn."

3

Bruce steered the rental car off the expressway onto the exit to the Pentagon with Robby beside him in the passenger's seat. He had not said a word since they left the airport, and had not told him any details about that folder from the President, only the location of the mission. But he was not going to hold back any longer.

"Robby, would you care to tell me what you learned from that meeting with the President?"

He faced forward as if he'd not heard his best friend, but he had filed the question in his mind until he sorted his own questions for the Admiral. Finally he faced Bruce; he owed him an answer.

"It's a historic document from the 2nd World War, mostly about the secret weapons the Germans were developing and could not completely develop in time to use them in the war. We are not speaking of Peenemunde weapons."

"I thought the V-2 *was* their secret weapon," Bruce replied with emphasis.

Robby smiled a correction. "Hold on to your hat. These files are describing flying saucers built by the Germans in the period of 1935-1945. Some scientists believe these are the UFO's seen today."

Bruce cocked his head. "Now Robby, that is a bit difficult to believe with all the talk of aliens from outer space."

He bobbed his head. "That's because the public has been the victim of lies since the 1930s," Robby shot back.

Bruce's brain massaged his reply as he parked the car in the front parking lot of the Pentagon. He switched off the key and rotated in his seat.

"You haven't convinced me with any solid proof."

"I expect to get that proof from Admiral McHenny," Robby replied as they exited the car.

The ensign checked his computer without finding an appointment for Admiral McHenny, and turned to his Lt. Commander with a frown on his face.

"Dr. Caruso says the White House made an appointment for him to meet with Admiral McHenny—I can't find a record."

"Check the Admiral's personal file," he advised.

"Can I do that?"

"No, but I can," he said annoyingly, punching keys on his keyboard. "Here it is, made for Dr. Caruso by Andrew Evans, chief of staff yesterday for 2:00 today."

The ensign swallowed embarrassingly, knowing he had wasted ten minutes. "It's ten past now," he added as he punched a button on the intercom. He heard the reply of the secretary through the tiny speaker, and raised his head. "Dr. Caruso, the Admiral is waiting—through that door," he gasped, pointing his long index finger.

Bruce touched Robby's shoulder. "I'll meet you in the cafeteria," he said pointing at the overhead sign in the hallway.

Robby took his hand. "Thanks for coming, Bruce. You have always been a consoling presence, and I appreciate your friendship."

His face bloomed with a blush. "Robby, what are friends for? We've been together too long for appreciation. We are blood brothers," he winked.

Robby shook his hand warmly, remembering the many times they had shed their own blood; Bruce had lost his girlfriend on one of the capers. Finally he released the clasped and they parted. Robby strode to the door against the far wall, a smile on his face put there by the challenge of his best friend.

Caruso entered a large foyer facing a desk twenty feet ahead. A pert young woman raised her head with a captivating smile.

"Dr. Caruso, I presume?"

Robby continued his stride to the desk. "That's what my mother calls me," he grinned.

She stood chuckling and handed him a visitor's clip-on badge. "The Admiral is expecting you Dr. Caruso—through that door at the end of the hall."

Robby pinned the badge to his shirt pocket as the secretary cocked her head. "I bet your mother is proud of you."

Robby smiled. "When I was eight my mother made fried apple pies, she called them apple jacks. I went back to get another and couldn't remember the name. I said, 'mother, could I have another Jack Ass?' She spanked me, asking where I got that word."

She spread a smile. "It's a good story, Dr. Caruso," she said crunching the bridge of her nose.

Robby winked, turned, and then walked toward the large 42-inch door, the emblem of the Navy anchor emblazed at the top.

He navigated the ten-foot long hallway noticing the historic pictures on each wall, mostly of the Pacific entanglement with Japan during World War II. He reached the door and gently twisted the brass knob,

swung it open and surveyed the room. The Adjutant stood and rounded his desk with his open hand extended, gripping Robby's hand with a sturdy grip. "Dr. Caruso, your vacation was pleasant, I presume."

The marine Adjutant's broad shoulders framed his six-two stance, a veteran of two Afghanistan naval missions. He led Robby to a door and swung it open.

Vice Admiral McHenny sat behind his glass-topped desk peering over papers that had piled up in his absence. Seated beside him was a handsome naval Captain. McHenny had just returned from the China Sea having commanded a small task force anticipating a missile launch from North Korea. His orders were to destroy any missile overflying Japan. He was signing several documents and dropped the pen as he stood.

"Have a seat, Dr. Caruso—the President has sent me your dossier: Marine Commander, retired—impressive record."

"Thank you, Admiral. I hope the President gave you some indication of my mission," replied.

The Admiral rounded his desk. "Captain Woolsey, would you get Dr. Caruso a cup of coffee?"

Edward Woolsey knew more about the UFO subject that any officer in the Navy, except Admiral McHenny, of course. As senior military officer attached to NICAP, now retired, he had investigated hundreds of sightings for the military while stationed in England. In those days he made it a specialty of ferreting out hoaxes that

had been swept under the rug. His graduation from the naval academy led him to extended service under Admiral McHenny and he received his Captain's license five years ago.

Woolsey saluted. "Begging your pardon, sir—would the Admiral desire a cup as well?"

"Bring the pot," he replied, and cast his intense eyes on a file lying on his desk, marked "Top Secret." He looked into the intelligent face of his visitor thinking just how he might explain this unusual mission. It would take a man with an open mind and strong convictions. After reading the dossier of Dr. Caruso it was his considered opinion the he was the man of the hour—as the President had confirmed.

"Did you read the file the President gave you," he asked as the Captain entered the office with a pot of steaming coffee, poured two cups, and then excused himself. The Admiral slid a cup over to his guest, and sipped a swallow and then opened the file.

Robby balanced the cup on his knee. "Yes, I read the file with guarded interest."

"How guarded?"

"In the since that the Germans had the technology in 1935 to build a functional flying saucer."

"I see. Well that is exactly your mission on this venture, to inspect one of those machines and bring it back for retro-fit," he said, and cast his eyes again on

the open file. He digested a few paragraphs and leaned back in his chair.

"Are you aware that the Roswell flying saucer was a German Unit?"

Robby choke on his coffee.

"Your reaction is typical," McHenny replied. "You have been in covert work long enough to know that the government covers up any and everything they judge justifiable or even vaguely related to national security."

Robby found the statement amusing but rather derogatory, since the President appointed him to a desk job. "Is the project codename "The Bell" related to national security?"

"You are referring to *Die Glocke*—most historians disagree as to whether it existed or was related to the German development of flying saucers—UFOs."

Robby drained his coffee cup. "Classified Polish documents are the only evidence that makes this research viable," Robby replied and looked squarely into the Admiral's eyes. "Do you think this Bell exhibited anti-gravity?"

McHenny dropped his gaze. "Walther Gerlach directed the project. He had conducted some surprising experiments with mercuric plasma which linked vortices with quantum gravity."

"I read that report; Gerlach became famous for his work on atomic nuclei spinning in a strong magnetic field. Nikola Tesla's experiments on wireless power

transmission were never fully developed before he died in 1943."

"That's a feasible connection. Agents of the Gestapo confiscated all of Tesla's notes, equipment, and files."

"Do you anticipate that *die Glocke* is the result of Tesla's notes?"

He bowed his head a moment and refilled Robby's empty cup. "When the Bell was first activated it exhibited harmful radiation and later research centered on that problem in the 1920s. It is an unconfirmed admission that Tesla's notes were used to perfect the electronic parts of the Bell. Imagine perfecting a system of anti-gravity using magnetic fields," he elucidated.

"Incredible. Is there any documentation on the "guts" of this Bell?"

"Only that it was about eight feet high and three feet wide and rounded at the top where high-voltage cables connected to an inside axis, or core, around which, two cylinders were spinning, one over the other."

Robby sipped his coffee. "That technology didn't just germinate in Gerlach's mind."

"Good observation," the Admiral deduced. "Hitler was dabbling in the occult—that elusive search for secret knowledge."

Robby sat back in his chair his analytical mind churning. There it was—that witchcraft stuff; as a chemist, Robby dealt with electrons. He could visualize those elusive cations discharging at the cathode. The

question he could not visualize was whether the Germans had advanced to magnetic fields and anti-gravity?

“Secret knowledge,” Robby snapped sarcastically.

“There is much we don’t know, Robby. According to the Bible angels are created beings that can heal, kill, and blind. They are awesome creatures. They possess knowledge beyond our comprehension,” the Admiral explained.

His forehead wrinkled revealing his remorse. “I thought angels were pledged to God,” Robby answered from his limited knowledge during his childhood days in Sunday school.

“Remember that two-thirds of the angels fell from grace when they followed Satan.”

“So?”

“So these fallen angels had that secret knowledge,” the Admiral replied.

“That’s a long reach, Admiral,” Robby responded. “I don’t know many people who have spoken with angels.”

The Admiral leaned back in his seat, bringing his palms together connected by the opposing fingers. “Hitler was in league with the Devil and regularly talked with him—daily. The Devil, Satan is an angel. Hitler and his SS occultists dabbled in the black arts and Hindu gods—searching for secret knowledge.”

Robby crossed his legs, his mind chewing on his scientific pride. Could it be more than just an intriguing

conversation, he thought? He shook his head, tired of sorting truth from myth.

"Okay, Hitler was a nut—give me a credible example." he suddenly barked.

"The Vatican has erected a telescope on Graham Mountain dubbed Lucifer; they are searching for anything that enters and returns from hyperspace in the atmosphere; they are looking for that secret knowledge."

Robby was out of his league. "Admiral, tell me who or what Hitler talked with—I can't buy this angel stuff."

"Men, but not just any man," he said. "What do you know of Nephilim?"

He'd heard the word but had not researched its meaning. "Okay, let's hear your definition."

"The Bible says in Genesis 6 the sons of God looked upon the daughters of men, they were fair, and they chose wives and had children. These children were giants--Nephilim."

Robby stood stunned. "Giants!"

"The sons of God were fallen angels."

"I thought angels were sexless."

"Angels can transform into men."

Robby was in a subject of which he knew next to nothing. "I'll take your word for that. But Admiral, the Roswell event of July 4, 1947, has the highest secret clearance available. Roswell is still classified—why?" he asked rather rhetorically.

The Admiral stared into space for a long pensive moment. His duty was to prepare Robby for a difficult mission; he'd try a different route. "What do you know of the Majestic 12?"

Robby's head snapped back, an eyebrow elevated; finally, a subject he was cognizant. "Know of it—it has been reported as a hoax since the 90s."

"Correct. And how does the government keep a secret."

"They lie," Robby smirked.

"In some respects you are correct. But the government is not that naïve."

"They aren't that smart, either."

The Admiral leaned back in his chair. "Some of these young MIT graduates, who enter the government, have been keeping secrets long enough to invent clever ways of hiding their secrets."

"You think?" Robby doubtfully acknowledged out of respect.

The Admiral appealed to the intellect of Robby. "Let me give you the anatomy of a secret invented by the Majestic 12: First you define your project as a national security secret and assign a secret classification. Second you create a Black Program, that is, a shell contract issued to an undisclosed contractor with a top secret clearance. And then you create a strategy of disinformation that says your project is a hoax. The skeptics stop searching for the truth," he said and gave

then an example. "The Manhattan project was such a secret, so is Area 51," he injected.

Robby sat stunned again, his mind returning to reality. "So the government allowed the Germans to discover that the Manhattan Project was a fraud, because the Corona-type used on the President's letterhead had not been invented—therefore it was a hoax. That's your Black Program?"

"Exactly!"

Robby swilled the last of his coffee, and sat it on the table. "It's too incredible," he mused aloud.

The Admiral stood and refilled their two cups. He slid one cup over on the desk to his disenchanted visitor. "This occult stuff, does it worry you?"

"I'm a realist, Admiral. And so far it has kept me alive."

The old navy Salt blew across the top of his cup. "I only thought you must understand what you will be going up against,

Dr. Caruso."

He smiled indifferently. "I have listened with that understanding and now I'm more confused than ever about my part in this mission."

The Admiral's eyes clouded with compunction. "I'll get to the point. Andrew has briefed you, I take it."

Robby nodded, "Yes sir—he has," his tone unassuming.

Out of respect for Dr. Caruso, his service to the President, the Admiral thought it necessary for a history lesson. He took a swallow of coffee and breathed deeply. "President Truman believed the Germans were staking a claim on Antarctica. He had no assurance that he might use the Monroe Doctrine to push them out. Truman was convinced that Hitler was alive and had taken residence in a South America—FBI reports confirm that much. Congress allotted $340,000 for Truman's project. Rear Admiral Byrd formed a task force and ran headlong into German UFOs," he said, and sipped his coffee, watching the sudden transformation in Robby's demeanor. "And now it is my duty, at the insistence of the President, to send you off on the same trek as Admiral Byrd. You will take over where Byrd left off. Your goal, directly from the President's desk: Find one of those flying saucers and bring it back for reverse-engineering purposes." It was the second time he had made this point, this time it was reinforced.

Robby sat stoic. The authoritative sound of Admiral McHenny's voice suddenly burst the fantasy bubble that he had been nursing; he saw the mission for the first time, and still had no clue where to start, only one last question.

"This habitat is actually tunneled under the ice?" he wondered, the thought fixated in his scientific mind.

He nodded affirmatively. "It's called *Neuschwabenland* or *New Swabia* on a map. It's a

transliteration of the name that the German explorers gave an area of Antarctica between 20° E and 10° W in Queen Maud Land. The first expedition ship the Germans sent into Antarctica was the *Schwabenland* that left Hamburg in December 1938. It was no secret the Germans intended to colonize a New Germany. A Nazi crew set up a base in Antarctica in 1938-1939, called Station 211. Most rumors agree that Station 211 and Neuschwabenland are synonymous." The Admiral stood. "As to logistics of your mission, Captain Woolsey will command an aircraft carrier that will take you to Antarctica."

Robby placed his thumb and index finger on his chin, thinking. Could this be a project where he might use Walter Nichols, he thought. His mind quickly filed the thought in his mental computer.

4

The Aircraft carrier received authorization to disembark from the harbor of Mayport, Florida, at 05:30 hours on a bright sunny morning. Arrows of sunlight bathed the smooth waters, pelicans precariously stood on ragged posts of a dismantle pier, keen eyes watching the gentle ripples of the surf for their morning food. Tiny ducklings swam near the shore in a tight row behind the drake. A trio of geese waddled on the shoreline, their beaks lazily pecking in the sand; these were the drake's cousins, a cross between a duck and swan. Groups of seagulls were squabbling together over the peaceful waters, eyes trained on the surf. The

limitless sky gazed down upon the dome of the sandy beach of Jacksonville, Florida.

Lashed on the carrier deck were moored four F-15 jet fighters. Also s+trapped to the deck, clear of the runway was a refurbished Sherman tank accompanied by a snowplow with tank-like tracks. Standing on rear deck, Bruce Allison and Robby stared at the thrashing water stirred up by the turbine props as the flattop moved out of the harbor into the turbulent waters of the Atlantic.**

Down in the bowels of the Carrier, Robby gazed at his best friend. "I hear that Consuela came over to the house to stay with Jenny Lynn," he said, facing him with admiration.

"Yeah, it was her idea," Bruce replied.

Consuela Montoya was the former daughter of the Mexican Ambassador to the U.S. He was killed on her inherited plantation, and Consuela hired Bruce, a former Navy Seal, to find his killer. It was the beginning of a Presidential mission related to the drug cartel out of South America. Bruce's girlfriend was killed, and he was wounded in that caper—decorated by the President with a purple heart for exposing the leader of the Colombian drug cartel.

The loud speaker blared from the top deck. It was the Flight Director calling Robby to the Captain's quarters.

They finally reached the level of the open Bridge situated over the Flight Deck, and Bruce tossed a cigarette butt into the breeze, turned and skip-hopped to catch up with Robby.

A weathered boatswain who volunteered for this mission met the two at the stairway and guided them down to the Captain's quarters. As they navigated the stairs to a landing, the boatswain turned to Bruce.

"Lieutenant Allison, it's a pleasure to serve with you again."

Bruce scratched his head. "Marty Kosaku, you old barnacle—thought you retired last year," he gasped, shaking his hand.

"Scuttlebutt said you and Dr. Caruso were off to Antarctica, I just had to go."

Bruce released his hand and slapped him on the back. "You always did have salt in your veins."

Marty turned to Dr. Caruso. "Sir, I followed your work for the President, even kept a scrapbook. Congratulations on your appointment as assistant director of Homeland Security."

"Thank you, Marty—how is the wife?"

He lowered his head. "She died last year, sir. That's why I wanted to go on this mission—the loneliness was about to scuttle me," he confessed, a pendant tear nestling in the corner of his cataract eyes.

Standing at the door, the ensign saluted, recognizing Bruce as a former Lieutenant retired. Bruce smiled a glance at Robby. The ensign opened the door, and Captain Woolsey sat seated beside a big, brawny sergeant.

"Have a seat, men. This ugly man here is Sergeant Kawasaki. He will pilot that snowplow strapped on the deck. Lieutenant Allison, I understand you have training on that Sherman tank. You will find both units useful," he said and opened a file on the table. "Gather around, gentlemen," he said and paused for the seat arrangement.

"This is a diagram of *Neuschwabenland,* the under ice city built by Hitler's SS and scientists in the 1930s. Submarines brought in the construction materiel and instruments, including the tunneling machines. There's an ice-free mountain located about here," he pointed. "Any questions?"

Two faces mutually flushed red.

Robby rubbed his chin with index and thumb. "You say the mountain is ice-free."

"Not logical is it?" Woolsey returned. "According to a Norwegian expedition between 1956 and 1960 that mapped most of Queen Maud Land, its surveys and air photos identified the mountain. Infrared photos defined it as being ice-free. Surprisingly it matches the rumored mountain where Station 211 was constructed."

Bruce stirred in his seat. "So what is the connection between *Neuschwabenland* and this Station 211?"

"Several historians have said that Heinrich Himmler believed it was important to ensure a remnant of the pure Aryan race survived. Even after the war ended in 1945, U-boats continued to shuttle equipment and materiel to a site labeled Station 211."

So Station 211 is just a code name for the construction of *Neuschwabenland*," Robby injected, recalling Admiral McHenny's briefing.

"That's correct. You must understand that Hitler envisioned a Shangri-La, in which his Aryan race would take possession of Antarctica—from there, the world."

Robby smiled. "Isn't that also the sworn mission of the illuminati?"

Woolsey nodded. "Hitler gained his knowledge from the same place as the Rothschild's—secret knowledge."

"Bruce pointed to a title on the map. "What is the title, *Terra Australis* doing there on the Antarctic continent?"

Captain Woolsey lit a cigarette. "Good question, Lieutenant. That's the title given to Australia before the South Pole was discovered. Myths about a land known as *Terra Australis* go back to 1500s."

Robby rustled in his seat. "Is there an opening into this ice city?"

"Its underwater about here," he pointed to a spot on the shoreline. "The water is held back by a *Biber Dam.*"

Robby's mind puzzled. "Then we are going to need a submarine to gain entrance."

"How right you are, Dr. Caruso. A nuclear sub is too large to enter. The navy has restored a World War II sub for this project. She should be standing by when we arrive."

Bruce slumped in his seat. "How are you going to get that tank and snowplow onto the icepack?"

"We should be able to offload both machines with the crane on the rear deck of the Carrier. Those machines may be quite useful on the top ice."

Robby deeply inhaled. "You expect trouble?"

Captain Woolsey dropped his pointer. "The worst," he sighed.

"You care to elaborate?"

Woolsey leaned back in his chair. "How much do you know about the Admiral Robert E. Byrd expedition?"

Robby's eyebrows squinted. "Only that, when he returned from Antarctica, he appeared on a news program, and disappeared."

"Your memory is correct, Dr. Caruso. Rumors about a secret German base in Antarctica rumbled in the press back during the war and continued after, and today there are stories of a host of "Nazis in the Antarctica." Those stories stem from Admiral Byrd's remarks after returning from the expedition.

Woolsey lit his briar bowl pipe and puffed brown smoke; the pungent vapors rose to the ceiling and dispersed into the air control system.

"The Congress was not about to allow the annexation of the South Pole by the Germans. They debated the use of the Monroe Doctrine which prompted President Roosevelt who originally tasked Admiral Byrd into the region. WWII cancelled Byrd's trip. After Roosevelt died, President Truman tagged Admiral Byrd again to take a task force into Antarctica. That's when all hell broke loose. Byrd lost three P-51s fighters and one cruiser was sunk by—you guessed it: German Flying saucers!

The room went silent.

"You mean UFOs?" Bruce injected.

Woolsey nodded affirmatively. "Those terms came out of Roswell. Area 51 was a closed subject until the 1950s—there were rumors that the government had captured a saucer and gossip spread about aliens from outer space."

"Could that have been a German flying disc?" Robby surmised.

Woolsey leaned back. "That's the view of some in high places."

"How high," Robby injected.

"Black-Program secrecy."

The refurbished and refitted aircraft carrier powered out of the harbor at Mayport and set a course to the open Atlantic. Down in the map room, a Lieutenant Commander plotted a course southward to Africa. The Vice Admiral sat in his flagship office and leaned back in

his chair, a picture of Antarctica projected on a large screen. The image was viewed from the axis of the South Pole. The continent of Africa faced *Queen Maud Land*. The area adjacent to the shore was *New Swabia*, the landing target.

Antarctic is unique. It is the coldest, windiest, and driest continent on Earth. The land is barren and mostly covered with a thick sheet of ice. Antarctica is almost entirely south to the Antarctic Circle (66.5S latitude). The continent is about one and a half the size of the United States. Ice shelves extend over the Ross and Weddell Seas. The little bits of land that are not covered by ice are very rocky. In several places under the ice sheet there are freshwater lakes. Temperatures can be very low. East Antarctica is colder than West Antarctica because it has the higher elevation. The Antarctic Peninsula has the warmest climate on the continent, however high temperatures still average slightly below freezing. The tallest mountain of the continent of Antarctica is called Vinson Massif. It rises 4,897 meters (16,050 feet) above sea level. This mountain and several other mountains in Antarctica are active volcanoes, including those on Deception Island and in remote parts of Antarctica.

The major oceans bordering the Antarctic continent are generally the Atlantic and Pacific. However, the Southern Ocean is a bit different. Many mapmakers do not even recognize it as an ocean. The Southern Ocean

has other names; sometimes known as the Antarctic Ocean or South Polar Ocean. It surrounds Antarctica in the South Polar Region extending to 60°S latitude. By definition, the boundaries of any ocean are usually those that surround continents. For example the Atlantic Ocean is bound by the North American and European continents in the north and the South American and African continents in the south. But the Southern Ocean does not have continents that define its boundaries. Therefore one may ask what makes the Southern Ocean an ocean. The big boys who make that decision is the IHO, and they say the Southern Ocean has distinct circulation patterns, and the waters are somewhat separated from to other oceans even without continents to form borders. In fact, the Antarctic Circumpolar Current is the strong ocean current that circles eastward around Antarctica. This circulation pattern makes the seawater colder. This colder and isolated water supports a unique marine ecosystem in the Antarctica. It's commonly inhabited by seals, penguin, and killer whale.

5

Captain Eugene Tunney stepped to the periscope of the restored WWII submarine. He was all Navy, the son of a captain in the Merchant Marines. Tunney was a Pennsylvanian who joined the Navy at the age of 21 years. He served on the John F. Kennedy and was commissioned on a nuclear Submarine out of the navy pens on the Atlantic coast of Florida. That was the occasion that brought him to the Deep South, and he never left, divorced—remarried to the Navy.

As he peered through the magnification lenses for a moment, he adjusted the focus. The scope rotated ninety degrees—left then right in a survey of the horizon. Finally he removed his eyes from the eyepiece, placed his arm over one of the grips and turned to his First Officer, Commander Stephen Coates.

Stephen Coates, a commissioned Navy officer and graduate of the University of Rhode Island ROTC induction. He served in the naval reclamation of the Titanic under retired United States Navy officer Richard Duane Ballard, a professor of oceanography at the University of Rhode Island. Coates rose in the ranks as the adjutant to Rear Admiral McHenny. When the Admiral served over Materiel Support of the Navy Department in Washington, he was his supply officer. More recently the Admiral was sent to the Japanese Sea, and Stephen served as the First Officer under Captain Edward Woolsey.

Captain Tunney gazed into the eyes of the man he had considered to recommend for the command of his first submarine, and suddenly dropped his gaze. "Antarctica is broad on the beam—down scope," he said. Commander Coates accepted the Captain's offer and peered through the periscope.

For a moment Tunney stood, rethinking the secret orders lying on his desk. A Navy Carrier was to arrive in four hours. It was his duty to send a scouting party on the ice at New Swabia. "Order the scouting party on deck," ordered the Captain.

"As you command, Sir," Coates said, and opened the compartment door and sealed it behind his exit. He snapped a microphone off a utility wall pressed a side button, spoke a few words into the speaker piped through the sub.

The hatch on the foredeck opened and a sailor exited followed by two other sailors. The last sailor was squeezing a camouflage kaki-covered package the size of a duffle bag from the manhole. He sealed the hatch, pulled a lever attached on the side of the package, and pressurized air inflated into a raft. He gripped a rope and slid the raft overboard into a turbulent Atlantic ocean. Three sailors stood with side-arms, descended a rope ladder, and got into the raft. The brawnier sailor gripped the paddle, and sculled the raft toward shore. There were no whitecaps at this hour, and Lieutenant wondered how long the waters would allow the use of this non-motorized raft. Then he consoled his curiosity recalling the orders for this one project: find the opening to the under the ice city.

The arctic bright snow was blinding. Fortunate that the three men donned dark sunglasses especially designed for snow blindness. Overhead the sky loomed grey, and a light mist was in the air, that stung the nose energized by the eternal breeze. The sailors were insulated with parkers, boots, gloves and hoods. One sailor, a Second Lieutenant finally stepped on the icepack with the raft rope gripped in his gloved hand. When the other two stepped out, he pulled the raft on the icepack. The

Lieutenant checked his location by the position of the sun, surveyed the horizon with his binoculars, and pointed. They trudged off toward a slight bulge in the surface, perhaps 500 meters in the distance. The surface was smooth as glass packed tightly, probably resurfaced recently with a snowplow. The idea that a snowplow was involved gave credibility to the story told by Captain Tunney last night. And suddenly the Lieutenant realized that other parts of this unrealistic story may also be true. German flying saucers were too similar to the Area 51 story of UFO's. Could that unconfirmed captured flying saucer have been piloted by a German? They finally reached the bulge and noticed it was, indeed, an opening beneath the surface of the restless ocean, a cavern entrance sixty meters wide and forty meters high. The Lieutenant recorded the position by the satellites. Scribbling a few notes, he motioned the twosome to head back to the raft. As they neared the raft, they were suddenly startled by a flying saucer that lifted from the water and flew over their heads! They stood in awe, but the Lieutenant quickly raised his radio.

"Mayday, Mayday. Admiral Byrd was right. The Germans have flying saucers."

The radio went dead.

The UFO roared overhead, a death ray exploded the ice dangerously near the trio, a melted hole opened in the icepack down to the ocean waters. The three men

urgently ran toward the raft, clutching injured arms inflicted by some type of pyrogenic laser. The flying saucer lifted into the bright sun, its nonstandard tail emblazed with a swastika. It soared at tremendous speed and arced downward toward the submarine. Again the radio squawked, the Lieutenant barking an urgent message over his radio.

"Dive! Dive! You are under attack by flying saucers!

Sudden water bubbled violently around the sub as ballasts released immense volumes of air, and the vessel sunk to the conning tower. Two successive bursts of a death ray splattered the water, angry waves rose in towers of froth around the submarine, the water a steam of pulsing pressure. The submerging sub rocked side-to-side, the emergency horns screeching blasts of penetrating sound from beneath the surface. Finally the submarine disappeared beneath the waves, and the periscope popped through the surface.

Two more blasts hit the water and dangerously rocked the submarine, releasing two torpedoes from its racks. The radio buzzed in the control room. Commander Coates steadied his legs answering the call; a sailor had been crushed by a falling torpedo. Curiously, the flying saucers seemed to call off the attack. They dove beneath the surface of the sea, the submarine sonar frantically tracking; the UFOs seemed somehow cloaked, no distinguishing pings returned to the sophisticated sonar. The control room was silent as

death as Tunney stared at the flushed face of his First Officer, visions of Roswell dancing in their startled thoughts.

Finally the submarine resurfaced to recover the sailors on the icepack. Tunney realized then that the Admiral had ordered F-15 jets into the air. Apparently the UFO pilots had never seen the maneuverability of modern jets. The rubber raft bumped the steel hull. The sailors were taken in through the rear hatch. The Sub immediately submerged. Captain Tunney ordered the three men to sickbay. All three men had badly burned arms; one's face had third-degree burns. The Lieutenant suffered from frostbitten fingers having lost both his gloves.

The Captain entered sickbay, slid his cap to the top of his head. He gazed at the medic, and then upon the somber three faces. "Men you earned your pay today—I'm proud of you," he said, and focused on the lead man. "Lieutenant, I'm recommending you for the Medal of Honor. Your quick thinking saved this sub and the men aboard. You other men will receive purple hearts and commendations. It was a wise decision under fire, making you and your men dispensable for the safety the sub."

The First Officer opened the door. "Sir, Admiral McHenny wishes you to transfer to the flagship."

The Captain glanced at the medic. "Take good care of these sailors, son," and turned to his First Mate. "Stephen, the Con is yours while I'm away."

The quarters of the aircraft carrier were roomier than the old refurbished submarine, but then Captain Tunney was a proud man, proud of his men and proud of the old sub. Having been ordered to the map room, an Ensign led him passed the cook's quarters for a cup of coffee. He thanked the compassionate Ensign, and followed him up a flight of stairs to the second level. They coursed a hall and finally knocked on a steel door. The ensign opened the door, and the Captain entered the map room. Admiral McHenny sat behind his desk. Two civilians stood, one Tunney knew, Dr. Robert Caruso. They had trained together; Caruso had joined the Marines, while he entered the Navy. They had not met in six years.

Caruso stepped out and met the Captain. "Eugene Tunney! It's been too long. I heard you devoiced, but your son is in the Navy now," he said warmly pumping his hand.

"Thank you Robby, yes Cooper is in Hawaii, married—I'm a grandfather by three months," he replied as they walked to their seats.

The Admiral lifted his eyes from a document he'd just signed and placed it under a stack of papers. "Captain Tunney let's hear your report. We picked up your Conversation describing an attack."

All eyes were on the Captain as he sat his coffee cup on a table by his chair.

Silence replaced the air in the room as Tunney gathered his thoughts. Finally he swallowed; his dry gulp was an audible echo. "My Lieutenant reported flying saucers emerging from beneath the ocean waters."

Hushed silence hovered.

An icy nausea coursed through his Tunney's body as he sat in numbed abhorrence and gazed into nothingness through his unbelieving eyes, recounting the event, "One saucer overflew the scouting party; they took fire, and then the Lieutenant frantically warned the conning tower to submerge. After firing some kind of laser ray at the sub, the UFOs broke off the attack and dove beneath the surface waters."

Gawking stares.

"That's incredible—injuries?" the Admiral blurted!

"One death, two purple hearts, and a Medal of honor."

"Explain."

"My Lieutenant warned the sub to dive, and they all received third-degree burns from that ray, and frostbite, one sailor crushed by a falling torpedo. They were all dispensable to save the sub," he paused. "There is nobody in Washington going to tell me that this is not war," Tunney boldly clarified.

The Admiral nodded with a deep breath that swelled the metals on his chest. "I'll back you on those medals,

Tunney," he said and turned a page in an open document, "is there any scouting information to report?"

Tunney ripped a sheet from his notepad and passed it by Robby to the Admiral. "These are the satellite coordinates of the submarine entrance to *Neuschwabenland.* We will need a few supplies and should be ready by 0600 hours tomorrow."

They all stood and gathered around Captain Tunney; the chatter was the sound of a group of nervous magpies. Robby congratulated Tunney for his brave action. Yet the Admiral nursed a hint of doubt about Tunney's readiness to captain the submarine on this delicate mission; however, owing to his action today he shelved the doubt.

The United States Coast Guard patrol plane was two hours into a dull routine eight-hour survey of icebergs drifting southward into the roaring Atlantic. There had been reports of icebergs in the shipping lanes as far as Bermuda, and a study was formed to survey the situation. Visibility was diamond-clear under a cloudless sky, and the wind barely moved the rolling swells—a unique condition for icebergs to drift from the North Atlantic to the turbulent waters of Antarctica. In the cockpit, the pilot and his copilot navigating the four-engine Boeing aircraft, while three others were in the cargo section watching the radar scopes. The pilot checked his Rolex wristwatch and then turned the aircraft in a sweeping arc, settling the nose on a straight course for Bermuda.

Suddenly he heard a scream from the radar section. He activated his mike, but received no answer. Quickly he set the autopilot and told the copilot to takeover while he went to the mid section. He stumbled over the door as he stepped over the transom, and caught his balance, gripping the doorframe. He heard live chatter in the corridor, and stepped into the radar section. The radar operator, stood with fear blazing in his eyes.

"Sir, there is a UFO tracking us," he stuttered.

The pilot couldn't believe his ears, even his eyes now focusing on the scope. A sudden swish zoomed by the window, and he stuck his head against the pane. "Holy Toledo, he whispered—a Confirmed UFO!"

Quickly he returned to the pilot's cabin. As he sat and buckled his seat, he saw the copilot frantically pointing at the windshield. There it was as big as day—a flying saucer 20 meters in diameter! Before he could reach the radio mike, a bright ray zipped from underneath the UFO and hit the left wing of the Boeing in a terrific explosion. Two motors ripped with the wing and fell into the ocean. The airframe dipped and began to rotate erratically spiraling downward. The copilot screamed, "Mayday, mayday!" The aircraft suddenly leveled under the lift of a rising surge of air. The pilot shouted through the mike. "Abandon ship, abandon

ship!" The side door opened and three men leaped out with parachutes. The pilot insisted that the copilot abandon ship. "An officer must escape to explain this UFO thing," he whispered.

The copilot reluctantly nodded and saluted, and then stepped through the door. As the damaged aircraft veered downward, the pilot confirmed that the copilot's parachute had open. The wounded aircraft crashed into the white capped waves of the Atlantic.

The radio in the aircraft carrier radar room had just picked up a Mayday, and plotted the coordinates. The radar officer urgently phoned the Captain. "Sir we have a Mayday, what are your orders?"

"Send those coordinates to the map room immediately," Captain Woolsey replied and gripped the phone. "Engine room, prepare to change course." The coordinates suddenly appeared on his computer screen. "Come to course six, zero, seven, Helmsman." Woolsey switched channels and buzzed the Admiral's cabin. The line chimed three times, and the Admiral dropped his pen on a form he was signing, glancing an 'excuse me' to his two guests.

"Yes, Captain Woolsey."

"We are responding to a Mayday off the port bow, just ten miles north."

Captain Tunney shot Dr. Caruso a withered look. Deep within the cortex of his mind he saw another incident with those flying saucers. He nudged Caruso.

"Want to bet we have another UFO incident?"

Caruso shook his head. "I'm holding my opinions for that submarine trip under the ice."

Admiral McHenny closed the phone. "Well gentlemen we may have something to confirm your report, Tunney. Robby, I think it's time we plan that trip under the ice. After we answer this Mayday we will conference," he said and lifted the phone once more, and punched a personal code to the cook. "Send up a pot of coffee—would you, and some refreshments."

The Admiral took a seat on the sofa next to Robby. "Has Tunney's report changed your mind concerning German technology and anti-gravity, Dr. Caruso?"

Robby formed his reply, but the door opened and the cook brought in a pot of coffee and some doughnuts. "I can accept anti-gravity easier than this angel business with secret knowledge," he replied, pouring three cups of coffee.

Eugene leaned from his chair next to the sofa and took a cup from Robby's extended hand. The Admiral seized his cup during the exchange. While they sipped the coffee, Eugene had a thought.

"Robby, I think it's wise to wait until you see these saucers," he advised, and crossed a leg.

Robby lowered his cup. "The President has charged me to bring one of these saucers back for evaluation, Eugene. I think you are exactly correct. I shall wait until I see one of these things up close."

The Admiral answered the chime of his phone. He listened intently, and then hung the receiver. "Let's go topside. There are four men taken aboard. One is the copilot of a US Coastguard aircraft that he says was shot down by a flying saucer by some sort of weapons ray," he announced with elevated eyebrows.

Robby glanced at Eugene, a sheepish look on his face. "Let's go—I'm game."

Four parachutes lay on the floor wet and crumpled; the men who wore them were sitting in the galley, with blankets wrapped over their shoulders, sipping on hot coffee. Captain Woolsey turned when the Admiral stepped through the door and saluted.

"Admiral, this is the copilot, Roger Stallings. Roger this is Admiral McHenny."

The Admiral released his handshake and offered Roger a seat in the next room, followed by Robby and Eugene. As Roger sat, he focused on Dr. Caruso, whom he thought he'd seen somewhere. Roger lowered his cup and rested it on his knee.

"I suspect you gentlemen would like to hear what happened to my airplane," he said and bowed his head in the steam rising from his hot cup, gathering his

confidence. "The captain went down with his ship after commanding me to parachute because he said an officer must be able to tell the story." He dryly swallowed. "We were on a routine survey of icebergs drifting south into the shipping lanes. We flew out of Bermuda—

Suddenly his eyes lit and he shifted his focus to the mystery man. "You are Dr. Caruso, the assistant to the director of Homeland Security—I have seen you in Bermuda," he shrugged.

Robby stood and touched his shoulder. "That's correct, Roger. I have a rented cabin in Bermuda. Now take your time and give us the story that your brave Captain died for us to hear," he said somberly.

A pendent tear formed in the corner of Stallings's left eye and rolled down his unshaven cheek. He brought his hand up and carelessly wiped it off. "We were shot down by a UFO with some sort of bright ray that tore off a wing. It happened so fast there was no chance to react," he replied and paused, the gravity of what had happened suddenly lodged in his mind.

He clasped both hands over his face and cried copiously.

The Admiral inhaled a deep breath. "Gentlemen, we shall meet in exactly one hour in the map room," he announced, stood, and went directly to his cabin.

The Admiral gazed at a map projected on a screen behind his desk; it was the familiar overhead satellite

view of the southern axis of the earth, a view that he had studied before. New Swabia faced the Atlantic toward Africa, dead on the zero longitude. To the west lay the Weddel Sea, to the east spread the Indian Ocean. Panning around the axis lay Tasmania, New Zealand, and the placid Pacific Ocean—a panoramic view of the South Pole: The land mass, Antarctica.

The door creaked open and Captain Tunney walked in ahead of Dr. Caruso.

"Sit down gentlemen. Tonight we will make a decision on the next plausible move," said the Admiral.

Coffee, orange juice and a plate of hot pig-in-blanket *hors d'oeuvres* were spaced strategically on a table directly in front of the sofa; strategic because the room was very tight. The Admiral directed they each take seats. Eugene sat first. Robby took a pig-in-blanket and a steaming cup of coffee, regardless of the exact placement, he had long arms.

"Aren't you hungry, Tunney?"

"Later, maybe," he whispered, seeing the Admiral smiling.

The Admiral took a pointer in hand and stood next to the screen. He tapped gently on the metal frame of the screen, and both faces steeled, focused on the images.

"The Americans were not treating the Nazi activities in the Antarctica as something innocent. In 1939 Roosevelt tasked Admiral Byrd to go to the region and gather information on what was going on there. Even after the Congress appropriated funds for the expedition, the investigation was cancelled because the US had entered WWII. Between 1943 and 1945, the British launched a secret wartime Antarctica operation, code-named *Tabarin*. So, you see gentlemen, the British assumed that something is under the ice; perhaps these flying saucers are staged there."

The Admiral reached for a cup of coffee, and Tunney seized the opportunity to ask a nagging question involving his mission. "Sir, I understand this ice city is entered by submarine."

McHenny sat his cup on the table steam rising before his eyes. "The Germans built and resupplied this city by submarine. U-boats, meaning "undersea boat," these were numerous. However there were super submarines, as well. You may recall the U-530 was surrendered to Argentina. Her submerged speed was reported at 30 knots, unheard of at that time. Some historians' belief the U-530 was in service only in the South Atlantic, which could have made her a workhorse for the construction of Neuschwabenland. I suspect she was a prototype of the XXI U-boats."

Robby leaned forward in his chair. He was familiar with the U-530, but had not read the intelligence report on the super submarines. "Admiral, what can you tell us of this XXI type sub?"

He stared into space as if reprogramming his mind. "Officially, only two of type XXI U-boats was launched. Yet there is some truth in the fact that three were in service building Neuschwabenland, even after the end of the WWII. In fact, France had one XXI in service, and the Soviets had at least four, Britain had one put in active service. Hellfire, gentlemen—our own Navy has one, the U3008."

The Admiral leaned over his desk and punched a button. A projection focused from behind the wall over his desk. "Gentlemen let me call your attention to a photograph snapped by surveillance aircraft of three Type SSI U-boats and one Type VII boat in Bergen, Norway on May 1945."

A silence of introspection persisted in the room for an undisclosed moment. Finally Robby stood and took a ham and cheese sandwich from the plate, reseated, and leaned back in his seat, munching a bite. He chewed exactly twenty-one times and swallowed. "Admiral, is it correct to assume that these super subs resupplied the construction of Neuschwabenland and the world had no knowledge?"

"That's plausible, Dr. Caruso. It is even plausible that Hitler took residence in this city beneath the ice."

Stunned faces stared blankly, all except Robby. He had confirmation evidence in the files of his office. Even President Eisenhower said that nobody knew the truth of whether Hitler was alive or dead. Otherwise he would be relaxing at this moment in Bermuda with Jenny Lynn in his arms.

An icebreaker had joined the task force at the insistence of Admiral McHenny. With its armored nose and turbine props it broke the ice in and around the landing site. Other service ships maneuvered the floating ice sections out of the area, leaving a clear working space. The carrier moved slowly up to the deepest shore with only two fathoms of water beneath her keel. Marty operated the controls on the crane and sat the tank in the water just above its tracks. The snowplow was half in the water, but sufficient to drive them both onto the packed ice. Bruce walked knee-deep in the cold water until he reached the tank and crawled up on the rear. Sergeant Kawasaki mounted the snowplow sitting in its open cab gazing over at Bruce and the refurbished Sherman tank. Kawasaki had a solid resolute face flanked by oversized ears. Beneath heavy black eyebrows, the dark unmoving eyes peered through a pair of thick-lens rimless glasses. No smile ever crossed his tight lips, except the day he met Bruce. He was a man's man and he had changed Kawasaki's life.

Kawasaki dropped his gaze and turned the ignition switch key. It growled and groaned then cracked, smoke blowing from its three-inch exhaust pipe. Bruce had little trouble cranking the refurbished tank and drove it onto the icepack. Both machines were driven further from the shore.

Bruce and Kawasaki both got into the tank fitted with a heater, and waited for instructions from Robby. The Admiral instructed Captain Woolsey to stage the task force in the Weddel Sea, where it could monitor the operation and may not be readily seen by one of those flying discs. Woolsey called in the icebreaker to lead the flattop and open a pathway. The Aircraft carrier and three service ships steamed away at the top speed of 30 knots. Below the Aircraft decks resided a small city of 6,000 sailors including officers and pilots for the F-15s.

The old rustic WWII submarine floated motionless like a sea monster from the great deep. Robby stood beside Captain Tunney in the conning tower watching their only contact with human life steaming away in the distance, the moonlight playing on the wings of F-15s strapped on the carrier's flattop. The moon was like a wraith-silver salver hanging in the lonely Atlantic sky. Tendrils of moonlight, as bright as diamond-flame, turned the sea aglow like melted platinum. It was if they were watching a scene from an old fable stepping off the page, and they were beguiled by its beauty. The Chinese called the May moon the dragon moon and Robby could see why. The turbulent waves were aglitter like the dragon's curved scales, and Robby became momentarily lost in the haunting lullaby of their swell and sigh.

Tunney nudged Robby's shoulder. "Let's get below. I seem to hear a lullaby from out there somewhere."

His voice awakened Robby, an eyebrow elevated. "You heard it, too?"

Tunney said nothing, perhaps they were both crazy, he thought.

After Bruce and Kawasaki were ordered aboard, Captain Tunney gave the order to blow ballast, while he checked the coordinates given by his scouting party. Seaman First Class Butch Hadley stared intently at the radar set, his face reflecting an unearthly green glow from the scope. Dr. Caruso surveyed the highly sophisticated periscope and the bright new equipment. His eyes focused on the astounding state of art instruments that had been installed in the tight control room of this old World War II relic. Air and surface research radar, the latest Loran-type navigational equipment with medium, high, and ultra-high frequency scanners. His curious eyes squinted at the HP Pavilion computerized plotting computer, the array of dials and switches adorning the shiny new monitor.

Tunney caught Robby's eyes studying the equipment. "Very impressive, huh?" he smiled.

Robby dropped his gaze. "I haven't seen this type of equipment since the days of shuttling to the moon."

Tunney's face demurred and he hung his head. "Did that moon out there sing—I mean did you hear

something?" he quizzed, embarrassment flushing his pink cheeks.

Robby sighed. "Suck it in, Tunney. The sea always sings to its travelers, the moon is its orchestra," he chuckled.

He inhaled. "Thanks, Robby. I needed that."

Robby slapped him on the shoulder. "We all need something, pal."

Tunney snapped a microphone from the turret. "Take her down to 50 fathoms," he said to the Helmsman, his voice echoing through the ventilation system.

6

Tunney turned to Robby with a tightened face. "Let's see what the entrance looks like at Station 211, he said, and trained his attention on the tubular periscope projecting from the floor to the ceiling of the control room. Space was scarce because of the room needed for all the equipment required by a submarine.

"Up Scope," he commanded.

He could smell the new oil in the well as the winged arms unhinged on each side of the optical tube. He placed his eyes against the soft surface of the eyepiece, both hands gripping the arms. He scanned a ninety degree quadrant, zeroing in on the Aircraft carrier with

its sister ships now just tiny dots on the horizon. He swung the instrument to the icepack; the tank and snowplow in view. He thought of Bruce and Kawasaki who would be using those machines, perhaps soon—not too soon, he hoped. He drew back, repositioned the scope arms.

"Down Scope, come to course five-three-nine; settle at fifty fathoms under the keel."

He stepped to the hatch, turned. "Join me with a cup of coffee, Robby," he said, and descended the stairs.

Robby watched his old classmate as his mind digressed. Tunney was only 24 when they were classmates at the University of North Carolina. He hailed from upstate Pennsylvania, and had hated the noise in his neighborhood, mobster gangs terrorizing the neighbors. When he finished high school, his parents sent him to live with his uncle in Rocky Mount near Raleigh, NC. He later learned that the house where Eugene was reared had been demolished by a pipe-bomb and his parents were killed. That incident had never left his troubled psyche, always nagging. He and Tunney were both members of ROTC, and after graduation Tunney joined the Navy, and Robby took a doctorate in chemistry, and entered the Marine Corp.

Tunney sat in his office with two cups of coffee as Robby enter and sat, his back against the fold-up bunk; a position that had suited him well, his eyes always on the door wherever the President had sent him. Tunney

handed him a cup. They sat quietly sipping, and Tunney lowered his cup.

“Do you remember when the guys on the dorm squeezed toothpaste on your face while you slept?”

“Do I ever?” he smiled. “My resident wiggled a feather on my nose and I wiped that toothpaste over my face.”

They both broke out laughing, a great reliever of tension. Robby sensed that Tunney was a bit nervous—a mission like this could do that to anyone. Yet the Admiral had confidentially mentioned that he had seen that same issue. Robby thought how glad he was that he did not have to make the Admiral’s decision.

Tunney stared for a moment in the distance, his mind racing back thirty years when everything was black and white; no grey area at all. “We students were all so proud of you Robby—that rocket you built in the dorm, and set the asphalt parking lot on fire while testing the escape parachute—what did you rescue, I’ve forgotten?”

“A cockroach in a litmus vial: launched it 8,000 feet and retrieved it alive with a parachute,” he beamed.

Tunney’s tired face relaxed. “When Dr. LeConte got you that summer job in Huntsville, Alabama, we marveled at the stories you told the class about how solid-composite rockets were produced.”

Robby casually nodded. “It all seems so far away now, and we suddenly discover that the Germans were decades ahead of the world in technology; in fact, the

Russians captured several German scientists which gave the Soviets the lead in rocketry when they launched the Sputnik," he gleaned from his busy mind and the reports in his locked file cabinets back in Washington. The President was adamant that he should bring back one of those German flying saucers for retrofitting. It seemed clear that Bruce would be his best bet in securing the UFO.

Tunney nodded. "You have been briefed on this project, Robby and I'm so fortunate to have you aboard. My mind is so cluttered I can't think at times. What in God's name will we find in that place under-the-ice?" Tunney felt a bit dizzy, probably the medicine he was taking for malaria prescribed by a stateside private physician, he thought.

Robby leaned back in his chair. "Well, there is one eyewitness report from our British friends. In the summer of 1944, British scientists and commandos found what they called an 'ancient tunnel.' Under orders, thirty SAS commandos went through a tunnel but only two returned. These two survivors made absurd claims about Polar Men, ancient tunnels and Nazis."

"Incredible!" Tunney sighed.

"The report went on to say that the Nazis power source was volcanic, which gave heat for steam and produced electricity. Apparently there were a number of people living in a vast city beneath the ice."

Tunney breathed a dry sigh. "Then you think we will find a living city down there?" Again his nervousness returned, even a twitch of one eye. Yet even with this new symptom, he felt more in at ease around Robby.

"I can only repeat what I've read and heard. In the face of this advanced technology, we do have some documented evidence. History tells us that Hitler envisioned the survival of a race of Aryans, and Germany's claim to Antarctica was the answer."

Tunney downed the last drop of his coffee. "It's going to be a bit hairy taking this submarine into that tunnel. I'm told there is a dam that I don't quite understand the mechanics."

Robby nodded. "It's called a *Biber Dam.* Think of it as one of those ingenious beaver dams. It holds back the thrust of the main water source—the ocean—and creates a controlled water system by a moat around the complex where is connects to whatever use required. One example would by desalinization of ocean water for potable drinking and cooking water."

Tunney absorbed the response. "Could this dam be structurally sound after so many years?"

"Hard to say, we will just have to wait and see."

Tunney's eye began to twitch erratically. He stepped away reaching down into his right pocket, pulled out a pill bottle, unscrewed the cap and swallowed two capsules. The pills seemed to take effect more rapidly than before, and he felt dizzy. He reached for the mike and called Commander Coates to the control room. When Coates climbed the ladder into the control room, Tunney gave him the Con and went to his cabin.

The old World War II refurbished submarine approached the target coordinates. Captain Tunney was called to the control room. He excused himself from a conversation with Dr. Caruso and climbed the ladder. After a short conversation with Seaman First Class Butch Hadley, he stepped to the pedestal of the upgraded optical system.

“Up scope,” he said. The periscope lifted smoothly from its well, the smell of oil obvious. The arms hinged down and he rested his eyes against the eyepiece. After a focused look at the shore, he gripped the arms and rotated the scope through a 90-degree quadrant. The only thing in the magnified view was a few specks on the horizon—Admiral McHenny’s task force. The entrance to the Station 211 was dead ahead.

“Surface,” he commanded. “Cut speed. Let’s crawl into this ice tunnel,” he said.

The nose of the submarine, wrapped around the bow with its arrayed sonar, pushed into the tunnel. Tunney cracked the hatch cover, a gush of water drained and he climbed the short distance to the conning tower. He eyes were seized by the great tunnel, obviously drilled through the ice with large tunneling machines. The submarine eased slowly along, still 40 fathoms under her keel. Suddenly Tunney's head snapped back, eyes wide-open.

"I'll be damned," he whispered stoically, his eyes clear and unmasked, as he seized the mike. "Dr. Caruso to the Con STAT!"

Tunney dropped his head. This *New Swabia* stuff was over his head. He never believed in UFO's and even considered removing his name from consideration for this mission. The dizziness returned.

Dr. Caruso stuck his torso through the hatch. "What's on your mind, Tunney?"

"You won't believe this. I see tall buildings in the background beyond that dam. There is a city of living, breathing humans—look for yourself. I want confirmation," he said in a rasping tone from his dry throat, the malaria dizziness concealed by his determination.

Robby curiously climbed up into the conning tower. A long silence pursued as he gazed out thought tie ice tunnel before he spoke. The unpredictable had occurred. There was the enigma broad on the beam. What would the President say if he could see this? He turned and faced Tunney's quizzical expression.

"Confirmed—tall buildings rise in a huge cavern under the ice, people milling about!"

Tunney knew he couldn't relax now, anymore than Seaman Hadley sitting with his gawking eyes. The trickiest part of the entire voyage was the Biber Dam.

"All stop! Send up Ensign Honnewell to the Con," he spoke into the mike.

He turned to face Caruso standing adjacent to him. "I think it wise to inspect that dam," he voiced.

Robby face ballooned in a smile, placing his hand on Tunney's shoulder. "Brilliant, adroitly clever," he said, his face twisted in mirth. "We have traveled three thousand miles to be stopped by a beaver dam with an Aryan city in the distance."

Tunney smiled. "Nobody's perfect," he shrugged helplessly, the dizziness gratefully had subsided.

Honnewell reached the Con and saluted the Captain. Tunney turned from his conversation with Robby, and gripped his chin with thumb and index fingers.

"Ensign, take a look out there."

The Ensign moved to the rail, his eyes blinked twice, the expanse an enigma in his mind.

"That dam is your target. I want you to select a partner and inspect the stability of its structure. Your duty is to take a sample for analyze—if that's even possible. I shall expect your report."

He came to attention. "Aye aye, Captain."

Tunney and Caruso watched from the conning tower as Ensign Honnewell exited the foredeck hatch. The second man, a Yeoman closed the hatch. Dressed in skin-tight, insulated diving skins, they slid into the icy waters and swam away probing the beam of a quartz

lantern in their path, its reflection on the frozen surface of whalebone white. As the two sailors submerged, the movement of lantern light seemed eerie under the water like a sea monster groping in silence. The brilliance of a camera flash silently exploded underwater, not one but two, then a third. It seemed like an eternity but only ten minutes had passed, and the two divers started their swim back to the submarine. Honnewell had a watertight bag looped on his wrist.

Robby descend into the hatch and Tunney followed and sealed the hatch, pulling the rope tight, and then rotating the locking wheel.

"I'll meet you in my cabin after a few minutes with Hadley," Tunney said to Robby. But it was a fib; he needed to take a pill. Dizziness had returned more eerie than before. The malaria had taken a stand to drive him nuts. When the foredeck hatch was closed Tunney ordered the ballast blown and the submarine settled to 20-fathom under her keel.

Robby sat in the Captain's cabin drinking a cup of coffee he had secured from the galley after he left the control room. For some reason the ice city was not on his mind, but the evasive tactics of Tunney.

Tunney stepped into the cabin. "Sorry I'm late. It took longer than expected—Hadley was a little rattled by circumstances." It was a rhetorical response answered only by silent stares.

Robby held his gaze on Tunney's face. "Eugene, something is bothering you—I saw that bottle of pills."

Tunney cowered, and sat. "It's that malaria I contacted when in Japan with Admiral McHenny.'

Hell, Tunney. The Admiral's worried about your fitness. Tell him about this malaria."

"The Admiral has enough on his plate."

"What about your fitness exam?"

"Avoided it; a private physician issued the pills."

"You're playing with fire."

The intercom buzz pierced the conversation. Tunney gratefully lifted the receiver and pressed it to his ear, facing Robby with a frowning face. A twenty-second pause slipped by and Tunney hung the phone.

"Should be about thirty minutes and the pictures will be ready for presentation," Tunney said. His tired eyes settled on the stern face of Robby, but fortunately Bruce stepped into the cabin.

"Hi guys, any reports on the dam?"

Tunney had an relative thought. "Bruce, do you have any idea about the strength of cement under water?" he asked with haste, avoiding Robby's stare.

"I know it continues to harden in water—never really chemically dries. A water analysis should tell more about its properties."

The intercom buzzed again, and Tunney answered. He listened for about ten seconds. "I have just the man right here," he said, and handed the receiver to Bruce.

Bruce pressed the phone to his ear. “Bruce Allison.” The message was tantalizing. “Be there right away,” Bruce said, and turned to the Captain. “Which way to the machine shop,” he bellowed.

“Down two levels, you can’t miss it.”

Bruce reached the machine shop and found Ensign Honnewell waiting with a bottle in his hand.

“These are borings six-inches into that concrete wall. How do we analyze it?”

“Depends on what equipment we have,” he said, scanning the room—machinery analysis equipment, nothing for serious chemical analysis.

He turned, and Honnewell held a ceramic mortar with pestle in his hand. “Is this useful?”

“Perfect!” Bruce exclaimed. He took the ceramic unit and sat it on the counter, and then selected the midsection of the boring. He pounded and crushed it with the pestle into a sandy granulation. “Did you notice the color of the damn?” Bruce asked.

He bobbed his head. “It was uniformly grey with a light greenish shade,” I think.

Bruce nodded. “Strength reduces with age.”

The Ensign rubbed his bent index finger under his nose. “Will litmus paper help?”

“Perhaps—the calcium content in cement is a reasonable indicator of strength—it’s worth a try.”

The Ensign opened a drawer, and handed Bruce a plastic vial. Bruce held the vial up to the light. He saw a ribbon used for iron presence, and a thought lodged in his mind. He wet the granulation with distilled water taken from the condenser of the heating unit. Stirring into a paste, he rubbed the mixture paste between his fingers—sniffed it. He wiped the ribbon across the top of the paste. The color changed to dark black. He dropped the ribbon into the trash container.

"We may have an deductive answer, Honnewell," he said as he ran to the ladder and ascended to the level of Tunney's cabin. As he drew the entry curtain aside, two faces were staring intently.

"Two items," Bruce announced to their absorbing expressions.

"Let's hear it," a duet said in chorus.

"The strength of cement decreases with age."

"It was poured about 1937 I would guess," Tunney theorized.

"That's old," Robby replied.

Tunney leaned back in his seat, almost unwilling to ask about the second item. "Then you think the dam is unstable?"

"It's still holding back the water," Bruce grunted. "My guess is the Germans reinforced it with iron bars—a litmus test for iron was quiet high."

Robby stood. "Eugene, I suggest you call Admiral McHenny and inquire about a civil engineer onboard, and what supplies they might have to strengthen that dam, if required."

Bruce advanced his final thought. "Hitler boasted the Third Reich would last a thousand years—his messianic dream. I suspect that dam was built to last a long while."

It was his final answer, like or not, Bruce thought.

The Submarine had backed out of the ice tunnel, allowing a small motor boat to dock against its hull. Tunney was in the Galley drinking coffee, his thoughts on the approval of the Biber dam. Two civil engineers were inspecting the dam at present. Robby was in the conning tower with binoculars trained on the entrance to Station 211. Tunney had conversed with Admiral McHenny on the dam problem, and he had ordered inspection by two civil engineers followed by a report on their recommendations.

Robby saw the motor boat finally exit the ice tunnel and it motored over to the submarine. Two sailors assisted the two engineers on deck and secured the boat to the deck. Robby left the conning tower, and locked the hatch cover. He snapped the microphone off the control room rack and buzzed Tunney. The Captain sat his cup on the table and reached for the phone hanging on the wall.

"Yes, Robby."

"The two engineers are coming aboard.'"

"Bring them to my cabin, Robby. Maybe we will finally have an answer on this Biber dam."

"Right."

The two engineers had removed their diving suits at the entry hatch, and one engineer unloosed a watertight bag from his wrist. A Yeoman led them to the Captain's cabin and ordered a pot of coffee from the Galley. As Tunney navigated the narrow passage, a cook stepped out of a door ahead with the coffee.

"I'll take that pot for you, Jim. Thank you."

"It's all yours, Captain," he said, and handed him the tray with cups.

As Tunney approached his cabin he saw Robby standing in the doorway, the curtain stretched against the jamb, his arms crossed over his broad chest.

"Let's get the verdict, Eugene."

He nodded and entered ahead of Robby.

Four men in the cabin were a bit constricted but they all had seats, accept Robby who stood. Tunney poured four cups and extended a cup to Robby. The two engineers seemed pleased to be in a warm cabin with hot coffee. One engineer, the one with the watertight bag, sat his cup on the table.

"I suppose you want to hear our report?" he said and leaned back in his seat.

Tunney grinned distastefully. "Give the man a cigar!"

The engineer shrugged, he'd dealt with crabby officers before. "We took borings at the top and bottom of the dam. Personally, I think the dam is sturdy as the

Hoover. Our drill hit reinforcement bars and rocks. Not only that, there seems to be some sort of plastic synthetic admixed in the cement. We won't know much beyond speculation until we can do an analysis."

Tunney glanced at Robby, a frown on his face. "Do you have any thoughts about that synthetic?" he asked impatiently.

His fingers massaged his chin. "Again its speculation you understand. The Romans had a substance similar to these borings when they built the aqueducts; the Hebrews used straw in the bricks. If it's what I'm thinking, it's some sort of advance adhesive that chemically bonds the iron bars stronger than wire, which otherwise loses its strength by rusting. Not only that, the iron bars may also be coated with the plastic substance to prevent rust."

Robby smiled and sipped his coffee. "If the Germans can devise anti-gravity, certainly they can build a dam that survives," he grinned.

The face of the lead engineer frowned. "What anti-gravity?"

Old cautious Tunney ignored the engineer's remark. "Thank you for your professional opinions gentleman. I'll wait on the test results and a call from Admiral McHenny."

Tunney sat his cup on the table, stood with a question marring his countenance. "I'll take the Con," he said and wiggled out of the room, and turned down

the narrow hallway. He stepped over the transom of the oblong steel door and pulled it shut. He inserted his hand into his pocket and took a pill from a plastic bottle. He swallowed it. Tunney mounted the stairs to the conning tower. He stood with binoculars pressed firmly against his eyes and surveyed the ice-free mountain under which lay the entrance to Neuschwabenland, as he mused. Was this mission viable, he thought? Was there really an issue of national security as Admiral Byrd surmised? How many would be killed or maimed? These nagging questions unnerved him to the point of intimidation.

Robby sat his cup on the tray. "You boys can find your way out. Give my regards to Admiral McHenny," he said and mounted the stairs to the control room where Hadley stood by the radar.

Hadley turned wistfully, cautious of the words forming in his mind. "I'm worried about the Captain," he said, a remorseful overtone in his voice. "He seems aloof, the mission weighing on his mind."

Robby weighed his assessment, and just before he spoke. The sound of Tunney's voice over the PA system shattered his thoughts.

"This is the Captain. Take her down to 50 fathoms."

Two civil engineers were in the flattop laboratory analyzing the boring samples. One engineer had a

crucible drying in the oven, while the other engineer was examining a slide under the microscope. The crystalline structure of the plastic material was indeed synthetic but there was no data for comparison. His bespectacled eyes suddenly brightened, and he turned to the shelf behind the counter, pulled down a large index volume. He opened the front cover to the contents page and ran his finger down to a section on synthetics. He lay the large book open on the counter and flipped to the page where he thought he might find some information. He was in luck! On the right column of the page were very clear and well-focused diagrams of the crystalline structure of several synthetic compounds. Suddenly he smiled.

"Hey Stan, this darn synthetic has a patent number!"

"This dried sample has adhered to the crucible—permanently; this is not standard cement."

The Chief engineer ran to the radio room and sent a telegram to the patent office in Washington D.C., and then went to the Admiral's office. The Admiral was at his desk reading a report. He heard a rap on the door and the adjutant cracked open the door.

"The civil engineer wishes to speak, Sir."

"Send him in."

Roger Stanton, chief engineer, stepped into the flagstaff office with professional excitement written on his unshaven face.

"Sit down Roger. Have you finished your analysis on the samples?" McHenny questioned.

He sat with the smile of a college chemistry student who had just aced his final exam. "Sir, we have some rather unusual results. First the cement in that dam is not standard cement. It has the normal ratio of sand and rocks but the reinforcement bars are coated with a synthetic substance that renders the cement a rather long life."

"That is remarkable. Can you identify this synthetic?"

"As soon as the patent office in Washington answers my telegram we will know the structural components."

"You mean the synthetic has a patent?" he inquired skeptically.

"That's exactly right, Sir."

"Let me know soon as that telegram arrives, Roger."

Roger Stanton finally received the patented components of the synthetic, and removed his spectacles. The patent was issued in 1956 to a Johann von Valier, a German scientist who arrived in America with the *Operation Paperclip* scientists. According to documents, Valier died in 1969 with no relatives. Beyond those facts he could safely surmise that the dam was built using these advanced synthetic components and he recommended the Admiral authorize the submarine to continue its mission.

Admiral McHenny sat in his flagship office staring in disbelief at the faxed patent and recommendation from Roger Stanton's desk. He sat there; it seemed for a decade, while his brain worked to explain the telegram from the President lying on his desk. He reluctantly called Dr. Caruso to the flagship.

Caruso finally opened the door to the Admiral's cabin. McHenny stood and invited him in. Neither said anything. Caruso sensed disturbing news written on the Admiral's face, but decided to wait for his explanation.

"Sit down, Robby," he advised, and handed him the telegram.

Robby's face frowned as he read the message. "Henri's lungs are scorched?" he whispered disbelievingly.

"I placed an overseas phone call. Henri is in the hospital, apparently recovering. Someone set off a pipe-bomb in his apartment."

Captain Tunney received a call from the task force flagship. The results of the concrete tests were more than positive—astounding! Somehow the gratification of this success calmed his demeanor and he was glad Dr. Caruso had returned from the flagship. He deeply sighed, and immediately patched a call to the Con where he had left Dr. Caruso in charge.

"Well Robby, it seems that Bruce's hunch was on the mark. There is a specific synthetic component that

bonds the cement system in a form that gives it an indefinite strength. In fact, I'm informed that the stuff has a patent!"

"That's a helluva note. So, when do we enter that ice tunnel again?"

"I think 0530 tomorrow morning. That gives us time to meet for breakfast. I'll inform the cook to prepare something early."

"You're on. I'll tell Bruce—better prepare a large plate of eggs. Bruce is a growing boy and who knows what Kawasaki can eat."

All day Tunney exchanged phone calls with Admiral McHenny who approved his decision to enter Station 211 at the coming dawn. Robby occupied the conning tower most of the day, often accompanied by Tunney. They talked of tomorrow morning and their adventure. Would they face Shangri-La or a Nazi tempest? The conversational atmosphere loomed somewhat clouded by a silence, a silence that seemed intensified by Tunney's lack of realism. After that paranoiac spat this morning at breakfast, Robby was concerned how Tunney might react if he came under fire. He was proud of Bruce for his apology. Neither Robby nor Tunney had spoken for several moments, each lost in his own thoughts. They thought only of the unrealistic tall buildings built in the 1930's. Even more surprising was the large bored-out tunnel for the entrance to the city beneath the Antarctic ice.

Before they retired for the night Robby suggest a brief meeting. He remembered his discussions with the President and the Admiral. As they sat around a pitcher of lemonade, Robby opened a discussion.

"The tunneling equipment and supplies were shuttled to Neuschwabenland by submarines larger than those used in the war. There were documented reports and even pictures of these large subs. In fact, a type VIIC U-boat U-995 is on display in Norway. The German type XXI U-boats were so advanced that captured submarines were used by Allied navies. The USA Navy's captured sub was designated U-3008."

Tunney seemed surprised. "How advanced were these subs?

"The XXI U-boats had a crew of 57 and a length of over 251 feet."

Bruce sighed. "That rivals even today's modern subs."

They would not get much sleep on the evening prior to dawn.

7

The sun hid its face somewhere beneath the horizon, the yawn and stretch of day in the making. Dawn was in its genesis, the solar energy rising to its peak. The Atlantic would soon emerge in its ebb and flow, until turbulent clouds formed in the east, and a tempest exploded in a heavy storm. The turbulence of the Atlantic returned to is whitecaps and high waves. Yet, at this southernmost latitude the dreamy sea was its own master. The waves were carelessly drenching the edges of the icepack. The palpitating pulse of the waves were steady and even peaceful, the wave-music enthralling.

Of all the oceans of the world, only the Atlantic is totally impulsive. The other oceans around the planet all have their peculiarities but have one trait in common: they seldom fail to provide a hint of their coming moods. Not so the Atlantic—she is the lady with an attitude. Heavy winds, heavy seas during the night may give every intention of a Force 5 hurricane, yet when the dawn comes, there is nothing to see but a glassy, azure sea beneath an empty sky. And so it was for the men aboard the World War II refitted submarine.

Captain Tunney leisurely ambled down the narrow aisle to the galley energized by a false euphoria; the dam was secure, but no indication of what they would find beneath the ice. The cook had already fried the sausage and bacon and a coffee pot sat in the center of the table with a pitcher of OJ. Robby stepped into the gallery with Bruce in the rear and Kawasaki behind him. No sooner had they all sat, than the cook entered with a large platter of scrambled eggs, and a plate of buttered toast and biscuits and grape jelly.

Conversation was nil, the noise of chewing and gurgitation overshadowed the familiar smells and tastes. Bruce had forgotten his experience as a bosun eating an early breakfast in the cramped quarters of a submarine, with ears ringing at certain pressure levels. Once you had had a meal beneath the sea, there was something exotic about it that lodged in your cortex. Kawasaki never talked when he ate. Ever since the days as a

young Boy Scout he ate alone, but now with a friend like Bruce. Yet he was still a quiet eater, eating each item as he rotated the plate, finishing with water. This quiet uncouth moment allowed Bruce time to plan and make his decisions. Bruce munched on a biscuit stuffed with sausage and two pieces of bacon broken neatly to fit the biscuit. "I hear the dam is acceptable for entry, Captain."

His eyes took on a thoughtful look. "It seems that your assessment was quite accurate, the civil engineering report confirms it. We will enter Station 211 after breakfast, Mr. Allison," he replied, and scooped up a fork of scrambled eggs. That was his apology, and now the moment of truth lay out there in that icy tunnel. What would they face? Who would be there, and how long would stay or could they stay? These were unnerving questions.

Robby grinned over the glass of OJ. "Are we carrying side arms or is this an altruistic venture?"

Tunney caught his drift and the consoling euphoria cracked. "With all that has happened—none of it peaceful—we will be armed," he replied, staring piercingly over his coffee mug.

Bruce swallowed the last bite of biscuit. "You guys talk as if you know something that Kawasaki and I don't."

Tunney swiped a napkin across his mouth, an adamant look on his face, the euphoria burst in rapid

statements. "There is a thriving city on the other side of that dam. If our information is correct, the population is a group of Aryans with the mind of Hitler," he said, slamming his fist on the table.

The air dissipated from the galley and floated on a cloud where all wrong remarks vanished.

Bruce cringed, not his style, but he realized that he had struck a nerve. Besides, he respected the Captain because he had practically grown up with Robby. Yes, he was out of step and he knew it, as he cast a glance at the affirmative face of Robby. Bruce winked and faced Tunney.

"No offense intended, sir," Bruce said equably.

The sun emerged on the horizon exposing the mammoth expanse of the Atlantic; no dawn is like that upon the sea. It has a rhythmic pulse unmatched by any other part of nature. It forges its own sounds and kindles its own symphony. If one can find himself visualizing its glorious vastness, its dreamy surface, and strain to hear its metronomic wave music, then one might understand the fascination of the neighborhood fisherman—the bass boat he purchases at the consternation of the spouse.

Bruce was in his cabin dressing. After his conversation with Robby concerning that second little testy spat with the Captain, Robby decided it best that he and Kawasaki man their positions on the icepack. If one of those UFOs popped out of the sea, the tank turret

gun might have a chance to score; or if by land, the snowplow could be useful. As Bruce stood inserting a leg in his insulated trousers a slight grin crawled across his unshaven face. "Tank by sea, plow by land—if only Paul Revere were here," he whispered, and maybe he was, he suddenly thought. Robby had the mind of a freedom fighter; he had seen him rise in victory over impossible odds during the years of their lifelong friendship.

Kawasaki had received the word from Bruce and showed no reaction; he had been too busy eating to have seen anything. His unblinking eyes never left Bruce's face when he explained his actions. In his mind, Tunney was not the leader of Captain Woolsey's. He had first met the Admiral when he commanded a task force in the Sea of Japan, his orders: shoot down any missile launched from North Korea. Admiral McHenny smoked a cigar and cursed like a sailor on leave. Kawasaki was no submariner: he was Sergeant Major of the USA Marine Corp, and Bruce was his kind of man: he followed orders, and never backed down for anyone in the wrong. He reached the rear section of the submarine ahead of Bruce.

Bruce smiled when he saw the brawny Sergeant sitting on an insulated pipe dressed in his insulated duds, his hairy hands wrapped around the barrel of his hot mug, its steam kissing the brim of his cap. The *précis* of this guy was topnotch; he could fight on his team anytime.

"I've got a dingy top deck," Kawasaki said.

Bruce closed the oblong steel door and locked it with a twist of the wheel. "Good. We should take our positions on the icecap ASAP."

Kawasaki sat the cup on his knee, a finger in the hole of the handle, while thoughtfully tapping the fingers of his right hand, convinced that he could trust this man. "What or who are these Aryans I keep hearing about?"

Bruce sat on an insulated duct warming his buttocks, rehearsing all that he had learned from Robby. "Hitler had hoped to produce a Super Race. And you are aware that he and certain members of the Third Reich where occultists. They dabbled in the dark arts of ancient Hindu mysticism, and formed mystical societies. For example, in a nutshell, the Thule Society, established by Hitler believed that an ancient alien civilization left survivors called Aryans, supermen of the Nordic Caucasian race. This European ideology was necessarily anti-Semitic; the reason for the holocaust under Hitler."

Kawasaki removed the rimless glasses and laid them in a safe place, his broad forehead approvingly wrinkling. "Thanks, that's quite a studious explanation, Bruce—thank you," he said. Kawasaki had left high school and joined the Marines; big for his age, and he easily passed the rugged physicals.

Bruce gazed at his new firend. "If you hang around Dr. Caruso for any length of time you pick up a college education," he grinned with a wink.

"You two have known each other for a longtime, I gather."

"From high school days on the football team; Robby was quarterback, and I was a fullback—we have been a team ever since."

He stirred his buttocks nervously on the hot pipe, almost embarrassingly. "I do covet that kind of relationship. I was always the bully in my Bronx neighborhood," he confessed, and bowed his remorseful head in the steam rising from the last cup of coffee.

Bruce gently slapped Kawasaki on the shoulder. "Let's break out that dingy, pal—time changes everything."

The sun broke in a myriad of bright shafts of radiant light, casting shadows on the jagged snow banks dancing like little fiery demons. They were clad in insulated jackets and boots including snow goggles. Kawasaki rhythmically paddled the dingy straight as an arrow, rotating strokes on either side of the rubber raft. Little wintery ripples of icecap water parted the gently waves, as the last whimper of darkness faded into the brightness of the new day. Kawasaki dismounted the dingy and gripped the lanyard, as he heard the two diesel engines of the submarine crank and roared to life.

They each trudged to their respective machines, Bruce to the Sherman tank, Kawasaki to the snowplow. As Bruce stepped up on the turret, he waved at Robby standing in the conning tower. His only thought was that his best friend was safe, remembering his promise to Jenny Lynn. No one knew exactly what they were up against on any covert operation he had been with Robby. This mission was a first, and he wondered what they really might find beneath the ice. He settled in the warmth of the driver's seat, after inserting a shell in the breach of the turret cannon. He sighed deeply, reached for the microphone and buzzed Kawasaki.

8

The Biber dam appeared in the periscope as the submarine entered the icy tunnel with 50 fathoms under her keel. The tall buildings were like icy shadows in the eerie distance. As the submarine drew nearer, it was clear that the buildings were of standard German architecture from the 1930s. It was only then they grasped the realism of how the Germans had accomplished this remarkable achievement of hauling in all the materiel and equipment on U-boats. Robby remembered the Admiral's discussion of three Type-XXI U-boats, and one Type-VII, both advanced submarines. The Type XXI had a smooth sail instead of conning tower and the engines were substantially quieter while rigged in silent running. The guns on deck were housed behind a metal sail to increase submerged speed.

Tunney called, "All stop." The periscope image revealed no possibility that the submarine could cross over the dam. He seemed puzzled until he realized that wide concrete landings were on each side of the tunnel. He assumed these were the off-loading ramps the Nazis must have used.

"Zero bubble," Captain.

He called Robby to the control room and Tunney invited him to the periscope pedestal with outstretched open hand.

"Tell me what you see."

Robby placed his forehead against the soft headrest and peered through the eyepiece magnification. He dropped his gaze and faced Tunney.

"Concrete pads on either side; we can get off here on these pads."

Tunney nodded, and called the First Office to the control room. As he waited, he settled his eyes on the man he respected.

"What do you really expect us to find under the ice, Robby?"

Robby sensed his apprehension. "Frankly, I don't exactly know, but all the information gleaned from those historic documents in the President's files point to a

Neo-Nazis people isolated from reality sitting on a ton of advance technology."

Presently, a new voice stood in open hatch, his lean proportions and straight back erected in a tall, impressive frame, only his torso visible. The oak-tanned face, the hard, almost cruel features, the penetrating brown eyes suggested that this wasn't a man to resist. Clad in official navy blue, watchful yet detached, he spread a patronizing grin.

"At your service, Captain," replied the First Officer Stephen Coates.

Tunney stared down at his youthful face. "You will take the Con during this invasion; remember you have 70 enlisted men under your command. You are the captain of this boat. Stay submerged and run silent. Keep your ears glued to the radio."

"Aye, Aye, Captain," he said, and stepped up into the control room, erecting his tall frame.

Robby stood in the rear section of the submarine selecting equipment from stores. He chose what he thought they might need: Side-arms, extra-clips, binoculars, two-way radios, flashlights, a camera, and insulated gear, including night-vision goggles. The sailors placed the equipment on the rear deck through the hatch. They offloaded the items on the concrete pad to the port side. Tunney and Robby stepped over the gangplank to the concrete pad, and each took their items. The stood face to face, without moving without

replying. They each knew they were not off to see the Wizard of Oz—the Devil, maybe. Robby led out, each with a pack strapped to their backs.

As they trudged along, Robby remembered Byrd's first reported journey to the South Pole was in 1947, Operation Highjump. He went 1,700 miles "beyond" the pole and into the center of the earth. He seemed to have disappeared, reported as being in a mental intuition until 1955. He led a second expedition again into Antarctic in 1956 going 2,300 miles beyond the South Pole only turning around for lack of fuel. Yet he reported what he saw on both journeys as an iceless area beneath the ice as big as North America with trees, mountains, lakes, and animals both familiar and unfamiliar; a paradise within the earth with an Eden-like landscape and unlimited scientific discoveries! Unfortunately, Byrd brought back no photographs or samples. Thus we have a Jules Vern story *Journey to the Center of the Earth* or that of James Hilton's *Lost Horizon*. Robby dropped his muse; could the earth be hollow?

He stood in reality, this was no dream—yet here before his eyes was an under-the-ice city with the vastness of a small continent. Many people were walking the sidewalks, couples standing in conversation, people entering and exiting the buildings. It was a thriving city. Could this be Byrd's discovery? He expected Tarzan to step out and take them to his tree

abode, and perhaps meet Jane, and Boy, surely Cheetah. He could visualize in his mind's eye the ape man of Edgar Rice Burroughs swinging on vines through the trees.

Tunney stood mesmerized. Yet he realized there was no sun, no sky, just the ragged projections of what might be stalactites of dripping frozen ice from the ceiling. Perhaps they should try to find the utilities room or whatever. Pictures would tell a thousand words, the error of Byrd's expeditions. Robby saw the indifference in Tunney's countenance and touched his arm.

"What's on your mind, Eugene?"

"I was thinking if we could find the utility room it could answer a lot of questions."

"I agree. Where do we look? I recall a report that power was taken from a volcano."

"Well an active volcano emits smoke," he said and suddenly pointed. "Look yonder to the right—isn't that a volcano?"

"It's no Vesuvius and this is not Italy, but it is certainly smoking. Let's check it out."

For the first time Tunney seemed engaged and even led the two-mile trip to a rising medium-size mountain. Robby saw something unusual, or was it just out of place. He left Tunney taking pictures of the volcano and walked around the circle of its base. Suddenly he saw the anomaly: A steel and concrete bridge over a type of

moat around the city. And as he investigated further, another anomaly: A door in the base of the mountain! Robby had the curiosity of an anteater, but he was quick to investigate professionally. As he walked closer to the door, he heard the regular pounding of a machine or large pump deep below the surface. He could hardly wait to test the door. He gripped the brass handle, slowly twisting counterclockwise; no success, he reversed the turn, and Eureka!

It opened.

He waved to Tunney, who replaced the lens cover on his Nikon camera and ran, crossing over the steel/concrete bridge, while stuffing the 35-mm in a bag hung around his neck.

"The first signs of human ingenuity," he said as he approached Robby.

"Appropriate—let's enter," Robby smiled.

As the door swung open, the pounding sound increased. They stepped out on a metal stairway, gazing deep down into the bowels of hot magma, churning in rolling embers, the heat noticeable. The stairway descended in five levels to the bottom; a distance of probably fifty to sixty feet. Tunney stepped down to the first level, while Robby studied the huge pump at the base. It had stainless steel insulated pipes running to an udder system of transfer lines that exited into the walls: ingenious, he thought. Tunney stood not exactly mesmerized but impressed nevertheless, he took the

Nikon from a bag and snapped a half-dozen color pictures. As he tuned he saw Robby descend the stairs. A door on his level suddenly swung open.

Robby swirled.

Standing in the seven foot door was a tall, blonde hair man at least six-eight in height. He was clad in dark blue trousers and a light blue jacket—unlined. He stared directly at Robby, who did not move. Then the man strolled calmly over to Robby and spoke.

"You are not one of us," he said in perfect English, his face stoic, his eyes sedate, empty.

Robby carefully extended his hand. "My name is Dr. Robert Caruso from America."

His unexpected smile reinforced the Nordic look of his face, his hair, his complexion—and the blue eyes revealed intelligence. Somehow Robby's words registered.

He took Robby's handshake, yet there was no strong grip. "I am Henri Weismann, glad to make your acquaintance."

'Glad,' Robby thought reaching into his mind searching for the proper words. "Is there some place we can talk?"

Quite surprisingly, if not astonishingly the tall man nodded. "Follow me," he said, and strolled on a concrete sidewalk to a building two blocks away, Robby at his side. They went into a café. The people were all blonde and many had blue eyes. Not only that, they all

wore the same type of dark blue trousers and moved about lethargically, glancing indifferently at his entry. Henri sat at a table and offered Robby a seat. His blue eyes were very disarming and Robby leaned back in his seat and thought for a moment. What could he say?

"Henri, you said that I am not one of you—what does that me?"

He only stared rather detached for a moment, as if he was a million miles away, but somehow his mind said this was reality. "Look around you, Dr. Caruso. Everyone looks like me."

Robby dropped his gaze. Henri was exactly right. "Should I ask you to follow me, could you—I mean would you?"

"That all depends on where we go and if I can return."

Robby touched his shoulder. "Of course you can return—I shall be sure to bring you back myself. Could you tell me if you have family?"

He sat still as a mouse; his hands crossed in his lap as if he were in an 18th century schoolhouse. "What is a family?" he replied, no ambiguity in his question.

"Parents, brother or sister—those you live with."

His face soured. "No one, I come here and eat, and to the library and read; we sleep in communes."

Then it dawned on Robby. Henri is a clone!

They sat peering into each other's face, Robby analytical, Henri stoical. Finally, Robby stood.

"Could we leave now, I want to introduce you to a new world."

His forehead wrinkled as if he understood something. "I have heard of a new world, but I have never seen it." Then somehow something within his mind prompted a reply. "Look at the emblem over the counter," he pointed.

Robby immediately turned. It was a swastika—a German swastika. Hitler had boasted of a thousand year reign; he thought he was the Messiah, and this must be the new society of Aryan people his SS men had created here under the ice. Yet, there must be leaders here who directed this operation from 1933-45, some type of government. If Henri could come back to the sub; perhaps there were things in his mind that would clarify a few anomalies. Should he dare take Henri out of this environment, he suddenly thought.

He turned and asked if Henri would follow him. Henri pushed back his chair, looked a moment at the man behind the counter, and then stepped out beside Robby.

"You will bring me back," he insisted.

"The moment you want to return—that's a promise."

Robby was surprised to find Tunney standing outside the café. But he said not a word, his eyes scanning Henri head to toe. The threesome set their course for the submarine at the dam. Henri took them a

different route directly to the tunnel. As they walked along the cement path to the submarine, Henri clamped his teeth together, jammed his fists two inches deep in the pockets of his jacket. He was beyond what he had dreamed.

"We are not allowed to venture into this tunnel," he remarked without any disagreement of being there, only relating orders indelible in his mind.

Tunney stared at Robby, a frown on his confused face. Robby stepped beside Henri. "It is much warmer in the submarine."

He eyes seem to display something in his deep consciousness. "We are told that our founders first came to this place in—what you say—submarine."

Tunney shook his head; his mind told him this young man had been brainwashed.

The group walked over the bridge from the icepack to the submarine, and stepped on the rear deck. Tunney saluted the First Office standing in the conning tower, his face screwed in a surprised mode. Tunney unlocked the hatch and swung the heavy steel hatch cover back.

Two sailors were waiting at the base of the ladder; neither had seen the young man until he stood nearly ten-inches over their heads. Robby followed Henri down the ladder, conscious of this unusual meeting, and gratified that Henri was so amenable.

"Gentlemen, this is Henri Weismann. He has come to visit us a while."

The two sailors exchanged frowns, neither ventured a response.

They sat in the galley and the cook brought them refreshments. Tunney restrained Robby at the door of the galley and pulled him into the hallway.

"What are your plans?"

"I'm flying under false colors, there is no plan."

Tunney wagged his head, and left his conversation with Robby, his face unveiling the surprise that registered starkly when he learned that Henri was a clone. They sat with Henri between the two "foreigners."

Tunney decided he had best say something. "Tell me, Henri how many citizens live in your city?"

Henri gripped the barrel of his cup of coca, staring into space. "I don't know the population, but think about eight hundred in my village."

"And do you have a government?"

"We are governed by a committee with offices up on the hill."

"And what of your people—"

Henri instinctively interrupted, his mind leaving the question unanswered as if he had had a distasteful experience. The wheels of his subconscious were turning at top speed, and he had never experienced such perplexity before. Finally he spoke by rote a message extracted from his genes.

"You will find the citizens of Neuschwabenland friendly. We are born into an isolated environment, yet we are not permitted to leave; we can understand each other's thoughts before we speak. Life and love are commonplace; death is merely an accepted occurrence." He dropped his head, an eyebrow arched. "Out in the valley there is a graveyard—our founders are buried there."

Robby paused, sensing too many questions all at once. They swilled on their drinks, a moment of perspective.

"Do you have a military?" Robby asked.

Henri placed his hands around the warm barrel of his cup, his eyes set in space. "Our founders were highly trained in violence, but killing is not permitted now. There are those who are trained from childhood to be pilots, but we citizens are not told what goes on outside our world."

Tunney glanced at Robby looking for a clue if he should speak. Robby finally nodded.

"Henri, is there an airfield?"

He deeply sighed; the rush of air into his lungs sent a familiar signal of distant pleasant scents. "No land-based field—I understand that our aircraft land in the water outside; I'm not privilege to that information, but there is a place in the south valley where the pilots come in, I believe."

The cook poured refills and sat a plate of sandwiches on the table, dropping his embarrassing gaze on the face of the stranger. The visitor studied the platter for a moment and reached out and took a tiny sandwich. He cautiously brought it to his mouth, smelled it like a raccoon before he eats, and clamped his teeth down on a tasteful substance spread between triangular-shaped bread. He chewed three times.

"What is this," he asked.

The cook wiped his hands in his apron. "We call it chicken salad."

"Chicken?"

Robby answered the question. "It's a domesticate bird, quite common on the "outside," which he emphasized.

"Chicken is good," he replied and turned. "Robert Caruso, I must get back, before the military sends out someone to get me. If I leave Neuschwabenland, I can never come back. And I understand someone on the outside will hunt me down. I'm not sure what happens beyond that."

9

Robby thought it necessary to invite Admiral McHenny to a conference, Tunney agreed. After hearing an astounding story over the radio, the Admiral left the flagship in a Zodiac motorized F470 CRRC craft, under guard. Two armed guards were both alertly watching the sky. They had had reports on those flying saucers, and wanted no part in any exchange without proper weapons. Overcast blanketed the sky, and there was a suspicion that one of those flying saucers may shoot out from behind that heavy mist.

The motorized trip over was thankfully uneventful. The limitless vault of misty blue peeked through the

flimsy clouds. Seagulls lazily looping and diving into the tiny wavelets fringed with a frothy white were the only scenery, except an occasion group of penguins on the icepack. Admiral McHenny raised his binoculars and surveyed the boundless horizon. He spotted the Sherman tank and snowplow sitting on the icy pack. The submarine was still submerged, and then suddenly he caught the telltale bubbles breaking the surface as the ballasts blew.

As they finally floated up to the steel hull, the coxswain secured its lanyard to the deck, and assisted the Admiral. Both guards came down to the rear hatch where an armed sailor stood watch. The Admiral descended the ladder ahead of the last sailor standing on the deck. He took a last look at the sky, stepped through the hatch and secured the steel lid. Out on the icepack Bruce and Kawasaki both huddled in the Sherman tank, received calls to attend the conference. The First Officer was in the conning tower waiting for the arrival of the two men on the ice.

Bruce boarded the dinghy ahead of Kawasaki and cranked the outboard motor secured to a wooden transom. He steered the dinghy over to the submarine, both shouting with joy thinking of entering a better environment. It was a short trip from the icepack with the submarine, but Bruce kept his eyes focused on the sky with one eye, the other on the submarine. Finally the rubberized dinghy bumped against the steel hull of the submarine, and Bruce secured the lanyard to the deck, and assisted Kawasaki out of the dinghy. As soon as they came down the ladder of the rear hatch, the scuttlebutt was humming with news about a "seven-foot man from that city beneath the ice." When they finally reached the Captain's cabin, this story was that the man had "green eyes and horns."

The Admiral sat facing Robby, Tunney at the end seat of the small table. In his mind Robby was surely the right man he had appointed, but something still bothered him about Tunney; perhaps he needed a rest.

"What can you tell me about this Henri Weismann," the Admiral asked, chewing down on a cigar.

Robby leaned back in his seat. "Eugene, would you bring those photos from our cabin for the Admiral?"

Tunney pushed back his seat and stepped out of the office. The Admiral removed the cigar and the smoke was sucked into the air conditioning system. He again asked an unanswered question. "What's your take on this ice man?"

Robby chose his words carefully. "After you talk with him a while, sir, you will sense the lethargic manner in which he talks almost aloof as something within his genes are prompting each word, each movement." He paused and looked directly into the Admiral's eyes. "Sir, I think Henri is a clone."

The Admiral gawked, removing his cigar. "You don't say?"

"According to Henri they live in communes, all dressed alike, all appearances quite similar. There is a graveyard when the former leaders are buried. Pilots are trained from birth. The flying saucers enter the ocean and there is apparently another tunnel harbor over in the south valley."

The Admiral chewed on his cigar. "This is incredible!" he said through puffs of cigar smoke. He laid the cigar in the ash tray. "Do you suppose we can investigate these places?"

"Would the Admiral wait to see the photos—then we can make some decisions."

"Of course, Robby you are quite correct."

Tunney shoved the curtain aside and stepped through the open passage with a packet of photos gripped in a nervous hand. He spread them on the table before the searching eyes of the Admiral, glancing at the somber face of Robby.

"Admiral, this city under the ice is a time capsule of the Third Reich, a Fourth Reich of new Germany clones."

The Admiral heard but wasn't listening as he leaned forward, his keen eyes surveying the strange photos. The quietness was unnerving, the smoke of the cigar pungent. Data blazed into his mind as the camera of his eyes flashed one image after the other projected on his retina. The buildings were clearly from the 1930s, the faces of the people Nordic. Could the SS have decided

the best way to preserve Hitler's 1000-year reign was by genetic cloning? Intriguing, he thought!

The Admiral laid the last photo on the table. "Where is Weismann now?

Robby rose from his chair. "I'll get him, sir."

As Robby left the cabin, Admiral McHenny gazed upon the tormented face of Captain Tunney. "Tell me about this Biber dam, Captain?"

He deeply sighed, at last a subject he could verse. "The concrete is reinforced by some sort of synthetic matrix—you saw the analysis. A submarine cannot progress over that dam. There are offloading pads on either side." He paused. "Admiral, the Germans were decades ahead in technology even in the 1920s," he said, unable to conceal the symptoms of malaria.

It was clear that Tunney was suffering under the stress of unreality. It may be that he would have to be relieved, and the Admiral's mind robotically considered promoting the First Officer. The decision return to the secret compartment of his mind, as Robby entered the office with Weismann.

"Henri, this is Admiral McHenny. Admiral, I'm pleased to present Henri Weismann."

Henri said nothing only extended his handshake. If this Admiral was a friend of Dr. Caruso, then he was satisfied it was permissible.

The Admiral released his hand. "Henri, thank you for being so kind as to meet with us," he said. His demeanor was just as Robby had described: stoic, even lethargic, aloof, and detached. His eyes were distant, as one blind from birth. The Admiral carefully selected his words. "Mr. Weismann, does the name, Hitler suggest anything?"

An eyebrow elevated, the eyes ballooned. "Hitler's picture is enshrined in a locked building, no admittance allowed except on special festival days," he replied, as if reciting.

"What have you been told about the Third Reich?"

He glanced at Dr. Caruso for confidence. "Only that Hitler had a dream for his people to live in purity and safety for a thousand years."

"Did you know that Hitler was responsible for exterminating over six million men, women and children?"

A frown crossed his face, his eyes squinted shut, and he covered his face with both hands. All the pictures of glory and pomp, the recordings of marvelous speeches of a rising empire of hope flashed before his eyes.

"Is this true, Dr. Caruso?" he said, revealing the first evidence of rationale.

Robby touched his shoulder, nodding. "I'm afraid it is, Henri."

Henri searched his mind, the daily classes under a language instructor, weeks of Aryan studies—all indoctrination! Finally he dropped his head. "I am undone, I have been living a lie—a terrible truth of violence and death has been hidden from my people," he muttered remorsefully.

The Admiral saw the shame written in his face. "We all have been deceived, Henri. When men decide to hide the truth from the citizens there can only be chaos."

Henri unfolded his hands from his eyes, and faced McHenny. "What would you have me do, sir?"

"I cannot ask you to deceive you people, Henri."

"But kind sir, they are already deceived."

McHenny stared at him with an impossible question on his tongue. "Would you be willing to guide us around in your city?"

His eyes returned to the staring mode upon Dr. Caruso, and then the Admiral. "You wish to see the aircraft harbor and that Hitler shrine, I suppose," he said in measured words.

McHenny stood. "Exactly, Mr. Weismann."

Weismann was taken to the galley and the cook prepared him a chicken dinner. The Admiral called a meeting in the Captain's cabin.

The cook left the galley with Weismann eating his chicken dinner, and brought a platter of refreshments and a pot of coffee with mugs to the Captain's office as instructed. As he entered, the men were studying a map on the wall, and he entered quietly and sat the platter in the center of the table. He placed the pot next to the Admiral's chair and the mugs in a grouping, and excused himself, leaving the room.

As the men gathered around the table, the Admiral poured three mugs with coffee. "The layout seems viable, but we have no idea where all the people are," he said sliding a mug in the direction of Robby.

Robby seized the mug. "The only place we visited was that volcano and a coffee shop on the edge of a street," Robby replied sipped his coffee. "Come to think of it, I didn't see any traffic vehicles at all—just two people in the shop," he added.

The Admiral massaged his mandrake beard. "I hesitated to tell Henri about Hitler. You remember the Volkswagen bug? He built a factory to assemble the people's car, and issued a green card on which the people recorded every *deutsche mark* they spent. When the card was complete, they turned it in to the government and received a Volkswagen. It was a sham to raise money to build war weapons. Instead, the people walked, many rode bicycles?"

Silence was the response.

Tunney rubbed his hands nervously. "This place is so uncommon, it gives me the jitters."

The remark increased the Admiral's concern about Tunney's fitness for command under these circumstances. The buzz of his cellphone broke his chain of thought. "This is Admiral McHenny," he spoke into the tiny speaker.

"Captain Woolsey here, Admiral: I have scrambled the F-15s, sir. Three flying saucers just entered our airspace."

10

Two nervous sailors including Marty Kosaku were fitting themselves with side arms and grenades in the aft section of the submarine. Tunney and Caruso, with Weismann, stood at the rear hatch ladder, the hatch cover open for their ascent. The Admiral leaned against the oblong bulkhead; his hands surrounding a hot mug of coffee.

"Gentlemen, you have your orders. Remember no amount of information—ancient of modern, is worth your lives," he said and faced Mr. Weismann. "Henri, let me thank you for your corporation, we are indebted to your bravery," he said, gently patting his hand on Henri's back.

His stoic eyes seemed to understand. "Admiral, I would like to see that world out there where you live."

He nodded. "Perhaps you will, my brave friend."

As the men each mounted the ladder and stood on the deck, the Admiral looked down from the Con realizing that he must return to the flagship. The First Mate had been given the Con of the Submarine. With flying saucers in the air, it was his duty to the 6,000 sailors aboard the Carrier. As the hatch screwed shut, he left the aft section of the submarine and went to the galley where the coxswain of the Zodiac was waiting with his two armed guards.

"Jonathan, are you ready to brave the open waters over to the flagship?"

He stood at attention; his lungs swelled to full capacity with reconditioned air. "Admiral, sir—I've been hankering for the open waters—these close quarters is giving me the jitters."

The Admiral's face exploded with laughter. "I guess you can blame me for this. Grab your gear and let's get up on deck," he said, and turned to Stephen Coates who stood at the ladder to the control room. "Well, Coates, the boat is your command. I'd recommend that you submerge in case one of those UFOs decides to enter this tunnel," he advised, extending his handshake.

Coates gripped the outstretched hand. "Admiral, God speed to you, sir. It looks like we will be fighting World War II all over again."

He released the hand. "You know, Coates, you may have something there."

The air was frigid, the darkness eerie, but the overcast was a blanket of security for the long trip over to the flagship. A flock of seagulls loitering in the sky gave some assurance of life. The coxswain stepped onto the aluminum deck floor plates of the Zodiac F470 Combat Rubber Raiding Craft (CRRC), and made his way to the stern. The Admiral straddled the gunwale and sat. Two sailors occupied the bow, one armed with a bazooka; the other with a high-powered antiaircraft machinegun strapped over his shoulder. The coxswain cranked the 55-horsepower two-cylinder engine, and swung the tiller of the Zodiac, easing away from the sub at idle speed. As they course through the icy tunnel, images of flying saucers danced in the shadows of their minds. The Admiral pondered the reality of an ice city of cloned neo-Nazis. The submarine submerged as the Zodiac pulled out of the tunnel and set a course along the shore, purposely avoiding the open waters.

The boundless crescent of the horizon loomed in the distance, the clouds in the process of dissipating by the heat of the sun. The flagship was a speck sitting precariously on an astral blue arch. Up in the measureless sky the cloak of stratosphere-blue was threaded with flimsy shapeless clouds as seen through the misty dissolving overcast. Done on the thankfully calm sea, the shuddering waves seemed to hold back its latent power. As the Zodiac motored close to the shoreline, the sea spray rising from the bow showered the icepack beach in a sudden gust of Antarctic wind.

The Admiral gazed out on the icepack and caught the familiar shape of the Sherman tank where Bruce and Kawasaki were hunkered down in the warmth of the newly installed heaters. He filed a note in his mind: inform Bruce of the situation. It may be that the cannon on the tank would have the opportunity to disable one of the flying discs. The prime directive of the President was to bring back one of those machines for retrofitting.

The trip to the flagship was without incident. Perhaps the flying discs had abandoned the attack on the aircraft carrier. The sky was vacant of F-15s. As they neared the flagship, the Admiral trained his binoculars on the flight deck. The F-15s were neatly in a row for takeoff. He dropped his gaze. No need for speculation, he thought. The flagship was intact, that was enough.

Finally, the Zodiac motored along the open parts of the carrier beneath the flight deck, its bow bumping against the side, cushioned by the fender hung over the bow. One of the sailors tossed the lanyard up to a sailor who tied the boat to a capstan. The Admiral exited after the two sailors at the bow, assisted by one sailor, as he stepped into the flight deck. He saw the waving hand of Captain Woolsey up on the bridge, and entered a door, opened by a saluting sailor. The door closed behind him and the sailor took his knapsack and guided him to the galley where the cook had prepared the Admiral's favorite hot food. Captain Woolsey stood by the door to the galley when the Admiral stepped through the steel door.

"Good to have you aboard, Admiral."

"You can't image how good, Captain."

He sat and removed his cap, coursed his fingers through his thinning hair, deeply sighing. A cup of hot coffee slid before him, and he wrapped his hands around the warm barrel.

"Captain, what of the F-15s scramble you mentioned?"

"Wasn't much at all, the F-15s chased them away as if the pilots of those saucers had never seen them before."

The Admiral fingered his chin with thumb and index finger. "According to all the reports, these saucers have speeds approaching 1,000 miles per hour, and they could easily outmaneuver our jets." And then it hit him. "From their perspective they had only seen the conventional P-51s that Byrd took with his task force, not the F-15s. Perhaps they had abandoned the attack, not wanting to tangle with those Sidewinder missiles," he envisioned.

Henri Weismann led the party of new friends to the area he had seen many times when his mind often wondered who he was and what this home beneath the ice really meant. For some reason he had always felt different from the other people here. Perhaps that's the reason he sensed the closeness to Dr. Caruso when he saw him the first time. Oh it was so confusing to him now, the Third Reich a monstrous invention by Hitler and the SS. Yet there was something about these "aliens" who had entered his world that attracted him. He dropped his musing, and pointed.

"Down there is the harbor where our aircraft land. I don't know where they go. I had never seen the outside until you came," he said facing Dr. Caruso.

"Thank you, Henri. I think it best if you guys stay here and keep out of sight. Henri and I will check out this harbor. Tunney, would you come with us?"

Tunney said not a word and stepped out with his knapsack shouldered. He followed directly behind them as they reached a sidewalk that led to the harbor. Downward the sidewalk meandered to several levels. When they reached the lowest level, Henri nodded in a direction over a ways.

"That's the office building where the leaders reside," he whispered.

Robby scanned the area. People were out walking yet they seem indifferent to their presence. He saw the building; it was one of the smaller buildings, only three

floors. He decided then that he would have to investigate, although he had some reservations about endangering the lives of those with him.

They stood deep in a shaft carved out of volcanic rock, an opening to the level of the sea, an embankment of concrete that amounted to a seawall. A smooth runway perhaps only fifty feet long; apparently these discs landed vertically. At the end of the runway was a tall building with large rollup doors; Robby immediately recognized it as an aircraft hangar. The question now was whether or not they should investigate. Tunney snapped several pictures with his Nikon camera.

"Henri, could you lead us down there? I'd like to see those aircraft up close."

He nodded and gestured forward. He led them to the side of the building on an icepack where they would be shielded from the pilots who had rooms in the back. Finally, he pointed to a door.

"That door is the only way in except through the roll up door in the front," he whispered.

Robby gripped the knob, rotating it slowly, and cracked it open. He pressed one eye against the crack: A hallway thirty feet long; two doors, one on either side at each end of the hallway. Robby pressed an ear against the crack—nothing, no noise of any kind, except the low hum of the air conditioning system. He entered the hallway, and motioned only Tunney to follow. Henri waited outside.

Robby cupped his ear at the door, and nodded. They continued slowly down the hallway and stopped at the last door. Again Robby cupped and ear; silence. They reached the end of the hall and he peered through a window in the door. He gently rotated the knob leading to the hangar. His face turned pale in the yellow half-light. With numbed apprehension he realized the size of the flying saucers.

There staged before his eyes were the Haunebu I and Haunebu II, flying saucers 42-feet in diameter. Tunney snapped pictures and Robby studied every detail. There was a central cockpit surrounded by rotating adjustable wing-vanes forming a circle. In level flight the angle would be adjusted to a smaller angle, he reasoned. This was similar to the way helicopter rotors operated, he thought. Robby ceased his musing, his mind rapidly storing information. The synapses stopped on a file in his office, the title clear: The Vril and Thule Societies. So this is where the project disappeared, his thoughts confirmed.

Suddenly a noise emanated from the hallway of the building. Tunney quickly placed his camera in his sack, having completed a series of photos. They crouched behind a large crate. Their eyes could not believe what stepped out of the hallway. Tunney immediate retrieved his camera and snapped one picture after the other. Two tall men dressed in 1933 German flight attire walked casually toward the two discs, each taking his

seat in the flying death machines. Tunney snapped pictures worth a fortune in the present world.

Suddenly the whir of rotating vanes, high pitch sounds rising in the scale unheard by human ears, then almost total silence. The great door hinged up. Two mammoth flying saucers emerged out of the darkness. The Haunebu I rolled out and rose into the night, followed by the Haunebu II. The crude hanger door rolled down and locked.

The two flabbergasted intruders crouched numbly! No one would believe what their eyes had seen. Tunney tapped Caruso's shoulder. "Did I see what I thought I saw?" he whispered. With partisan eye Caruso realized that Tunney was not privy to the Nazis esoteric societies. He made a mental note.

Despite the cool damp air and temperature dropping, Henri led the men back up the sloop near the locale of the three-floor building. The lights in the cavern seemed to have extinguished. Henri explained that sometimes the electricity developed by the magma flow ceased to function for a few hours. Robby turned to Tunney and gestured for a flashlight. He thrust his hand into his knapsack, and handed a halogen battery-powered light to Robby. He and Tunney slowly walked up to the building on a pathway lit by the halogen lamp. The building was built on a jagged slope and the pillars beneath it were several heights. They cautiously ascended the six concrete steps to a porch. Robby peered through the window of the entry door. Again he saw a hallway. But before he opened the door, three tall and blonde men opened hall doors and stepped out into the hallway, heading straight for the porch. Robby turned and gestured to Tunney; both jumped off the pouch and hid beneath the steps. Tunney retrieved the camera from his sack. As the men descended the steps he snapped pictures. Apparently the men were heading for the large building for some kind of meeting.

Robby and Tunney took the opportunity to move up the sloop to where Marty and the others were waiting. When they finally navigated the sloop, Marty reached down his hand and assisted their slippery ascent. Henri informed that the building was the meeting place of the village. Tunney wanted to go over and take pictures. Robby overruled the idea because it was too dangerous, no windows in the building, and they would step right in before everyone. When Tunney replied in defense of his idea that Henri could introduce them, Robby conferred with Henri. Instead, Henri agreed with Robby, and led them to the graveyard where the founders of Neuschwabenland were buried.

Out behind an embankment and down into a flat surface on the packed ice, they approached a small graveyard enclosed with a wrought iron fence. Slowly, unhurriedly Robby walked up to the fence, his mind trying to make sense of all that had transpired this day of enigma. And then his love of history pushed him to the entrance, and he causally, though cautiously kneeled at the first tombstone. The name carved into the limestone seemed washed out and blurred, and he squinted inquisitively. Suddenly his eyes streaked red, his throat raspy as he swallowed dryly.

Emblazed on tombstone were the words, Adolf Hitler!

Despite the shock, his mind rushed back to the historical evidence of Hitler's burned body. Flashing before his eyes a snapshot of events streaked across the retina in a tablet of four years of Hitler's movements from 1933 until he vanished in 1945. The Soviet Union had captured the German Reich Chancellery as well as Hitler's Bunker in Berlin. They confiscated documents from Hitler's headquarters, even much of the staff living in the Bunker, including Hitler's SS adjutant, Otto Günsche and his valet, Heinz Linge. Officers of the Soviet Army may have thought they'd found Hitler's charred remains, only to later discover it was one of Hitler's doubles, Gustav Weller.

He counted six tombstones, as Tunney snapped a picture of Hitler's stone. Curiosity took over his mission, pushing him to the other five tombstones. One bore the name Hans Kammler who was in charge of the V-weapons at Peenemunde, another George Klein, overseer of secret projects for Albert Spear, another Herman Klaas, actually involved with German flying saucer projects, the last tombstone that of George Lusar, who worked in the German Patent office, cognizant of many flying saucer patents.

Tunney completed taking pictures for later analysis, as Robby paused for a moment of reflection. His analytical mind reviewed the evidence, and he came to the conclusion that these were the German leaders who established Neuschwabenland. No doubt they had trained the remaining people, developed the flying saucers, and taught the pilots to fly them. Their sole mission was to establish a new Germany here under the Antarctica ice. There were SS scientists that made this trip; could it have been their decision to clone the survivors—the New Germany?

The submarine Captain shoved his camera into his sack, taken aback by his lack of involvement, and touched Henri's shoulder. "That little building over there, what goes on there?"

Henri nodded, his mind revisiting the birthplace of the people in this carven. "Yes, I will take you there."

Robby sighed. It was going against his better judgment. He considered for a moment, a tantalizing thought of introspection wrestling with a deep feeling of foreboding. Introspection won out. "Okay let's do it," he agreed; every ounce of his being suspicious that it was the laboratory where the clones were fabricated?

The five inquisitors and their guide trudged up the icy sloop to the building. Henri ascended the four concrete steps to the smallish porch, turning to the five men standing behind him, and ended his survey on the face of Dr. Caruso.

"I enter with much chagrin. No one has ever willing explained our existence in this icy cavern or who we are, why we are here," he confessed with a bowed head. Robby touched his shoulder.

"It's a question we all have at one time in our lives. That is why it is so important to have friends that we trust."

Henri placed his hand on Robby's arm. "I trust you, Dr. Caruso."

Robby gulped silently. It was an important responsibility, and suddenly he thought of Bruce and Kawasaki, Captain Woolsey, First Officer Stephen Coates, and Admiral McHenny, yet his eyes were drawn to the sophisticated equipment in the room. Several microscopes were staged along two counters, cages where test animals were kept; his eyes were drawn to one of the cages, his eyes squinted. Lying in the cage was the dead carcasses of two penguins. Robby shook his head in disgust, continuing his observations. Many Petri dishes lay broken, distillation flasks, and metric scales. Over against the wall he was stunned to see a B&L Atomic analyzer. Above the analyzer pinned to the wall was the familiar Periodic Table of atoms with their number of electrons and activity number, ranging from gas to solid. Beyond the B&L unit, stood a rudimentary

Gas Chromatograph—a completely stocked Biogenetic Laboratory.

His attention was directed to Henri who had just opened a door into an antiseptic room, and motioned for him to come. As Robby entered, what he saw reminded him of a funeral home with tools for extracting organs and bottle of chemicals. There were coffin-like units hooked up to heavy electrical wires. And he recognized the genetic charts that were used for—cloning! Somehow the German hierarchy had constructed this ice city from whence to establish the Fourth Reich. And then it occurred to him how dangerous it was investigating the building were neo-Nazism was taught for the rise of a New Germany based on Hitler's passion for an Aryan race. As he turned to Henri he noticed that Tunney was snapping pictures.

"Henri, is it safe to take us to the Officer's quarters?"

He slowly shook his head in retrospect. "I am willing to take you any place in this carven, my dear friend. However, they will arrest you since you are from the outside. I suggest we leave while we have a reasonable chance. Tunney, Marty and the two sailors agreed, and Robby did not disagree. Henri led them back toward the tunnel where the submarine was submerged.

In the warmth of the submarine galley, Tunney sat nursing a hot cup of coffee cuddled in his hands. Caruso slid back the curtain suspended by the overhead lintel; his mind flagged a mental note. He walked over to the large urn and rotated the spigot. Hot coffee filled his ceramic cup. He had seen the confusion in Tunney's face and remembered that same confusion when Admiral McHenny dumped this esoteric information on him. He sat across from Tunney.

"Out there you asked me if you saw what you saw. How much do you know about the German Society for Metaphysics?"

Tunney rubbed his thumb around the rim of his cup. "I don't believe in this esoteric mumbo-jumbo," he replied.

"Well my friend, you saw it in that hanger when those two jumbo flying saucers went airborne."

He bowed his head sulking, and then raised his morose face. "I'm willing to listen, Robby."

Robby leaned back in his chair. "Back in 1921 this metaphysics society was formed with an all-German membership to explore the origins of the Aryan race."

"Wasn't Hitler into this Aryan race stuff?"

"It's the idea of a pure German heritage, a select group called *Ahnenerbe* formed by Hitler. They were studying alternative energy, the Black Sun. Are you familiar with *die Glocke*, the bell-shaped experiment," he asked warily.

"Only that it was reported as being suspended in midair by opposing force fields," he admitted.

"It goes deeper than *die Glocke.* A female group of physic mediums led by Maria Orsitsch highly influenced Hitler and a few SS officers, who claimed to have received communication from Aryan aliens living in *Alpha Tauri*, the *Aldebaran* system."

"You've lost me now."

"Allegedly, these aliens had visited earth and settled in Sumeria."

"This is where these theories get the idea of planetary aliens," Tunney guessed.

"Those who are members of the Vril Society also have this belief," Robby added.

"How so—I'm not familiar with this society?"

"The word Vril was formed from the ancient Sumerian word VRI-11, which means "like god." The Vril Society teaches concentration exercises designed to awaken the forces of Vril. The main goal was to achieve spaceflight to reach *Aldebaran.*

"Now tie this mumbo-jumbo into the Hitler motif, would you."

"Himmler and Goring were involved with the Vril force. In 1922 the joint societies of Vril and Thule influenced the Nazi scientist in advancing the technology with the bell experiment—*die Glocke.*"

"It's still as clear as mud. What is this Thule Society?"

"Occult black arts, the keepers of the Aryan race oracles."

"Satanism."

"In one word, that's not a bad analogy. What you think you saw today was the result of a long project. Using satanic powers, fostered by their occult practices, Nazi scientists constructed Germany's first flying saucer, the JFM (*Jeneits-flugmaschine*) in Munich conducting flight testing. The project was led by the Technical University of Munich under Walther Gerlach, but the project was halted in 1924, with the machine dismantled and shipped to the Messerschmitt Augsburg facility, where it was stored for future research."

"Now it gets clearer."

Robby nodded and faced Tunney with the Ace Card. "This research actually developed levitation—pure antigravity! With Hitler in power in 1933, both Thule and Vril Societies received official state backing for continued flying saucer development programs aimed at spaceflight—*Aldebaran.*"

"And your contention is this technology was transported to *Neuschwabenland.*"

"It's only a theory.

Tunney stood. "After seeing those two giant flying saucers today, I say it's a damn good theory, clarifies a host of mumbo-jumbo," he responded, suddenly laughing.

11

Since the heating system was in repair, the cold ice city of Neuschwabenland somehow seemed uninviting, but Robby sensed the coldness wasn't just the heating system; Henri had been gone a long while, even had warned that he should get back into the city. He worried incessantly that they may be discovered.

Henri explained a turbine somehow harnessed the heat of the volcano and channeled it through ducts over the city. Suddenly, the lights were operative again; the shadows gave the icy blue snow a foreboding appearance. The investigating entourage could see the tunnel now in

the near distance, the water lashing up over the Biber dam. The moaning of the wind echoed from the tunnel like a pipe organ and bounced off the snow pack. Five men were within 200 meters of the tunnel and Henri was out front leading them, his head rotating from side to side. These were his newfound friends and he would not let them down.

"Hurry, we must have been detected by now," he whispered.

The sudden sound of a siren blared over the city, its echo reverberating off the tall buildings in the distance. Several men peeled out of a building and charged toward the tunnel, weapons in hand.

Henri's prediction suddenly came true.

A fire brigade of tall, blonde men stormed down the icepack arming German Lugers and nasty looking automatic weapons with holographic sights. Dr. Caruso directed the group behind a large boulder beside the moat, the wide bridge almost directly behind them. As they positioned themselves, he thought of Admiral Byrd and the men and equipment they had lost during the flying disc attack. Sudden zinging bullets ricocheted off the boulder, grenades splashed into the moat.

Robby yelled, "Fire!"

All hell broke loose!

The retreating group laid down a line of fire that dropped about six or seven of the advancing horde, opposition weapons barking, sparkles of grenades exploding. Robby began to see the number of weapons challenging his meager group, glancing at the active fire from his men. Henri crouched horrified. Marty was a one man army firing two weapons simultaneously; adjusting the odds more evenly.

"Good shooting, Marty."

The two sailors were firing, one gun jammed, and he threw grenades instead. Robby crouched on bended knee, fired and dropped the one nearest. Automatic fire zinged over their heads and splattered into the moat. Tunney fell, hit in the gut. Suddenly rapid fire barked from behind them, and three sailors from the submarine joined with automatic weapons blazing.

It seemed the onslaught had ended when the last German soldier fell. But Robby was busy wrestling the Lieutenant who had led the charge. Robby's firmly muscled body, with broad shoulders and straight back, was reenergized, and he moved with a catlike grace that seemed poised for action. There was razor hardness about him that even a stranger could sense. This tall, blonde German would soon respect his prowess. He moved quickly as a cat and disarmed the German, twisting his arm behind his back.

"Okay buddy, we didn't come here to harm anyone."

"*Wie kommst du hierher ihn Täter?*" he sneered.

Robby turned to Henri for a translation, but Henri was lying on the icepack; he'd been shot! An unrepentant frown crossed Robby's forehead. The scene

maddened him with revenge, and he slugged the German Lieutenant in the jaw. His head snapped back unconscious. Robby dropped him on the icepack and instructed Marty to watch him as he rushed to Henri. He kneeled beside him; he was wounded, but alive.

"So sorry . . . Dr. Caruso," he groaned. "I would like to have seen America . . ."

"Hold on Henri, we'll get you out of here."

Robby turned to Tunney. He was gut-shot. He leaned over him, lifting his motionless torso into his arms. His eyes weakly opened; conscious for a moment, staring up at Robby. "Take care of Coates. He's young—needs your council," he weakly whispered. Then he trembled and his lungs emptied in a final gasp.

Eugene Tunney was dead.

Robby could do nothing more for his friend, and gently laid him on the icepack. This had been a costly project, and he didn't appreciate it. He allowed the unwelcome pain sweep through his body. Deep unconsciousness should have sustained Robby, but a distant alarm from the synapses of his brain instinctively pushed him to his feet. He resolutely walked over to the German soldier who had gained consciousness, his jaw bruised.

"Have you got any idea what the Third Reich did?"

The German's blue eyes glanced at Henri, the traitor who probably didn't know what he did, and faced Robby with a deep sneer. He spoke in perfect English.

"Hermann Goring answered your question in 1938. He said, we will go down in history either as the world's greatest statesman or its worst villains," he smiled.

Robby stared at his grimy face. "Well dumdum, which is it?"

Marty stepped up. "I can answer that question, the worst villains who ever walked on the face of this planet," he said with a smirk, and spat in his face.

Robby spun him around, and ripped off the strap of the German's gun, and tied his hands with it. Finally he tossed the automatic gun into the icy waters. "You are coming back to the real world and see for yourself what the Third Reich has done."

The Nazi airman swelled his large chest with cold air, his blue eyes beaming. "*Nein! Wei ist einen Flieger der Luftwaffe*," he replied in a devious denial. He suddenly turned and leaped into the icy waters, his hands tied behind his back, loudly laughing as he sank beneath the briny deep.

Robby stared into the dark abyss of the churning waters; it seemed ravenous for this body that represented all the anguish and death caused by the Third Reich. Quickly he kneeled down beside Henri and inspected his wounds. He was shot in the upper shoulder, broken rib that may be affecting his breathing. He stood and instructed Marty to fashion a stretcher. Marty stepped off looking for the right materials. Robby removed his scarf; using his knife he split the heavy

insulted jacket off Henri's shoulder. He tied his scarf under the armpit and over the shoulder. He stood and removed his jacket and draped around Henri's shoulders. It was more important that he was kept warm. Robby was still stewing over Tunney's death waiting for Marty's return.

Marty returned with two rifles used by the attacking force. He removed his jacket and fashioned the stretcher, each rifle thrust through a slit-open sleeve. Robber gently stood Henri, and laid him on the makeshift stretcher. The two sailors managed the stretcher. The other sailors who came to their rescue assisted with their Captain's body. They headed over the bridge and toward the submarine. Robby followed, his mind tormented by the cruel events. Tunney would get a seaman's burial, and Henri would be turned over to the pharmacy mate until they boarded the flattop and the physician would attend to him. He was determined to get Henri to America.

Stephen Coates stood on the submarine deck as the group approached, saddened by the sight of Captain Tunney cradled in the arms of one of the sailors. Two other sailors came on deck and assisted their climb up the net-ladder. Coates stood at the Con saluting the Captain out of respect, not tradition. When the last man descended the rear deck hatch, and the steel lid close,

Coates gripped the microphone staged in the conning tower.

"Ease back, and take her down to twenty fathoms," he said, as he hung the mike, and stepped into the hatch hole. He grabbed the rope of the heavy steel cover, pulling it shut, as water doused his shirt. He rotated the locking handle with the other hand. Robby stood in the control room when Coates descended the hatch ladder.

"Care to tell me what happened?" Coates asked, as he stepped to the pedestal, and took the mike. "Bring her up to periscope depth."

Robby squared his feet. "We were discovered as we reached the tunnel. Tunney got it in the gut. His last words concerned you, Stephen."

His forehead wrinkled. "He was a good man, taught me his experience—I owe him."

"He thought highly of you, and you can repay him by being as good a Captain as he. He deserves a sailor's burial," he said, then continued his report. "Henri came forward and gave all the information we needed, even took us around the city at great risk—we owe our lives to him. And I shall see that he gets to America."

Tunney's body was prepared for burial at sea, and Marty and a seaman brought the body to the deck through the rear hatch. It was bandaged like a mummy, proper for burial authorized by the tradition of seamen everywhere. Robby offered a prayer and reviewed briefly the epitaph of his lifetime friend. He had known Tunney the better part of his life. The enigma of death suddenly chilled his body as if a million bees were stinging his skin. Death was merely a separation—they who went before us are still here in our memories, he thought. He sniffed, raised his head in the peaceful moment, staring at those around him.

"Let no one say this boat did not have a helluva Captain," Robby said finalizing his epitaph.

Just as the body slid into the ocean, two flying saucers circled overhead. Out in the distance two more were attacking the aircraft carrier. Captain Woolsey had scrambled the F-15s. Captain Stephen Coates ordered everyone off the deck. He seized the mike, as the rear deck hatch closed.

"Dive, dive!" He glanced around; everyone had descended. He grabbed the rope, closing the Con hatch, and turned lively to the central pedestal rising from the floor of the control room. "Take her down to periscope depth," he ordered.

He placed his eyes into the viewfinder and focused on the flattop on the horizon. Two saucers were diving on the bridge. Surprisingly two F-15s were on their tails. He spun the periscope around and focused on the icepack. The Sherman tank was active, its turret was elevated. Kawasaki was manning the snowplow. He saw a circular shadow displayed on the icepack, a flying

saucer diving on the Sherman. Then smoke and sparks; a shell silently leaving the muzzle of the tank cannon.

He pitched the periscope at the limit of its sky view. Again he saw smoke, a flying saucer wobbling with smoke streaming from the pilot cabin. Bruce had scored a hit and an F-15 pilot was on its trail with Sidewinder missiles. Two Sidewinders roared from the wings of the F-15. One Sidewinder exploded just beneath the saucer, the other missed, and the saucer vibrated, still airborne, and gliding directly toward the icepack. It impacted on the ice thirty meters from the Sherman tank. The snowplow had already repositioned with its blade elevated tracking directly toward the saucer. The blade struck hard and pushed the unit off the icepack into the ocean.

The periscope swung back to the Weddel Sea. The flattop radar had been damaged and she was navigating by instruments. The last flying saucer hovered over its decks, beginning its dive toward the bridge. One F-15, the last of the squadron, set its sights on the saucer. Two Sidewinders leapt from the wings, and the F-15 watched his scope as the missiles soared toward the saucer heat-seeking the exhausts. The UFO exploded: direct hit, debris tumbled into the ocean. The lone F-15 miraculously landed on the damaged flattop deck, exercising expert piloting.

Captain Coates had ordered the submarine submerged to 50 fathoms. The last position of the flying saucer that Kawasaki had pushed off the icepack had been entered into the radar computer. He waited for the radar operator to provide a search pattern.

"Dr. Caruso to the control room," he spoke, and replaced the mike.

Hadley raised his head. "Captain that saucer is lying near the icepack at 40 fathom. We don't have diving equipment for that depth."

"Copy that, Seaman. The flattop has diving equipment," he replied. "Engine room; bring her down to 40 fathom."

"Aye, aye, sir—40 fathom."

Dr. Caruso poked his head in the open hatch. "You called, Captain?"

"Join me for a cup of coffee in my quarters," he grinned.

Robby descended the hatch ladder and as he turned, he saw the cook with a pot of coffee in the narrow hall just ahead of the captain's quarters. The cook entered the chamber and exited prior to Robby's arrival. Robby swung the curtain against the doorframe and entered a tight space. He focused on the coffee pot sitting on the small fold-down table, and scooted up a chair. He poured two cups just as Captain Coates stepped into the office, and closed the curtain behind him. He sat and gripped the cup as Robby slid it over.

"It seems we will need diving equipment in order to salvage that saucer," he said as the snapped the microphone off the wall behind him. He punched a code, and reached for his cup. Robby leaned back in his chair swilling a gulp of black coffee.

"Any report on the damage of the Admiral's flagship?"

"Thought I'd ask if someone ever picks up the phone . . . this is Captain Coates. Is the Admiral available?"

"One moment, Captain, the Admiral is topside inspecting the damage. Captain Woolsey can take your call."

"Put him on," he replied and gazed down at Robby. "Now we may get some information," he advised, and sat his cup on the table. "Yes, Captain, we were inquiring on the damage."

"We lost three F-15s to that reported death ray, the amidships is a mesh, the bridge is intact."

"Casualties?"

"Four sailors—we are fortunate. The deck should be repaired by tomorrow evening—how did the sub fair?"

"We buried Captain Tunney at sea. No other casualties—we, too, were fortunate," he said sighing deeply. "Henri Weismann is alive and going back with us."

"That's something at least. The Admiral will be pleased."

"So are we. Listen Captain, Dr. Caruso needs to raise a flying saucer at the depth of 40 fathom. I understand you have diving equipment."

"That's affirmative. In fact we have the latest thing in Navy deep sea diving. You'll need a crane to lift it to the surface and place it on the flattop. Amidships is being repaired now, the crane is undamaged. Why don't you come over and get this new scuba outfit. While you are attaching cables to it, I'll bring the Carrier over to your location. We can depart for Mayport on the morning tide."

"Copy that!"

12

The submarine coursed over to the icepack after contacting Bruce. As they approached, Captain Coates focused the periscope on the two men dragging the dinghy to the waterline and decided the sub was close enough; only about twenty meters from the icepack.

"Down scope, and surface," he said, glancing at Robby as he closed the arms and the unit slid back into its oiled well.

"It was very considerate of Admiral McHenny giving you a commission after Tunney's death. I think you have a career with the Navy," Robby said.

"I think it's wise to stay in the Navy in these uncertain times. We could be at war any day with that nut in North Korea rattling his nuclear sword."

"What are your plans for the salvage of that flying saucer?" Robby wondered. He had seen the sonar record, and knew it was too deep for snorkeling.

"As a matter of fact we are taking the sub over to the flattop after we pick up Bruce and Kawasaki," he replied.

"I'd like to assist on the removal of the saucer from the deep. I talked with the President last night, and he is quite anxious to speak with Henri. Although he didn't mention the flying saucer, if I don't bring it back there will be hell to pay," he thought aloud.

Coates leaned back, suddenly laughing. "I understand Andrew Evans is a plateful."

"I wouldn't cross him, you'd lose this sub with a demotion in grade," he said smiling.

"I'll get that saucer for you, Dr. Caruso no matter what Evans tells you."

Caruso smiled, yet concealed his doubt that Coates actually knew the deviousness of Andrew Evans.

The rubber dinghy bumped against the steel hull and Bruce leaped out and tied the rope. The rear deck hatch opened as Kawasaki deflated the dinghy. Bruce stuffed the folded rubber unit into the hatch and allowed Kawasaki the first descent down the hatch. As he

descended the ladder, Bruce stopped, his torso exposed, somehow mesmerized by the bright moon hanging in the winter sky. That same moon had been lodged in his youthful mind back when he and Robby were in high school. His mind digressed in a moment of reflection. It was Thanksgiving, much like this harvest moon. Our teacher had read a story that still stuck in my mind. How did it go? *"The wolves howl mournful outside the village, slinking between shadows and the dark shape of the tents. A bitter winter-white moon hangs in the sky and the smoke from dying fires still lingers in the air. A pile of buffalo bones lie to one side, gleaming silver and attracting the ravenous wolves. It is January 16, 1621. In exactly two months to the day, an Indian named Samoset will walk into an encampment at Maine, New England with the words: "Welcome, Englishmen!" They give him a coat and he will trade furs and fish with the pilgrims of the Mayflower. Life for the Indians will never be the same again."*

Suddenly Kawasaki poked his head in the hatch. "What's going on up there, Bruce? The Captain is anxious to leave."

Bruce's mind snapped to reality. Reminiscing that far back could get him killed, he chided himself. "Coming right down—" a sudden huge explosion shook the sub and great white-capped waves rocked it side-to-side. Bruce snapped around gazing toward the tunnel.

The entire mountain was aflame at the top, magma flowing down its rugged sides. Neuschwabenland was buried under millions of tons of rock and ice.

Suddenly he heard the emergency dive horn and a voice from the conning tower scream, "Dive, dive!"

He jumped into the hatch and down the ladder, gripping the rope and pulling the hatch closed. Captain Coates simultaneously closed the conning tower hatch—seawater doused his shirt.

"Take her down to periscope depth," Coates said and the smell of oil filled his nostrils as the scope rose from its well. He spun the scope around, the top of the mountain had blown apart and molten lava was flowing into the ocean, steam rising from the turbulent meeting of hot and cold.

"Dr. Caruso to the control room," said Coates and rotated the scope to the icepack. The explosion had separated the land mass from the volcanic mountain.

Robby stuck his torso in the hatch. "What was that explosion, Captain?"

"Get up here and see."

Robby ascended the ladder and stood, and before he could say anything the Captain rotated the scope. "I think somebody activated a self-destruct button—the mountain is spewing lava, and the icepack is split open."

Robby gripped the periscope handles. The tense moments passed in total silence, minutes before Robby could bring himself to say anything important. He

dropped his gaze, a frown on his forehead, and then replaced his forehead against the eyepiece. The Sherman tank was at that moment rolling into the sea, and the snowplow was dangerously hanging on the edge. His only thought was that the loss of these machines could make the recovery of the saucer more difficult. When at last he did say something, his voice sounded to him like a vague whisper. Why whisper? He thought. "There she goes. The snowplow just slipped into the ocean."

Coates nodded. "Helmsman set your course at five-eight-seven. That should put us dead on the flattop," Coates ordered.

"Aye aye, Captain—five-eight-seven it is."

As they stood in the control room, Robby thought of raising the flying saucer. His best chance was to discuss it with Bruce and Kawasaki. The rescue depended on repair of the flight deck of the flagship.

13

Coates nudged the submarine dangerously close to the hanger deck of the Aircraft Carrier. Bruce and Kawasaki paddled the rubber dinghy the short distance with Robby in the mid seat. Finally they secured it to the Carrier for their trip back within two hours. They had come over at the specific request of Captain Woolsey, and Robby was to report to Admiral McHenny on the current plans.

Captain Woolsey met them on the hanger deck and escorted the three quests to his cabin. The cook had coffee and sandwiches prepared and sitting on the small table when they entered the cabin. As they sat, a Seaman First Class brought in a rather cumbersome

outfit and lay in on the Captain's bunk, and then left as quickly as he came without a word. Bruce's inquisitive eyes scanned the suit, and thought he recognized the pieces of an outfit he had tested for the Navy when was an active Seal.

Captain Woolsey caught his gaze. "Does it look familiar, Bruce?"

"Somehow, it does," he replied, a smile crawling over his surprised face.

"It is the prototype of the Navy's new deep scuba diving unit. I think you had something to do with the first testing. When the scientists at the Naval Surface Warfare Center in Panama City, Florida heard that you and Dr. Caruso were on this mission, they called the Admiral and sent out two of this unit, suggesting you use it and report any changes or improvements you think necessary."

Bruce searched his mind. "In the developing concept we studied the standard diving dress, that is, the hard hat or copper hat or heavy gear developed in the 1800s by the Deane brothers and Augustus Siebe. It was used extensively for deep diving by the Navy, marine salvage, civil engineering, and even pearl divers. If you notice the unit carefully it looks very much like a miniature version, especially the diving helmet, though considerably lightweight. The most significant change is the unique way this prototype conserves helium. Off course it features double tanks for the most cubic foot of

air. This is the modern change from surface supplied air pumped into the helmet. "

Robby smiled. "Bruce, your public follows you."

He returned the smile. "I'm glad they sent the prototype. It's the only way we can dive and recover that flying saucer."

"Ouch; flying saucers," Woolsey quipped. "That reminds me the repairs amidships are complete and Admiral McHenny is anxious to see you, Dr. Caruso."

Bruce donned the Navy's new prototype deep scuba diving helmet with its associated suit complete with integral gloves and the helium contents of the air tanks plumbed to the helmet. The last item was the heavy watertight boots that kept him upright. The genius of the unit was its savings of helium gas so necessary for deep diving. Kawasaki led him to the rear hatch of the submarine, and attached a high-powered battery light to his belt. He handed him a familiar item—his hunting knife in its scabbard. Bruce clipped it around his thigh with its Velcro strap. Robby slapped him on the shoulder and winked. Bruce mounted the ladder, the boots heavy as lead. His mission: Access the situation and determine the salvage criteria.

Captain Coates had positioned the submarine as close as possible to the spot where the flying saucer had been pushed off the icepack. And now it was obvious that half the icepack had floated away in three sections,

joining the floating surface ice. Robby recheck the air gages and cleaned the moisture off the face glass. He looked through the glass and winked again, his way of offering his "smooth sailing" goodbyes. Robby tapped the helmet, and led him to the rope ladder extended off the side of the submarine. He descended the ladder into the briny deep submerged up to his shoulders and waved. He push off the ladder, holding a rope laced through a loop on his belt that kept him attached to the submarine down in the dark waters.

As he descended through the floating ice, he saw jagged projections extending under the icepack like giant stalactites. The open water was darker now than when he had entered. Downward he descended in the creeping darkness in an elevator of bubbles. Then he focused on a round mass contrasting against the silt. The telltale circular object below his feet had to be the flying saucer, exactly on the 40-fathom level as Captain Coates had advised him. His heavy boots finally settled in the bottom silt. He cast the light on the tail section: A swastika. This was indeed the unit, he ascertained. He kicked over to the gun turret mounted on the top, forward of the pilot seat. Suddenly the filtering surface light glittered off the pilot's window. Bruce reposition himself. And then it was clear, a head and eyes; no, a skeleton of the pilot, not aged, but cleanly eaten by tiny creatures of the deep. A bone analysis of this creature would be interesting, he surmised. Not only was this

saucer easily accessible, the Sherman tank was on its side ten meters away, the snowplow ever further sitting upright, its tracks buried in the silt. But fate wasn't playing the game. He discovered no lifting lungs where they should have been on the saucer. Bruce slammed his fist on the saucer casing in frustration. It was useless to look further. He knew that modern large and heavy equipment and machines always had lifting lugs. As smart and inventive as these Germans were, someone had forgotten a very important item. The chill of the water calmed his frustration. Then it struck him: this is a flying machine; anything producing drag would be eliminated from the design. He pressed his gloved hand against his forehead, how stupid, he thought.

Suddenly an ominous shadow coursed over his head. He rocked back and stared up in the blurry darkness. Swimming in the near distance, it was no mistake—a killer whale! Bruce's mind raced back to his training as a Navy Seal: ***There are three examples of marine life in the Antarctic: Seals and krill live in the Southern Ocean. Penguins live on the Ataractic Continent and rely on the ocean for food. The third example is the killer whale. Although there is little known about these ecotypes, the killer whale plays a major role in the Antarctic marine ecosystem.***

This killing machine hailed from the Kodiak waters and swam the Atlantic to the coast of France in search of prey. On his way to the Antarctica he had battled two

sharks and three porpoises. His battle scars made him the King of the Southern Ocean. He was cruel and worthy of his name as a killer whale. He never considered why the humans called him by that name. For centuries his kind had instilled fear in the hearts of mankind. In all their ferociousness they were dubbed wolves of the sea, whale killers, killing demons and fish tigers. They are found in every ocean of the world. Males such as he, reached up to 32 feet and 22,000 pounds, a battering ram of Roman class. They could dive as deep as 1,500 feet and could swim over 30 mph. They were strict carnivores and wonderfully adapted to flesh, caught and ate a wide variety of marine animals. Usually they seldom roamed beyond a relatively small home range. Others, however, traveled greater distances searching for their preferred prey: whales, dolphins and other mammals. This orca was a different breed; while on the long trip to France he had tasted human flesh. The palatable taste was still in his memory.

Bruce gulped and deeply sighed, gripping the safety rope as he followed it up toward the surface, he reluctantly, but approvingly, stopped at prescribed intervals to prevent the bends, resisting nitrogen infusion into his bloodstream. Finally he climbed the net ladder hung off the deck of the submarine. Robby and Kawasaki assisted him onto the deck.

“That was fast work, Bruce,” Robby smiled, removing his helmet.

Bruce sucked in a lungful of open ocean air. "There isn't a lifting lug anywhere on the perimeter of the 24-foot circle," he negatively reported.

Robby massaged his unshaven chin with index finger and thumb. "That's not odd—aerodynamics."

Bruce grinned; Robby knew it, of course, he thought.

"If we can position a large cargo net under her, we could fashion the cables at the top," Bruce envisioned.

"It could work. Maybe the Carrier has one the size we need," Robby surmised.

"Help me get out of this monkey suit," Bruce almost begged.

Kawasaki mused, thinking of the great relationship of Dr. Caruso and Bruce. Perhaps he had an idea that could assist the salvage of that saucer.

Admiral McHenny sat behind the desk in his flagship office on the Aircraft Carrier, when the intercom buzzed. He dropped a pen on the files he was signing and gripped the receiver, pressing it to this ear.

"Yes, Captain."

"Sir, Captain Coates just docked the submarine at the hanger deck. Dr. Caruso would like a meeting STAT."

Send him up—and have the cook send in some refreshments."

"Will do, Sir."

An ensign directed the entourage of Dr. Caruso, Captain Coates, Bruce, and Kawasaki up to the flagship office. The Admiral stood and rounded his desk.

"Well gentlemen there must be some pressing news," he said clamping his teeth a notch tighter on the corncob pipe stem. It was a relic of his days at Annapolis. He had retrieved it from his desk drawer where it lay beside a letter from the President during the entire mission. Only this morning had he taken it out; it calm him in difficult decision matters.

Dr. Caruso sat as did the others. "Quite pressing, Admiral," he replied almost jovial. His eyes took on a thoughtful look. "We have had some difficulty raising that flying saucer," he added, and turned to Bruce. "Why don't you brief the Admiral, Bruce?"

He shuffled in his seat. "I inspected the entire periphery of that saucer and there are no lifting lugs."

"I see, and what do you suggest."

"Cargo lifting net, sir."

"Ingenious. We have several down on the hanger deck," he replied, impressed. "Captain Woolsey tells me he issued you the Navy Prototype Scuba diving unit. Was it useful?"

"Absolutely, sir there is no other way to work in that 40-fathom environment."

Robby leaned forward in his seat. "Sir I don't think we have dealt with the real issue."

"How is that, Dr. Caruso?"

"How is Bruce to get that net under the saucer?"

The chatter related several ideas but reached no viable conclusion. In the height of frustration, Kawasaki placed his fist over his mouth with an audible cough.

"Ah, sir—if I may."

"Speak up Kawasaki, what's on your mind?

"That snowplow is battery powered, sir. She will crank underwater."

Mute faces panned each other with arched eyebrows and goggled-eyed!

Bruce spread a grin. "The snowplow is upright."

Robby stood. "What are we waiting for?"

Woolsey stood in the door and overheard the last of the discussion. "Gentlemen, I think Bruce will need a little assistance in placing that net beneath the saucer."

Kawasaki spoke up again. "I am your man, sir."

"Come with me, Sergeant," Captain Woolsey said, and escorted Kawasaki to the hanger deck and instructed a seaman to provide him with the second Scuba Prototype Diving suit. While the seaman was away, Woolsey located a cargo net of the largest size onboard.

They all met on the hanger deck, discussing brief plans. The rising dawn would be the time for the mission in raising the flying saucer. Woolsey told Bruce where the cargo net was stored, and looked at the somber faces.

"Well, since nothing happens until dawn, why don't you stay for a hot meal?"

No one disagreed.

Dawn, that yawning moment the rotating earth awakens from the previous night, the stars and moon lose their hemispheric brilliance and fade behind the brightness of the sun replaced by God's morning star: sunrise on million horizons. This particular sunrise kissed the anarchic-white with a wondrous array of celestial magic. The icy shadows dancing on a thousand ledges of snow beneath the feet of waddling penguins.

Yet all that brilliance disappeared in the icy waters beneath the surface, only a dim ray of sun piercing the murky darkness. The dark waters beneath the floating ice were deceitfully foreboding, Bruce thought, as he and Kawasaki descended into the deep depths, both dressed in the Prototype Scuba Diving units. The freedom granted the by the helium air from the tanks strapped on their backs was the only compensation for this dive. There was much work ahead before they might signal the flattop to drop its crane cables. Without this helium air, it would not be possible.

The silt bottom loomed ever closer. As their weighted boots touched the bottom, Kawasaki moved over to the snowplow for close inspection of her condition. He gaped in astonishment at the snowplow sitting upright in the silt. Suddenly, he froze in horror

should it not crank. Bruce positioned the cargo net at the base of the flying saucer, and studied the situation, visualizing the operation. Suddenly he heard the whirring, hissing sound of the massive lithium batteries spinning the drive wheels of the delta shaped tracks on either side of the snowplow. The engine had cranked.

Kawasaki sat in the large open cab admiring this beast. She was built for the Navy by a subcontractor, modified with front blades. It featured a four-track, positive-drive system, the only factory integrated drive system of its kind in the world. The two-seat cabin sat high above for visibility. It flowed smoothly with equal-sized, independent oscillating tracks. It had delta-shaped drives an either side with a large drive wheel running the two drive tracks. Delivering more usable power than any oscillating track snowplow, it had the largest lithium batteries ever built in the U.S.A., grouped with six batteries in series.

He pushed the clutch and the tracks nudged forward tracking through the silt. He aimed the steering mechanism toward the flying saucer and lowered the front blade to ground position. He stopped in front of the saucer, checked the position of the blade, and released the clutch. The powerful oscillating tracks eased up and the blade engaged under the lip of the saucer. Kawasaki hit a lever and the sauce tilted up about eight feet. He leaped out and assisted Bruce spreading the net beneath the saucer. They rolled the

remaining half of the net snug up against the saucer in the silt. Kawasaki jumped back in the cabin and lowered the blade, reversed gears and tracked to the opposite side of the saucer. He engaged the blade and raised the saucer up once more. Bruce was already under the saucer unrolling the second half of the net, when suddenly that familiar shadow passed over his head.

He turned.

The killer whale had returned.

He roamed his kingdom not so much in search of prey but as the King of the ocean not only feared but revered and respected. Deep below at 200 feet his tundra-cold eyes spotted a strange movement. His senses told him it was no seal or penguin, its shape completely different from any animal he had hunted. He circled the object.

Bruce screamed, waving his hands, but Kawasaki neither saw nor heard his warning. The whale suddenly rammed its menacing head into the cab opening, twisting, thrashing, its jaws chewing and gnawing the air as Kawasaki glued his body against the opposite side. Orca's powerful, muscular body finally squirmed headlong into the cabin.

A chilling sound of pain and agony reverberated through the waters just as Bruce arrived, his hunting knife poised. He stabbed the 20-foot monster's waggling body three successive times to the hilt, the blade tearing into flesh. It pulled back from the cab, its mouth revengefully open with torn pieces of Kawasaki's diving suit tangling from its teeth. Suddenly two shadows zipped overhead. They were about six feet in length, and then he recognized them as White Whale Dolphins who roamed the cold waters. They thrust their bottle noses into the whale's broad side at 35 mph. The whale recoiled and scurried away with the two dolphins in chase. The killer whale's top speed was 30 mph, and the two more speedy avengers badgered him as they vanished in the deep, dark shadows of Summer Ocean.

Bruce spun to the snowplow cabin. Kawasaki lay on the floor, his left leg mangled. He tried to open the door, but the whale's head had bent the doorframe massively. He kicked to the opposite side and the door thankfully opened. He grabbed Kawasaki under both arms and pulled him out of the cab. He was unconscious and he felt his pulse through the rubberized suit, but could not get a positive check. He cut Kawasaki's safety rope and cut off about six feet for a tourniquet. He tied three loops around the mangled leg just below the knee, and then nestled him in his arms and ascended to the surface by means of his safety rope between his knees. It was imperative that he stop at intervals; the bends would kill Kawasaki if he wasn't already dead.

When Bruce finally popped to the surface beside the submarine, Robby and two seamen were waiting. He reached down and took Kawasaki's limp body under the arms and hoisted him onto the deck. The two sailors quickly took Kawasaki down to the pharmacist. Captain Coates was on the phone up in the conning tower watching the entire scene.

"Woolsey, Kawasaki needs a surgeon pronto, Bruce just surfaced with him; he has a mangled leg."

"We are on the way at this moment. Should arrive is less than an hour. Over and out!"

The pharmacist checked Kawasaki's blood pressure. He needed a transfusion but he had no glucose in stock; hopefully the surgeon would have some when he arrived. He treated the wound with sulfur powder, having nothing else of use. He did have antibiotics and prepared a syringe with a broad-spectrum antibiotic, and injected it in his arm. He placed a blanket over his body and wiped his forehead with and alcohol wipe.

The surgeon from the flagship stepped into the pharmacist's office, his eyes focused directly on the patient. "What's his blood pressure?"

"100 over 60?"

"Quick, let's get a blood type. You check your men for his type. Meanwhile I will investigate my list. Surely we will find his type among this outsized population."

Kawasaki lay on a table, a cannula painfully fixed on his wrist with a sterile line extending from a pouch hanging on a tripod delivering fresh blood into his vein. The Pharmacist had had no difficulty finding the sailor with

AB blood type. A blood pressure device was hooked to the other upper arm with readouts on a computer screen. His left leg was suspended from a rod hanging horizontally over the bed.

The surgeon stood bedside conversing with Bruce. He had just told the surgeon the gruesome story of the killer whale attack. It was a first for him, having never treated wounds by a whale; a shark, yes. His blood pressure was steady now. The wound dressed sufficiently in healing mode.

"The quick thinking of the pharmacists saved your friend's life," the surgeon said. "I have searched my library, and there are no reported cases of a killer whale attack on humans."

Bruce glanced at Robby. "What about that movie starring Richard Harris and Bo Derek, 'Orca, the Killer Whale' gobbling up people one by one?"

"That's Hollywood stuff—Jaws."

"There is always a first to everything, doctor. I saw it happen and I will gladly give you an affidavit."

He sneered scornfully. "Too bad you couldn't have gotten pictures of those dolphins—what do you think the odds are that these two mammals were babies released from SeaWorld back into the wild?"

Robby didn't accept the premise. "That's a long stretch, doctor—perhaps beyond that of a killer whale attack," he said, a hint of sarcasm in his tone.

The pharmacist walked into the room and immediate chatter captured the conversation. Bruce stared into space. “I hope that cargo net doesn’t stretch,” he said, musing in a whisper. Without another thought, he left the ichthyology discussion and headed for the engine room where his diving suit was drying.

He entered the steamy area, and found that a seaman had draped his suit over an insulated heat duct. He donned the warm outfit, quickly passed through a bulkhead door, a man on a mission. He twisted the wheel that sealed the door, turned and entered the rear section of the submarine. Standing beneath the hatch, he cracked the steel cover. Ascending the ladder, he stepped up on deck. Robby poked his head through the hatch.

“Where do you think you are going?”

Bruce steeled. “Somebody had to hook the net and attach it to the crane cable.”

Robby sighed deeply. “Be careful Bruce. Don’t take any unnecessary chances,” he said, and closed the hatch.

Bruce cast his eyes on the flattop, the crane with its long arm positioned out over the side, and a cable extending into the water directly over the coordinates of the saucer. He dangled his legs over the side and slid into the dark waters feet first. No fanfare, no diving partner, only the opportunity to get something done for Kawasaki.

Down into the deep waters of the Southern Ocean where shadows rule the emotions, a certain killer whale lurks for food. Bruce reasoned that a rogue killer was loose, but he was not going to be its dinner. His heavy boots settled in the silt and he leaned forward half swimming, had strutting and finally reached the saucer. He climbed up on the top and gathered one corner of the cargo net and then the next, as he crawled around the metallic surface. With the last corner in his hand he gathered the loops of the four corners. He reached out with one hand and gripped the large hook suspended from the crane. With all his waning strength he snapped the hook through each of the cargo net loops. He breathed a deep sigh and sat on the surface of the saucer to rest.

Suddenly out of the darkness two dolphins darted in with playful chatter; that same dolphins that had saved Kawasaki's life. They had been watching from the distance, and Bruce believed they were now protecting him from that killer whale. As the dolphins swam off into the darkness, Bruce heard the faint whir of the crane motor and witnessed the cargo net pulling tightly at the perimeter of the saucer. The stretching sound lasted for but a few moments and the saucer lifted cleared of the silt, steadily rising upward toward the surface. Bruce gripped his safety rope and pulled himself upward almost in tandem with the saucer. Kawasaki was revenged, thanks to those two dolphins.

14

The task force weighed anchor and steamed out of Weddle Sea into the Summer Ocean heading dead north up the Atlantic, the flying saucer lashed tightly to the flagship deck. Dr. Caruso had recommended the saucer be covered with a tarp, and so she was. Captain Woolsey stood on the bridge conversing with Dr. Caruso. Captain Coates stood in the conning tower of the submarine stationed at a descent distance from the Icebreaker. The aircraft carrier led the task force. Bruce Allison was in the infirmary with Kawasaki undergoing a change of bandages. Henri

Weismann was in the gallery talking recipes with the cook.

The flying saucer weighed heavy on the aircraft carrier with one F-15 remaining from a squad. The task force had suffered many loses, but the mortal prize was Henri Weismann; the metallic prize a flying saucer. There would be doubting skeptics. The press would say this was the President's problem. There would be many skeptics as there where when President Truman had sent a task force to the Antarctica and lost a squad of P-51s and a cruiser. The big mystery was what had happened to Admiral Byrd?

The men of this task force were absolutely ready to head for home. They had achieved their mission at great cost. If the skeptics were smart they would wait for the evidence, and on this trip there was evidence. But would the public receive the truth? According to Admiral McHenny the real truth had not been heard since the 1930s. The government found it necessary to keep the truth about UFOs from the public since the Area 51 incident. What would they say now, when the press had publicized for years that aliens from another planet were piloting the UFOs? Yes, what would they say when Dr. Caruso told them they were flown by German clones?

Deep in the bowels of the aircraft carrier, the Admiral had called a conference. Seated in the

conference room were all the principles of the task force. These included Dr. Caruso, Bruce Allison, Captain Woolsey, and Sergeant Kawasaki, the only attendee that was wounded and lived; he was in a wheelchair. McHenny also had asked Captain Stephen Coates to attend the meeting, after approving his choice for the First Officer to command the con while the captain was away. He had left the agenda open because there must be discussion, and each of these men had something to report. He knew the apparent destruction of Neuschwabenland was heavy on their minds as it was his.

McHenny sat behind his desk, and punched a code on the phone system. "Please have the cook send up refreshments," he requested.

"Yes, Admiral," said a Lieutenant Jr. Grade.

The Admiral laced the fingers of both hands on his desk, and scanned the quests. "We must be prepared for a press conference, should the President decide to call it," he instructed. "The meeting is open for comments."

He was unsure just what might occur and was pleased that the door opened in that impasse, and the cook brought in a platter of finger sandwiches and a large pot of coffee with mugs. He sat them on a side table and left the room. The Admiral stood.

"Gentlemen get your refreshments and we will begin our meeting," he announced, wondering why he had not

opened with refreshments which would had given them all time to exchange ideas and review all that had happened. That was exactly what transpired before his eyes.

Kawasaki's wheelchair was surrounded by Bruce and Captain Coates. Dr. Caruso was conversing with Henri Weismann. Woolsey stood by the sandwich tray, munching on one in his hand and one at his mouth. Admiral McHenny joined Woolsey and poured a cup of coffee.

"Woolsey, what's your take on Weismann?"

He swallowed and poured a cup of coffee. "If Dr. Caruso is right; he will have a painful process of readjustment."

"I expect your assessment is correct. It is fortunate that Weisman has such trust in Dr. Caruso."

"If Weismann does not assimilate in the modern culture, I hesitate to think of the psychosis he will sustain."

He nodded and sipped his coffee. "Dr. Caruso has confided in me that he plans to talk with an anthropologist before seeking medical advice."

The steam rose from Woolsey's cup and was sucked into the AC intake, a never ending duct system. "There is much we could learn about human cloning."

The Admiral sat his cup beside the other empty cups. "This flying saucer is the pride of the mission, and the goal of the President. Our Dr. Caruso has a

monumental task when we dock in Mayport, Florida," he predicted. He stood and walked over to Dr. Caruso who was refilling his coffee cup.

"Well Caruso, I am surprised no one has commented on the destruction of Neuschwabenland—what's your thought?"

He lowered his cup, the steam massaging his thoughts. "I suspect the leader down there beneath the ice decided the secret was out and he had to terminate all evidence."

"You don't think this is the end of this cloning business, I assume?"

"Admiral my files back in Washington are replete with Neo-Nazi groups. And I don't think Neuschwabenland was a secret to them."

Commander Woolsey and Dr. Caruso both stood on the open bridge, the ocean breeze caressing their bronze faces. A dreamy sea has a rhythmic pulse to its wave action unmatched by any other part of nature. It forges its own sounds and kindles its own symphony. Somehow the sighing of the waves is mesmerizing. Out on the evening horizon, the limitless vault of halogen-blue is knitted with silver. The unfathomable drape of the sky, a color of plasma-blue is sewn with puffball white, accented by a tiny flock of seagulls heading home in the distance. A pair of dolphin breaks the water at the sharp bow of the flattop, the sea buzzing with its dormant

strength, gurgling metronomic. Their thoughts were nostalgic.

As the sun rested on the horizon on the second day of the voyage home, the moon was first to show its famous face. What face was she exposing tonight? Was she a Worm Moon so called by the trails that worms leave in the snow; a Dyad moon from the duo of the moon and sun together in the sky; or a Mead moon, the celebration of drinking honey and ale; or a Harvest moon, the medieval autumn, the last sheaf of corn; or a Wort moon, the time of growing healing plants of butterwort and woundwort; or a Sturgeon moon, the time the Indians caught huge fish from the Great Lakes; or was she a Dog's moon, the Roman title of Sirius, the time dogs went man from the heat; and finally was she the celebrated Blue moon, a calendar enigma every two or three years there is a "extra" moon, thirteen instead of twelve, the Saxon word "*belewe*" meaning "false" moon? Who was she tonight, that face smiling in the sky?

She was a Blood moon tonight, so named because she can appear red at certain times, and tonight was one of those times. Darkness increased and chords of moonlight beamed in a halo of iron red. It seemed that little fairies danced on the chords.

But no such peaceful welcome awaited this task force because the media had its spies within the White House. The poison pens of the press had been busy for

months writing cleaver false stories to boost their ratings, the same elites who had broken the story on Admiral Byrd and caused his disappearance. Yet they were up against another Admiral this time; one with guts. And they had crossed swords with Dr. Caruso once before and lost with plummeting ratings.

Across the Potomac in the quaint little city of Rockville, Maryland, a former CIA operative sat in the basement of a Ranch style home on Twinbrook Parkway, embittered and revengeful. He had been fired for perjury in a case brought by the FBI for tampering with evidence and refusing to reveal his sources. His supervisor was the key witness against him, protecting his own complicity. He had gone underground after issuing a contract on the supervisor's life, and was paid handsomely by his sources.

He rotated the tuning dial of his Elton Grundig Satellite 750 Ultimate AM/FM/Aircraft/SSB/Shortwave radio with external tower antenna to a frequent station in Miami. The speaker hummed and buzzed and suddenly came alive with a brawny voice.

"This is Dolphin calling Killer Whale, over."

"This is Killer Whale receiving you five by five, over."

"Where is the prey on the open sea, over?"

"She bears off the Straits of Florida, over and out."

There was nothing unusual about the man slouched in the backseat of a nondescript Chevrolet sedan driving slowly through the streets of Washington. To the uncaring pedestrians scurrying in front of the car at the spotlighted intersections, he might have been a clothing salesman being driven to a night job by his cousin. No one paid attention to the swastika on the license plate.

The driver, a neo-Nazi assigned by the local chapter parked the car outside the History Building of Georgetown University. The occupant in the backseat mused about the soon arrival of a task force from the Antarctica. It was the driver's job to get this passenger safely to an important meeting. The passenger was Wilhelm Kastler, director of *Neuschwabenland.* He was tall and blonde, with blue eyes, born and raised in Ohio yet attended university at Harvard. The driver shut off the engine, stepped out of the car, and opened the door of the backseat. Kastler slid from the seat, pulling his collar up around his neck, and walked over to the front of the building. He took an elevator just inside the door to the second floor. Crossing the hall on the second floor, he wrapped lightly on a certain door. It was unlocked as expected, and he stepped inside, took a seat and waited.

Presently, a professor left his class and entered his room down the hall. He removed his coat, and customarily hung it on the clothes rack behind the door. As he sat down at his desk, he heard the rustle of an

expected visitor in the outer waiting room. The door to the waiting room opened and the visitor stepped in and took a seat across from the desk of Professor Dietrich Shuster, commander of the Neo-Nazi group in the D.C. area. The professor smiled.

"Your arrival is timely. I have finished my last class for today. Yet I suggest we meet in the café just outside the university on the corner of Broad and Westland."

The visitor nodded, "I know the place."

They reached the café and took a booth by the window. While they waited for the waitress, the professor looked across the table at his guest. "I was saddened by the destruction of *Neuschwabenland.* I suspect you have your reasons."

He placed his hand on a thick file sitting on the table. "Our secret has been compromised. We must address a new direction."

"I see. Then you will want to meet with organization leader," he advised, turning his head toward a man who just walked into the café. The professor thought he had seen him somewhere recently. The man took a table across the way. The waitress arrived and took their orders. The professor gazed over again at the table, the profile now presented by the man still perplexing.

"Pardon me, madam, do you recognize that man seated at the table over there," he cleverly pointed.

She turned momentarily. “That’s Andrew Evans, the Chief of Staff to the President—eats here infrequently.”

“Thank you,” he said and faced the man seated opposite him, as the waitress departed with their orders.

“This is you change to satisfy a little of your anger.”

Kastler grinned and rose. He went to a hallway that accessed the restrooms. A door on the same hall had the sign: “Employees Only.” He cracked the door, and eased inside, took a white smock from the rack and slipped it over his coat. He stepped into hall and peered through the glass window of the kitchen door. He saw the waitress take Evan’s order, waited until the order was posted on a rack. He carefully watched the order being prepared and laid on a tray. Someone took the tray and sat it on the ledge of the pickup opening, went back for another order. He carefully sneaked over, took a vial from his coat and dripped six drops in the soup.

Back at the table Professor Shuster wrote a note in his Day Timer. Finally he ripped out the sheet, folded it and handed it to Kastler. “Memorize this address and burn it,” he said. “The master will not be available until the weekend.”

15

The President's chief of staff, a young man in his early thirties with the grandiloquent name of Andrew Evans entered his office and checked in with his secretary; he checked his Rolex with the clock over the secretary's desk: 11:49 AM. The President was due for a Press Conference at 6:00 PM sharp. Evans was medium height, elegantly styled, political science by trade, a graduate of Dartmouth. He had been the campaign manager for President Darcy when as the Chairman of the CIA, sought the office of President. He had also successfully directed his second term. He was amiable, never gullible on the bills of the Congress, and protected the President with a vengeance. Cross him

once and you lost your press pass, cross him twice and you went to the top of the political black list and was barred from the lobby corp.

Suddenly, he felt sick at his stomach, perhaps the chicken soup at the café was tainted, he thought momentarily. His head ached, and the tips of his fingers were blue. He told his secretary to hold his calls; he was going to Georgetown hospital on an appointment. His sweatsoaked face reflected the fear that he may he not be present at the Press Conference. He hurriedly punched his cellphone and left a note to his assistant. His ailing stomach suddenly reminded him that Admiral McHenny was also due to dock at Mayport today.

Evans finally reached the hospital and pulled into the parking lot, reminding himself that it was the only appointment he could get on short notice. He parked and checked his cellphone before he got out, disoriented and unsure he could stand erect. Taking a deep breath that almost resulted in regurgitation; he gripped the car door and stood wobbly. He wasn't going to make it, he felt it, and before he fainted, he punched 911 on his cellphone.

He collapsed beside his car, door open the warning signal loudly buzzing, his cellphone spilled on the pavement.

Deep in the backstreets of Georgetown, D.C., the windows of a rental house reflected a blazing fire roaring

in the fireplace. A grey-haired man with deep-blue eyes sat in a wheelchair watching the flames leaping erratically up the chimney. In his tired condition he was surprised that he actually heard the sound of a deep red ember when it bounced out of the flames and landed on the hearth, glowing ominously. Outside the window, streaks of lightning signaled a threatening thunderstorm as the old man reached for his glass of wine. He swilled a swallow and sat the glass on the table by his chair.

Hans Grübber commander of the National Socialist Movement groaned as if he had a vision of long ago, a night bred in hell, he thought. It was the night that news reached his office that Congress had passed a diabolical Law. It resulted from surges of Neo-Nazism in Germany, France, Russia, England, Canada and the USA. This legislation made it illegal to display symbols of hate including swastikas. Following World War II, Neo-Nazis still believed in Hitler's ideologies and sought to follow many of the same practices as the Nazis Party of Hitler's Germany. Therefore Grübber had formed a movement protected by the Fourth Amendment of the U.S. Constitution. And now his organization had spread into all the continental forty-eight states. He handled his books much as Al Capone in the 1920s but used reputable CPA's and lawyers. Everything was above board and completely legal, except for the cache of weapons he had concealed in a cave on acreage of property he owned in Tennessee.

Grübber, the aging grandson of immigrant parents who migrated to Michigan, was too smart to insist on publically displaying swastikas; although the local chapter did, because the mayor was a member of the chapter. Grübber could peaceably handout literature and hold meetings as long as he didn't show evidence of overthrowing the US government. His bylaws stated that Neo-Nazis desired the unification of all Aryans in North America—just as Christians believed everyone should accept Christ. Nazism believed that only those with Aryan bloodlines should be allowed citizenship. Other goals included the establishment of an educational system that emphasizes physical and moral development, the return of the family farm, strengthening of the family unit, the formation of a debt-free economy, and energy self-sufficiency. His meetings stressed policies that gave leadership only to the white Aryan race. These intriguing goals attracted a group of persecuted indigenous cultures which were flocking to the movement; white supremacists, Ku Klux Klan, African Americans, Jewish unorthodox, and Mafia-type Italians including patriotic Irishmen. And in Grübber's tormented mind he recalled the words of the telegram that his beloved *Neuschwabenland* was greatly damaged.

There came a knock on the door and his servant answered. The visitor was Wilhelm Kastler, director of *Neuschwabenland* who had called last night. Seems he

had just arrived from Antarctica with important news for the national leader of the American Nazi Party.

The servant pushed open the large sliding doors and rolled his master over by the warmth of the fireplace. He placed a blanket over his lap and legs and departed. The visitor strolled by the sofa and sat in a fireside chair opposite the leader. As he sat, the old man turned.

"Your message seemed urgent, Kastler," he said, the warm side of his face turning red. He removed the blanket and rolled back a few feet from the fireplace.

Wilhelm Kastler folded his hands in his lap. "Sir, our secrecy has been blown by Henri Weismann," he said angrily.

He stared into the flames. "Weismann," he whispered. "Is not that the man who had so many questions on the first day of training, and you suggested that the cloning process was flawed?"

He quickly replied. "I felt that using the same genes over and over would produce only males with the same flaw as hemophiliacs."

"Yes, I remember now—seems you were correct," he replied, dropping his gaze. "I have another correction for your consideration."

"You have only to command, mein Fuehrer.

"The American President, he too, has to be eliminated for sending that task force into Antarctica."

"It shall be done," he said, "and what of Weismann, mein Fuehrer?"

Another ember leaped out on the hearth. As he gazed at the dying glow, he suddenly responded. "They both must die."

Kastler finally left his house and Grübber deeply sighed. The collapse of Neuschwabenland would require a new location to train the new Fourth Reich. He had anticipated that this day would come with all his entanglement with the American officials. He had selected a site in Montana and would have his lawyers purchase a sizeable piece of property. The number of new German people produced in the cloning facility had exceeded 3,000 and they would be transferred to the new Montana facility. He reached for the telephone and placed a call to Professor Dietrich Schuster whom he had chosen to teach the recruits in their new facility. As he waited on the call he poured another glass of wine.

Mayport, Florida bustled with naval ships in dry dock and two carriers in port, one due for engine overhaul, the other loaded for its trip to Hawaii on the outgoing tide. Captain Woolsey eased the third aircraft carrier into the harbor with his radio tuned to the tower. He had received instructions to dock at Berth Four, held in reserve for his arrival today on orders from the office of the President of the U.S.A.

Captain Coates stood in the conning tower directing the submarine in a berth by the dock. Once she was

docked, he gripped the mike asked the cook to prepare lunch. He was not ready to speak with the Admiral just yet. He had many thoughts to examine. And then he heard the Admiral's familiar footsteps walking down the dock toward the submarine.

You could tell from his body, slim and a bit emancipated, that McHenny was a fitness fanatic. He was medium height and had a chest that stuck out like a bantam rooster. He often wore a straw hat when he was home, nattily dressed in a short-sleeve shirt. But on the ship he was all business. His attitude revealed his Irish temper. A cigar was usually stuck in his mouth, never lit because he chewed on it because it calmed him on days like this one. He had a meeting with the President this afternoon, and he had not been able to schedule Captain Coates and Dr. Caruso for a debriefing. Even Captain Woolsey's demeanor had changed on this expedition. The charisma of Dr. Caruso was not only mysterious, he even like the man. He had a double Ph.D. in chemistry and oceanography. Not only that, he had the President's ear and was appointed as the assistant to the director of Homeland Security. What was there not to like about the man?

Washington traffic was light on the approaching evening, only because the rush traffic was over. The sun was hidden behind a snow threatening sky. The time was approaching the six hour, and Andrew Evans was in his

bathroom vomiting in the commode. He had taken the prescribed medicine but it had not done much good, and he must get dressed for the President's press conference.

The nauseating feeling in his gut was beginning to return and yet his stomach ached as he stared in the fireplace, the flaming logs seemed to speak to him; was it the medicine or was he paranoiac, both probably true, he stoically thought. Funny, he suddenly remembered that Dr. Caruso had accused of being paranoia. ***The*** **flames began speaking in a vacant tone. And then it dawned on him. Get dressed, you fool!**

16

Reporters from around the world jammed into the pressroom, standing room only. Cellphones were ringing, busy fingers typing on laptops. Television cameras were panning the room, zooming in on the door where the President usually entered, although this President often came from side stage. Suddenly the door opened behind the stage and the people stood when the President walked up to the podium. Applause erupted and the sound was almost unbearable. He placed both hands on the sides of the podium scanning the audience. Before he spoke he opened a bottle of water and took two swallows, bent and placed the bottle on the shelf beneath the podium. He

deeply sighed, holding out his hands for the crowd to sit and silence.

"Ladies and gentlemen," he began. "I have the most astounding news. Most of you are aware that I sent Admiral McHenny to the Antarctica. Last night the task force returned with evidence that the world will find difficult to believe," he said and reached for the bottle of water.

The crowd buzzed with momentary chatter.

"Many of you do not remember World War II, some may recall Adolph Hitler. When the war ended in 1945, Germany had not produced the secret weapons they bragged about. Most of us thought the V-2 rockets were that weapon but President Roosevelt knew differently. But Roosevelt died, and Truman took up the project and sent Admiral Byrd into the Antarctica with a task force under a grant of $340,000 from the Congress. Today we have the evidence that Admiral Byrd failed to produce," he said, and punched a button that lit a large screen hanging from the ceiling at the back of the stage. "Here you see actual photos from the German Federal Achieves."

The silence was unnerving.

The photo onscreen revealed a Nazis crew of three Germans standing on an icepack, a Swastika flag staked in the ice, members of an Antarctic exploration during 1938-1939. Even in 1800 they had mapped the icy shores of the Continent and headed inland. The term

Neuschwabenland **blazed in huge letters across the screen.**

A reporter stood. "Mr. President, are you telling us that Germany had built a city beneath the ice in Antarctica?"

"I am."

A roaring buzz emanated from the crowd, echoing off the walls.

The President gripped the edges of the lectern. "They hauled the equipment using undisclosed submarines much larger than we expected. The German ship ***Schwabenland*** **transferred personnel and supplies on a regular basis between Germany and the South Pole during the late 1930s," the President added as he stepped from behind the podium. "Are you ready for the big surprise?" he asked, almost apologetically. "Gentleman, this is the secret weapon of the Nazis high command."**

He punched a button.

The screen lit with the pictures of the ***Haunebu I*** **and Haunebu II Flying Saucers with an average height soldier standing beside them to indicate the size of these huge UFOs.**

Stunned silence.

The numbed crowd sat silent as the President described unbelievable facts. "In August 1939, the first ***Haunebu*** **took off; it was a flying gyro of 25-meters across with a crew of eight and a speed of 2,982 miles**

per hour. In 1942 the Haunebu II was ready. It was larger, some 32-meters across with nine to twenty crew, and a speed of 4,349 miles per hour."

He paused surveying the silent crowd.

Finally a brave reporter raised his hand. "How is it possible to have that kind of speed in the 1940s?" he asked almost in a hush.

The President nodded. "German technology reached phenomenal levels of ingenuity in the 1920s. According to documents in the SS archives, the *Haunebu III* could reach orbital speed of 24,854 miles per hour, necessary to break the bonds of gravity and reach outer space. A crack team of scientists are busy at this moment attempting to understand the technology."

Andrew Evans stepped to the podium from side stage and whispered in the President's ear, evoking a buzz from the audience.

The President leaned on the podium. "Gentlemen I am told that we have pictures taken in the city under the ice, *Neuschwabenland*," he said, and pushed a button.

For thirty minutes the photos flashed upon the stage without a comment. The entire room was quiet as a church mouse. Finally, the President returned to the podium having been backstage talking with Dr. Caruso.

"Ladies and gentlemen we have a real treat. Dr. Robert Caruso whom you know as the assistant to Homeland Security has just returned from Antarctica

with a man he would like to introduce." He paused and stared over the podium. "I am told to warn you that this gentleman is indeed a clone."

The first chatter in an hour buzzed across the crowd, reporters crossing the aisles vying for a vantage of their cameras. At that disquieting moment a tall, blond man with blue eyes walked from side stage with Dr. Caruso beside him.

Caruso took the mike handed by the President, but said nothing as the crowd settled into their seats. "I am pleased to introduce to you a man that risked his life to reveal all that you have seen on this screen," he announced, turning to his guest with a smile. "Ladies and gentlemen may I present Henri Weismann."

Cameras zoomed in with their covered hoods, keys on cellphones were rapidly punched, and laptops were busy typing. A female reporter stood in the hum of electronic instruments.

"Mr. Weismann, as a member of the press corps, let me welcome you to America. I hesitate to ask anything that might embarrass you. Dr. Caruso, might you do that honor?"

A roar of approving applause pierced the guarded silence as everyone in the crowded room stood in agreement.

Caruso turned to Henri with a smile. "As you might know the Third Reich wanted to survive the war. This is why they built the city under the ice in Antarctica.

Henri somehow understood that Hitler's dream was evil. We are fortunate that he decided to do something about it. You must also understand that the neo-Nazis movement will do everything in their power to eliminate Henri." He turned and shook Henri's hand. "My friend, in this land we have laws that protect the innocent. We shall protect you, Henri."

Again the standing audience applauded.

The President stepped back to the podium. "There you have it, eye-witness evidence. It is up to you my friends of the media to tell the true story. We must rid this country of the evil that has been allowed to spread from shore to shore. We shall do it together as a free nation."

The reporters went wild with applause. Television cameras zoomed in on the smiling face of Henri Weismann, tears streaming down cheeks.

Had America and the world accepted the idea of a city beneath the ice staffed with clones?

Deep in the dark corners of the city of Washington, D.C. a man sat on his sofa watching the Press Conference from the White House on his television. Anger rose into his throat; acid dyspepsia boiled within his esophagus. Rage pushed his hand toward the glass of Vodka sitting on the table before him. He seized it, nervously touched the rim to his chapped lips, and swilled the glass dry, escaping droplets rolling down his unshaven chin.

Throbbing pain pounding in his head, active diarrhea churning in his gut screamed for release. With his last ounce of strength he hurled the glass into the screen of the television. The black screen imploded, smoke rose with a pungent smell that plugged his nostrils. Wilhelm Kastler stood. Visions formed in his mind, the vision of the moment he had activated the destruction of his beloved *Neuschwabenland.* And now it was time to execute the biding of *die Fuehrer.* Suddenly a patronizing grin crossed his tormented face; the word "execute," how appropriate, he thought.

He immediately left the room with his cellphone pressed to an ear, as he opened the door to his garage. He said a few words, closed the cellphone, and sat in the driver's seat of his car for a moment as he thought of the instructions he had just given the man on the phone. Finally, he pushed a button behind the sun visor, and the garage door opened. He pushed a button on the dash. The engine cranked, the powerful sound of pounding pistons gave him renewed courage.

The Cadillac backed out of the garage into the wet streets of melting snow, as the garage door closed automatically, water dripping from the synthetic rubber lip of the door. He activated the headlights when the setting sun suddenly dropped below the horizon, casting the road into a tunnel of darkness. Kastler set his course for a restaurant some five miles away where he had scheduled a meeting with a professional killer. As

he drove, he thought not of the meeting but of the meeting place. It was one of the first Gothic buildings built in the DC district, and he loved the atmosphere, dark with low light, and a pianist playing soft classical music. Suddenly he burped, the rumbling in his stomach had returned—too much western food, he reasoned.

The ghostly silver of the full moon broke through the clouds signally the storm had passed, but in his mind he envisioned a different kind of storm: assassination. He set his mind for what he had to do, yet the stars even thou dimed by the ghastly moon light were twinkling so brilliantly it was unnervingly eerie. The restaurant appeared in the streetlights and he forgot the beauty of the night sky and his nauseous stomach.

The exterior of the three-story stone restaurant was cold and morbid, like a setting in an Emily Brontë novel. He pulled into the parking lot and again admired the architecture as he silenced the engine. This ancient building was remodeled into a restaurant some ten years. He remembered the place because he had eaten there many evenings while he visited the old master, Hans Grübber.

Sitting at a table in the corner near a window sat a man who looked and acted like the archetype James Bond. The white cuff links glittered from the white sleeves of his black suit, his hair trimmed and slicked back with an immaculately creased left-hand part, a ramrod spine and precise correctness in speech and mannerisms. He was the classic assassin debonair.

"Sit, won't you Mr. Kastler?" greeted Sean Casey as he brought a champagne glass to his lips.

Kastler nodded as he pulled back a chair and sat. This was the man he had called to assassinate the President. He had been used by the master and came with his recommendation. Kastler sat; his demeanor calmed by the melodic sounds of Rachmaninoff's concerto floating over the room. A waitress approached the table, and he ordered a glass of milk. Casey grinned but said nothing, covering his mouth with the back of his hand. As the waitress left, Kastler casually straightened his tie and caught the smile on Casey's face.

"What's so funny?"

Casey glanced down, dropped his smile. "Nothing, just wondered why a man in your position comes to a place like this and orders milk," he said, suddenly laughing.

The pert young woman playing the piano leaned over glaring at the commotion, a frown on her face. She had seen the nerd before, but not the debonair young man. Her frown shifted to a smile.

Kastler stirred embarrassingly. "If your stomach was as queasy as mine, you'd understand," he barked.

The milk arrived, and the pianist waltzed over to the table, winked at Casey. "Pardon me gentlemen. Do you have a request?"

Kastler smiled, taking a swallow of milk. He wiped his "white" mustache with a clothe napkin. "Beethoven's Fifth would be nice."

She flashed her blue eyes at Casey. "What about you handsome?"

He dropped his gaze. "Do you know *I don't get around much anymore*?"

She caught his pun and cocked her head. "Beethoven it is sweetie."

Kastler shot a pointed stare at Casey. "You are a sourpuss," he replied dourly. "That girl wanted a date."

Casey returned the stare. "I don't date when I'm on a case," he snarled.

Kastler sat the half-empty glass on the table. "In that case, let's get down to business," he said, his ears collecting the staccato measures of Beethoven's Fifth. He took a deep breath, his stomach fit, and pulled a manila envelope from his inside coat pocket, and slid the envelope across the table. "This is satisfactory, I trust."

The debonair suavely opened the envelope and thumbed three $10,000 dollar bills. His dark brown eyes beamed. "This is but half the agreed amount," he replied with cultivated finesse.

Kastler's countenance exhibited the tactfulness of a poker face. "You will get the other half after you complete the task," he replied with the grace of a diplomat.

The black-suited man stood in the sizeable frame of six-two, deep tan, piercing brown eyes with his usual elegance. A guarded smile creased his five o'clock shadow, as his mind reminded him that the purpose of diplomacy was to prolong a crisis. Unless he received the balance of the payment, this crisis would be prolonged.

17

Washington City was the victim of a hazardous storm that had surged across the northeastern states bringing colder temperatures with the threat of unprecedented snow. Thunderstorms had flayed the trees, lashing the landscape with debris and had nearly flooded the Potomac. Raising winds buffeted the land and some alert person reported that the tall obelisk was swaying and required the Washington monument tied to the ground with metal cables and large iron stakes. The cherry trees leaned horizontal under the battering gusts of the windstorm.

There was a haunting feeling of helplessness, almost fear in Roger Dobie's mind as he worked late into the night, sifting through a stack of military documents for the chief of staff. The subject was Admiral Byrd and he had been in the archives all day, when this terrific storm had arisen. He decided he would at least keep searching until the storm subsided. He had just laid open a document file labeled *Phoenix,* declassified last October. Attached to the document was a handwritten note signed by the Chief of Staff for President Theodore Roosevelt just before he died in 1945. The note was explosive, a smoking gun for Andrew Evans. He unstapled the note, walked over to a copy machine and made a copy. He re-stapled the original back to the document and filed it in one of the rows of cabinets against the wall. He folded the note and stuck it in his wallet. As he walked to the hall door, he switched off the lights, and stepped into a hall dark as death. It seemed that the storm had deactivated a breaker in one of the electrical boxes. He was not qualified to search for the problem and made his way along the wall toward the door to the outside located some distance down the hall. As Dobie crossed over to the opposite side of the hall, he instantly felt something crash on his head. He collapsed on the floor unconscious, his thoughts lost in a dark abyss, and then there was nothing.

A man dressed in kaki coveralls stooped and viciously sliced Dobie's throat with a Bowie-styled knife.

The assassin let the body lay and lit a tiny flashlight, making his way back to the room were the file cabinets were staged. These were classified files and he had cleverly jammed the locking bolt preventing engagement when the door was closed. He easily pushed open the door and cast the beam on the row of file cabinets. He opened a selected drawer ran his fingers down a row of files. He stopped on a blue-labeled file, *White House Renovation, 1949.* He opened the file and his dark brown eyes gleamed at the architectural layout of exact dimensions and scale drawings. A color photo of Harry S. Truman sitting at his desk with the sign: *The Buck Stops Here* creased a smile on his face. Ole Harry knew exactly what he had to do, and that was the essence of his mission to assassinate the President. Now he had what he needed. The hours when the President left his home and went to the Oval Office, the dimensions of his office, and the hours of the secretary, including the chief of staff. The remaining information he would receive tonight when he watched the White House police movements. He unzipped his coveralls exposing a black tuxedo and shoved the file against his chest, then closed the zipper.

Andrew Evans sat in his office reading a report when his secretary buzzed the intercom. "Mr. Evans there is a police officer out here who says a murder has been committed in the North Entrance Hall," she gulped, her

face white as the snow now falling in the Washington area.

"I'll be right out," he gasped, annoyingly, and raced to the door.

Standing by the secretary's desk stood a police officer he quickly recognized assigned to the staff of the Secret Service. Harry O'Reilly was an Irish man who had been a guard in the Congress when President Darcy was with the CIA. He was a plump, balding character with a genial freckled face and rusty red hair.

"What's this about a murder, Harry?" Evans hurriedly asked.

"I think the victim is one of your staff, sir—would you follow me?" advised Sergeant O'Reilly peering over his Ben Franklin spectacles.

Andrew turned to his secretary. "Tammy would you phone Dr. Caruso? Ask him to check in with me?"

"Yes sir," she replied and punched several codes, as Andrew walked out of the door behind the sergeant.

O'Reilly and Andrew stepped into an elevator and the sergeant pushed a silver icon. Andrew's roving eyes focused on an obvious smudge on O'Reilly's sleeve. His eyes squinted. It was blood.

O'Reilly caught his glance. "The body had a slit throat; guess I got too close."

"Good heavens!" Andrew exclaimed.

They stepped out of the elevator and walked to the entrance of the North Hall. Standing near the corner

were two officers, one a lieutenant, the other a captain. Lying on the floor was a body covered by a blanket.

Andrew stooped and pealed back the blanket from the head of the victim. His face frowned in revulsion. "Why it's Roger Dobie! He was doing some research for me!" Andrew gravely exclaimed.

The lieutenant called the captain over to the door of an office. "Sir this door has been jammed open."

"Have you dusted for fingerprints?" he asked.

"Someone from the FBI lab is due any minute," he replied.

"Let me know the moment he arrives," he said, and turned into the dark shadow of someone outside the door toting a large case by its handle.

The door swung open and a young woman stepped into the hallway, to the great surprise of the lieutenant; he had surmised the promised agent was a man, pleasantly glad it wasn't. She was dressed in light tan slacks with a beige blouse fashioned with a plunging neckline. Her hair was pulled into a ponytail, her face accented by wide bream glasses. The heels of her shoes echoed down the hall as she strolled toward the people standing around a body. She sat her case on the floor looking into the deep brown eyes of the startled lieutenant. "Agent Stanley—FBI lab."

Andrew Evans sat at his desk swiftly answering two phone calls and adroitly shuffling papers from one bin to

another. The intercom buzzed as he had just begun writing a letter to Roger's wife. "Yes Tammy," he answered, dropping the pen.

"Dr. Caruso is here."

"Send him in."

The door opened and Andrew met Dr. Caruso with his hand extended. "Thanks for coming on such a short notice, Robby," he said in an aggressive handshake.

"No problem, I was in the area; what's on your mind, Andrew?"

Without an answer he turned and rounded his desk, facing Dr. Caruso. "Before we begin, may I get you something?"

"Black coffee would be nice," he said, sensing the troubled countenance of Andrew's face, but held his questions.

Andrew leaned forward and punched a code on his intercom. "Tammy would bring a pot of coffee into my office?" he said, and fingered a file lying on his desk.

"Right away, sir," the tiny speaker echoed.

Andrew leaned back in his chair, facing Robby. "Do you remember the Phoenix case, specifically that man who was his assassin?" he asked as he opened the file on his desk and pulled out the fingerprint file that had earlier arrived from the FBI lab.

Robby's mind raced back three years. "Sean Casey, the debonair," he said gazing at the open file. He stood and took the page handed by Andrew containing the

fingerprints. Printed beneath a thumbprint was the name: Sean Casey.

"He has struck again," Andrew said.

Robby sat, a memory struggling in his mind, the killer of his first partner, the months he had searched for Casey's whereabouts, the trust fund he had set up for his partner's family. Now the wound was opened again, the scar irritated; but this time he would not rest until Casey was brought to justice.

Robby walked through the large north entrance hall, the Oval Blue Room in view and stopped at a desk. Judy, the President's personal secretary spread a smile. "The President is expecting you, Dr. Caruso." She punched a code on her intercom. "Dr. Caruso is here, Mr. President."

A tiny voice spoke from the speaker of the intercom. "Send him in, Judy."

Winston Darcy sat behind his desk, his mind focused on a murder committed right in the West Wing of the White House. He had asked for Robby because Andrew called and updated him on the murder case. The Oval Office door cracked open and Robby stepped inside.

"You called, Mr. President?"

"Yes, thank your Robby. Please sit down."

Robby had never seen the President so depressed. Of all the years he had been associated with this President, now in his second term, he had been strong as a

mountain on political issues, meek as a lamb with his associates. However, the years of his service with the CIA made him hard as nails when the country was in danger. He wondered if the reappearance of Sean Casey was at fault.

Darcy fumbled momentarily with the corner of a document on his desk. "I assume Andrew informed you of the events of last night?

"Yes, Mr. President."

"I had hoped that the Phoenix case was closed," said the President lethargically.

He rose and began pacing. "Andrew informs me there was a note in Dobie's wallet."

"Yes, the FBI has it in their possession," Robby smiled, "apparently Dobie made a copy before he shredded the original."

"What do you make of the message?"

"It adds credibility to Admiral Byrd's news conference," Robby answered without elaboration.

"I see," he replied, and moved to the tall windows and gazed across the winter snow covering the White House lawn, saying nothing more, struggling with his thoughts. Finally he turned and stared directly at Robby. "Who else knows about Sean Casey besides you?"

"Bruce Allison."

“Let’s keep it to ourselves. You and Bruce can follow up on this assassin. No need to reopen this Phoenix case for a media nightmare.”

Winston Darcy sat and gazed across his French Empire desk at his appointee. “And you, Robby. What’s your perspective?”

Robby respectfully stood. “I’m a chemist, Mr. President. I steer clear of political involvement unless you tell me otherwise.”

Darcy smiled. The day this man came under his attention, there was something about him that stuck in his mind. And now he understood. Robby was a pragmatic man, not a politician. And he believed that his attitude was the exact reason he was so effective at his job.

18

The President stroked to the opposite side of the White House swimming pool and casually pulled himself up the ladder, water streaming down his strong body. No sooner had he had strolled to his chair and picked up his towel, Admiral McHenny and Captain Woolsey came through the hall door, followed by two guards.

"I hope this meeting doesn't upset your schedules," said the President, wiping his wet torso.

"Not at all, Mr. President. The matter seems worth our discussion," replied the Admiral.

Woolsey peered around the indoor pool room and up at the translucent cover. "I understand the last President who used this pool was Jack Kennedy."

"That's right, would you gentlemen care for cold lemonade?" he cordially asked, his peripheral vision revealing an aide bringing a pitcher and glasses. He sat the tray on a table under an overhead enclosure.

They settled in chairs around the table, and the aide poured three glasses, bowed and excused himself. The President draped the towel over his bare shoulders, and reached for a glass. He swilled a long swallow and sat the glass on the table. "I've called this meeting to discuss a suggestion made by Henri Weismann."

The Admiral sat his half-empty glass on the table, and swiped the back of his hand across his lips. "Henri is a wealth of information; the photos are priceless," he replied.

Woolsey took his glass in hand. "Cloning a new generation of Nazis to further Hitler's madness still mystifies me," he added.

The President sat his empty glass on the table. "You have informed me that *Neuschwabenland* was destroyed in an explosion," he said, and let the statement stir in their minds for a moment. "However, Dr. Caruso assures me this document reveals another entrance," he said laying a typewritten document on the table.

Two sets of goggling eyes focused on the swastika blazed under the title.

"What exactly is this document," Admiral McHenny inquired?

The President fanned a few pages. "It is a German to English translation of a document owned by Henri Weismann. When Dr. Caruso presented it to me I had it translated into English. Weismann has the original," he said, and tossed a second translated copy on the table.

A period of guarded silence pursued as the two men read the document. Finally the Admiral laid his copy on the table. "Mr. President, this document alone is worth a fortune in technical information!" he exclaimed.

The President smiled. "I quite agree."

Captain Woolsey closed the document on his index finger. "This term, *Ahnenerbe* is German for "Ancestral Heritage."

"Good observation, Captain. Hitler himself established the group. Heinrich Himmler was the apparent power behind the throne within the organization," the President clarified.

Woolsey pursued the opening. "Suffice it to say this group discovered a variety of unusual weapons and power sources that eventually enabled the creation of flying saucers."

Woolsey's words blew over Admiral McHenny's head. He sat blank, unbelieving what it implied. "What will

the Washington press corps print if you say cloned Germans are flying UFOs, Mr. President?"

"Strictly off the record," the President laughed. "What say we have another glass of lemonade?"

The President removed the glass from his lips and looked at his two guests. "Gentlemen, the alleged time span of the *Neuschwabenland* German base is coincident with the "golden age" of UFO sightings, the Roswell crash, and the Washington denial of the 1950s."

The two guests were mute for the proverbial moment. The Admiral leaned back in his chair, crossed his leg. "Mr. President, that statement is political dynamite."

"Be that as it may, the truth has been masked in the decades of lies—its release will clear the air. The public must know the truth. You and I know the truth has not been told since the 1930s."

This fact stopped the questions. The discussion centered on Hitler's obsession with the occult and the advance of German technology. The Admiral realized that this was a rabbit hole and brought the discussion back on target, and asked the pertinent question. "Where is this alternative entrance, Mr. President?"

The President seemed diplomatically thankful for the Admiral's prowess, and poured a third glass of lemonade. "To answer that question I have asked Dr. Caruso to attend this meeting," the President said, gazing at his wristwatch.

They each continued reading the document and finally Dr. Caruso appeared through the door beneath the undercover beyond the pool.

"Sorry, Mr. President if I am a little late," said Dr. Caruso, a briefcase suspended in one hand.

"You are right on time, Robby. We have already discussed Henri Weismann's document."

"Good," he said and sat at the table. Captain Woolsey poured him a glass of lemonade.

The President sat his glass on the table, a thought calculating its viability in his mind. "The question is the alternate entrance to *Neuschwabenland*," he began. "Is the city totally destroyed?"

Robby swilled a swallow of lemonade. "The alternate entrance is through the landing base tunnel used by the returning flying saucers. The answer to your second question is "a guarded no," the city should not be totally destroyed, only the utilities when the volcano blew. Walls will have collapsed, but basically certain buildings will be enterable. Granted, it is doubtful that anyone survived the toxic gases released in the city," Robby elucidated.

The Admiral leaned back in his chair. "Then that explosion and flowing lava we saw was only the volcano erupting," he surmised.

"There may have been some type of nitroglycerine device initiated—that's plausible," Caruso replied.

The President leaned back in his chair. "Well Admiral is your crew ready to mount another trip to Antarctica?"

He slid back his chair, his confusion shelved in his mind. "Only if I pick that crew, Mr. President."

"Most assuredly," the President beamed.

"Very well. I chose Captain Woolsey, Captain Coates, Dr. Caruso, and Bruce Allison," he said.

Caruso stood. "Good choice, Admiral. I notice you didn't mention Sergeant Kawasaki."

The Admiral stood. "I visited Kawasaki in the hospital. When I told him we might head back to the Antarctica, the Sergeant bowed his head and admitted he could not go."

Caruso smiled. "That's good enough for me. But may I request that Bruce remain stateside with Henri Weismann."

The Admiral nodded affirmatively, "I should have realized the situation—thank you Robby, of course Bruce stays stateside."

The President stood. "Well gentlemen I wish you smooth sailing," he said and faced McHenny, "Admiral, Andrew Evans will give your sailing orders." He paused, and reseated. "Dr. Caruso would you mind a few minutes of your time."

"Certainly, Mr. President," he replied and turned to the others. "I'll meet you for dinner tonight."

"Have a seat, Robby," Darcy advised and opened a file on his desk. "What proof can you provide on this scientific question of antigravity?" he asked point blank.

Robby crossed his leg and inhaled a deep breath. "Well every modern scientist will tell you that antigravity is impossible. German technology previous to World War II threw a monkey wrench into that paradigm. The code word is Magnetic Wave. Nicola Tesla did the basic research and spoke of a powerful death beam that generated interest in the FBI and the Soviets. When Tesla died, the papers on the death ray disappeared and other papers on magnetic waves."

Darcy interrupted. "Is this Canton-Einstein theory accepted today?"

"Yes sir, it is mainstream quantum physics. However, Canton experienced very weak propulsion with the quantum theory. The experiments with gyros have demonstrated that the anti-gravitational effect is much larger than realized—by several orders of magnitude. And the discovery of the separation of magnetic fields on the semiconductors makes the magnitude even greater."

"Can you give any clarification to this so-called death ray?"

"One word: soliton."

"Explain."

“That’s a bit difficult. A soliton is like electricity; one cannot define it but only describe what it does. It is a permanent electromagnetic, localized in its own medium, and can interact with other elements without changing by collision. You recall that the power of the hydrogen bomb was the result of splitting the atom. A soliton exhibits great power without changing form. If its medium is a laser beam, you can understand its possibilities.”

“That kind of mathematics is beyond me,” he admitted.

“Not many mathematicians understand it either, Mr. President.”

“Then elaborate if you may, Robby. How are we to understand this soliton?”

“We have in our possession a German flying saucer. In the retrofit project that question would be a good dissertation for a doctrinal candidate.”

The President stood. “Thank you, Robby. We shall talk again after your dinner meeting.”

The President had called a meeting in his Oval Office following the dinner hour. Dr. Caruso had been especially invited by the President. The President’s secretary had prepared a pot of coffee and finger sandwiches, and then was allowed to leave for the night. Andrew Evans sat in his office, not willing to leave the President alone at this late hour. Dr. Caruso turned the

corner of the hallway and strolled past Evan's door suddenly retraced his steps.

"Keeping late hours, Andrew?" he said quietly laughing.

"Step inside for a moment, Robby," he replied.

Caruso sat in a chair beside Andrew's desk. "What's on your mind?"

"This story about a death ray, the President disclose to me this afternoon. You can't believe that stuff," he blurted.

Robby shuffled in his chair. "How much do you know about Nikola Tesla?"

His forehead wrinkled. "Only that he invented the electric motor," he replied.

"What would you say if I told you he also invented the death ray?"

Andrew gulped.

President Darcy stepped from the Oval Office, two armed guards standing by his office door. "What's all this noise out here," he bellowed.

Andrew walked from his office door. "Dr. Caruso is here, Mr. President."

"Send him in," he replied, and stared directly at his chief of staff. "Andrew, go home!" he said.

Caruso looked into Andrew's worried face. "Between you and me those two guards and the Secret Service should be able to protect the President. Go home Andrew," he also advised.

Andrew shook his head, and walked past the two guards strolling to the parking lot. Caruso approached the Oval Office, smiled at the guards, and opened the door.

The President sat behind his desk drinking a cup of coffee. "Come in Robby, pour yourself a cup."

Robby gripped the handle of the pot and poured a cup, turned, and sat in the chair placed before the President's desk.

Winston Darcy opened a file lying on his desk. "I have here a report from the FBI concerning the days that Tesla worked for Thomas Edison," he said for openers.

"Does that report say anything about what happened to the personal boxes of Tesla when he died?" Robby quickly returned.

"The FBI seized them in 1943 under the Office of the Alien Property law. The outcry of the public was the fact that Tesla was an American citizen. This became the reason for so much suspicion of Tesla's death."

"We know that Tesla's 80 trunks are now found in the Nikola Tesla Museum in Belgrade."

"Not many people know that these items were shipped to Belgrade in 1952 under the pressure of Tesla's nephew. However, the government did not want to have Tesla's death ray invention available on the open market."

Robby stretched his legs. "Then that's why the government stopped the history books from mentioning Tesla's work."

"Hell, Tesla didn't receive the credit he deserved for the radio and telegraph and many of Edison's inventions."

Caruso shook his head. "The world is unfair today, Mr. President."

Darcy sipped his coffee. "Can we say the Germans got the death ray from Tesla's notes?"

"Excuse me, Mr. President; we don't have that proof yet."

He sat his coffee on his desk. "Well, Robby let that be your mission."

Over in Georgetown darkness had cloaked the city, pools of dark light hung from the ancestral trees. The only illumination came from the glow of the city across the Potomac. The early evening breeze blew steadily out of the northwest, the Potomac waters cold-blue from the approaching winter. The chilling wind seemed stuffed with tiny needles that jabbed exposed skin into numbness. The temperature had dropped to three degrees Celsius. The only light came from the headlamps of a black sedan heading to Constitution Avenues.

Night had settled over the White House, the eerie, blood-red moon of approaching autumn lit the browning lawn in sienna colors. Guards were at their posts.

Somewhere in the shadows stood a tall man dressed in black body-hugging skins with a black hood. A holstered Beretta was strapped to his right calf, a sheathed Bowie-style knife strapped to his left calf, and a small pack shouldered on his back. Sean Casey had been meticulous in selecting the means and place of killing the President of the U.S. Every drawback, however remote, had met his precise standards. The numbers of guards were in their assigned positions, the times of breaks, even the weather conditions were just as he had anticipated. Many long hours were spent in practice sessions. He was ready to collect the remaining $30,000. He had already purchased airfare tickets to Hawaii.

The steady hum of heat-pump compressors within the buildings concealed the sound of a grappling hook snagging the edge of a concrete wall at the roofline; Casey climbed the rope and crouched on the flat tarred-rock roof. He moved stealthily to the opposite edge of the building. Once again his keen eyes measured the distance of the open space to the adjacent building, as he had done with laser instruments in the practice sessions. With great confidence he leaped over the ten foot space with the dexterity of a cat. Fully extended he landed feet-and-hands on the slope of an obtusely gabled roof. He then crawled to the peak and down the opposite side where his ferreting eyes spotted the skylight that he had surveyed during the week.

He stepped to the edge of the glass fixture, crouched and inspected the area below and around him. Usually two guards were on the roof but they were not there after 1800 hours. He removed his shouldered pack and retrieved a glass-cutter. He secured a string to the glass with tape and scribed a two-foot circle. His black gloved hand tapped the glass, and it snapped along the circular scored edge. He gently lifted the circle with the string and laid it in a groove at the base of the fixture. He took a nylon rope from the pack and staked it to the roof beside the fixture, and lowered his body through the hole. Landing quietly on the floor with the prowess of a cat, he sneaked to the corner of the large North Entrance Hall, focusing on the positions of guards. One was standing twenty meters away by the entrance to the State Dining Hall; another was seated at a desk in the distant hallway that led to the current Lincoln Bedroom used by Lincoln as an office and cabinet room, redecorated by Truman into the Lincoln Bedroom. He made his way to the entry of the Oval Office.

A guard was standing at the entry to the open area where the Secretarial desk was staged; his keen eyes caught the movement of the shadow, but seemed to disregard it, rather didn't register in his mind, dismissed as the movement of the areca palms in the air conditioning.

The man in black crouched and crawled against the wall up to the secretary's desk and removed his pack.

He retrieved a bomb with timer, and crawled to the Oval Office door. The door was locked. He retrieved a set of pass keys from a pocket, inserted three, and the fourth key opened the lock. Quietly and discreetly he waddled into the darkness of the room. He reached the desk and then the favorite chair of the President. Gently he taped the bomb to the underside of the seat. And then he set the timer for 9:45 the next morning. His surveillance indicated that the President always came to his office at 9:00 AM, the secretary at 8:00 AM.

Taking one last look around the oval room, he waddled to the door, shut it and heard it automatically lock. He saw the nearest guard watching the open area, and tip-toed to the wall behind the secretary's desk where he'd left his pack. Quickly he shouldered the pack and crawled back to the hallway from which he came. As he turned the corner, a guard stood with revolver drawn.

"Hands up! This is the end of the line, buster!" he said savagely, leaning his head to a lapel microphone. "This is Fox 2, intruder at area six."

The intruder knew he had to move quickly, his dark eyes clouded with panic. Suddenly he slapped the revolver hand; the revolver flew over the desk. His left hand gripped the knife strapped to his calf and the right hand grabbed the back of the officer's neck in a deadly movement. The sharp blade sliced across his throat, his startled eyes revealing his demise, darkness faded in his

confused mind, the silence—eternal silence. The intruder shoved the body under the desk.

Quickly he surveyed the situation. The guards near the door were running toward him. He ran to the skylight. Quickly he gripped the dangling rope and hoisted himself hand-over-hand up to the hole he'd cut in the glass. Bullets began to ricochet off the frame of the skylight, several shattering the glass. He struggled through the hole; a sudden bullet expanded the glass opening, and he stepped on the gabled roof. He breathed deeply running to the edge of the building. Down below were three guards, revolvers drawn and blasting rapid fire. Splinters of concrete sprayed in the air. He leapt over the open space to the flat tarred-rock roof; a bullet clipped the heel of his boot. As he stabilized his body, he startlingly felt the barrel of a revolver stuck in his back.

The man with the revolver said nothing but gripped one of the intruder's hands. As he attempted to cuff his hands, it was the moment the intruder had contemplated. With the sudden move of a cat he swung around slamming a stunning blow of his elbow against the temple of the officer's head. A rapid move of his left hand gripped the knife and sliced the throat of the shocked officer.

He laid the body on the roof surface and ran to the far edge of the roof and found his grappling hook secure in its position. He placed one leg over the edge with the

rope in both hands and lowered his body fist-over-fist to the ground. He walked, half ran, and then casually strolled back to his parked car in the lot of a local all night restaurant.

Taking no time to disrobe he stood beside the car in the darkness, his head rotating left then right. The air was pierced by sirens on the White House grounds, lights flashing. He smiled indifferently as he unlocked the driver's door and sat. He pushed the ignition button on the dash, and the Cadillac engine roared to idle. He drove off in the night, as police cars zipped by, lights flashing and sirens shrieking. Several neighborhoods were awakened by the noise, the normal response of barking dogs echoed in the night.

The refurbished warehouse behind the Pentagon loomed gray and foreboding in the overcast, another weather front had moved into the Northeast. Snow was in the forecast, but the temperature was 40 degrees; that was understandable, but not the device sitting on the floor of the warehouse. A light shone through the high windows and a team of scientists were working overtime around a curious flying saucer that had arrived just before noon today.

Walter Slovak, chief scientist for the CIA and a master of Orwellian passion sat in the pilot seat of the UFO, a publicly denied existence. His puzzled mind was in a quandary of immense dimensions. The enigma was

circular, 27-meters in diameter, space for a pilot, one of the standard flying saucers in the German experimental arsenal! It was another enigma that the thing could fly. Yet he must somehow understand its power source and how it defied gravity.

A young scientist assigned from Slovak's MIT university class poured over the diagram he had made of the unit that somehow emitted a death ray; it featured a simple nozzle, its internal surfaces lined with a ceramic material. He had researched all the information available on laser beams, but none had the power reported by Admiral McHenny. Slovak looked down from his seat at the young student. Perhaps he had uncovered something useful, he thought. He released a latch and hinged up the windshield. He stepped out of the unit down a ladder to the floor and walked over to the student.

"Is there something we might discuss," he asked.

The student removed his wire-rim spectacles. "If we only had Nikola Tesla's notes," he surmised. "I'm certain this ray is a pulsating laser, but its power source escapes me."

Slovak raised his cellphone and punched a code to the Admiral's office telephone.

19

Admiral McHenny's task force pulled out of Mayport harbor on the outgoing tide the following weekend that President Darcy had given the command to go back to Antarctica. Captain Stephen Coates followed the flagship aircraft carrier commanding the refurbished World War II submarine. Dr. Caruso was assigned to the flagship, however, Bruce Allison remained onshore as Dr. Caruso had requested. The morning they left, the sea softly doused the sandy shores of Jacksonville Beach. The decks of the Carrier had six F-15s strapped to capstans just in case one of those flying discs was still hovering around *Neuschwabenland.* The ebbing tide seemed harmonious

with the murmuring of the waves as the task force moved ever southward over the whitecaps of the turbulent Atlantic.

Captain Woolsey commanded the carrier bridge standing with his binoculars trained on the horizon. Deep in his mind the orders of Admiral McHenny rehashed in his thoughts. The mission was centered on bringing back technology, especially any engineering drawings. On the list were any technical notes on the flying saucer power source and the death ray—specifically Tesla's notes. If at all possible, the President requested the exhumation of Hitler's grave and a bone sample extracted for DNA analysis.

Down in the galley, Admiral McHenny and Dr. Caruso discussed the mission. The primary topic that was the exhumation of Hitler's grave. The Admiral pushed back in his chair, inhaled a deep breath, and quietly sighed. "At the end of the Nuremberg trials the U.S. chief, Thomas J. Dodd declared that no one could say that Hitler was dead."

Robby sat an empty cup on the table. "I understand that the Soviets took charge of the bunker remains of the infamous graves of Eva Braun and Adolf Hitler."

"Quite true," he confirmed. "They also confiscated documents from Hitler's headquarters and even his living quarters. In addition they apprehended many of Hitler's staff," the Admiral added.

Robby shrugged. "Say we do obtain a bone sample, what would we compare it with?" he said good-naturedly.

"That's the jackpot question. Maybe we should let the geneticists tackle that question," advised the Admiral in a cement tone.

"One more question for you Admiral. The President has given me the mission to look into the death ray question. I thought perhaps you might be privy to something useful," Caruso offered.

"I might throw that question back into your oversight. Just before we sailed I received a call from the CIA. They have a MIT group working on the UFO power source and the death ray. Dr. Slovak, the man in charge has requested Tesla's notes."

Robby slid to the edge of his chair if not the edge of his patience. "The CIA should know those notes are missing—hell, I'm not at all unsure that the CIA didn't take those notes."

The steward came to the table. "Admiral there is an overseas phone call for you."

"Pardon me, Robby," he said pushing back his chair. He followed the steward, and took the phone in his office. Pressing the unit to his ear, he recognized the voice of the Chief of Staff to the President. His eyes bulged, he said nothing only listened. "Thank you for the message . . . I shall," he said and hung the phone, gazing into nothingness.

He made his way back to the galley seized by his thoughts. The course down the narrow hallway seemed an eternity as he coursed the conversation through the computer of his mine. Finally, he entered the room and noticed the mystified expression on Robby's face.

"What in heaven's name is going on?" Robby asked austerely seeing the grayish color of his face.

McHenny said nothing, the gravity of the message incredulous. As he sat, he shook the cobwebs from his thoughts, the message strangled in the webs of bafflement.

Robby's face frowned impatiently.

Then the Admiral spoke.

"There has been an assassination attempt on the President," he muttered in disbelief the cobwebs again in command.

Robby pushed back in his chair, anger marring his countenance. "Sean Casey," he whispered. "Were there any fingerprints?" he persisted.

Clarity returned. "No mention of prints. A bomb was placed under the President's chair—in the Oval Office of all places," he stammered. "The intruder sliced the throat of two police officers and somehow escaped their pursuit."

Robby stood angrily. "That's Casey's motif—the President, was he harmed?"

"He had just opened the door to his office when the bomb exploded. The shrapnel and debris broke his left arm, a few scratches and lacerations, I understand."

Robby was overwhelmed by the attack on the President; he left the Admiral's office and went to the bridge for fresh air to clear his mind. Woolsey had just received the message about the assassination attempt as he placed the mike in its cradle on the bridge. He glimpsed the anguish in Robby's face, and dropped the binoculars suspended by its strap around his neck. He thought of the President's wounds and the White House guards with slit throats. "Good God what kind of maniac could do this," Woolsey groaned.

Robby did not try to hide his feelings. Deep in the caches of his mind who could not escape that moment three years ago when he had Sean Casey in the clutches of his bare hands. Phoenix, the drug lord of Colombia laid unconscious on the floor the victim of Robby's strong uppercut. Casey had stepped from the shadows and stuck the barrel of his familiar Berretta in Robby's ribs. They wrestled. Within the skirmish Robby held Casey with his hands twisted behind his back, the handcuffs open. Suddenly, something crashed on his head. He helplessly sank to the floor, reality dissipated with the sound of two voices in the dark distance. Then there was nothing, nothing at all.

Caruso faced Woolsey. "It's not fair—where is justice?" Caruso tormented, slamming his fist on the rail.

Woolsey nodded. "Justice is a frail thing," he whispered, and looked once more at Robby's tired face. "Tomorrow is another day."

Robby lifted his head. "Yeah, days like those of Eugene Tunney." He peered into Woolsey's agreeable face. "That will be the epitaph of Sean Casey—trust me."

Most murderers followed a pattern, developed a modus operandi, and preferred a particular weapon. Casey's pattern was classic. He left no strings to connect him to his past—except one, Robby knew his past.

Woolsey understood Robby's point, but the real issue was still ahead. If only they could get the design drawings of those flying discs, we could unravel the secret of the Nazis, he thought. And it suddenly occurred to him that Robby had disclosed to him the Nazi fascination with the occult, the years in which the Vril-force had inspired Hitler, Himmler and the other SS officers. They were all involved in the inner core of occult lodges such as the Thule and Vril. And though one may not believe a word of all that this task force had discovered, the point is they believed it and built at least two very complicated societies that still plague America this very day.

Woolsey left his conversation with Robby and went to McHenny's office. The Admiral stood when he entered, a sour expression on his face. "More bad news, Sir?" he wondered.

Admiral McHenny sat behind his desk staring out into space. Finally he turned to the Captain. "You know, Henri Weismann may also be attacked. It's only a thought but lately things are happening that made no sense." He said almost in a whisper.

"It's an interesting thought. Suppose there is a Neo-Nazi group directing these assaults," Woolsey replied.

Just to clear his mind, he opened the drawer on his desk where he'd placed his copy of Weismann's document that the President had translated into English. "Perhaps there might be something helpful in this translation."

McHenny and Woolsey both realized they were grasping at straws, but there just may be a clue in the document.

Bruce parked his Jeep beneath Henri's apartment in Georgetown. He stepped out and placed a pizza on top of the cab and closed and locked the door. Taking the pizza, he strolled to the steps opposite the swimming pool and navigated the twenty eight steps to the second level. As he walked the several strides to Henri's room, he noticed a car that just pulled in beside his Jeep. If not for the foreign tag he may not have noticed, but

disregarded his curiosity; the pizza would not be hot. Henri met him at the door, a smile on his pleasant face, and took the pizza from Bruce's outstretched arms.

"Excuse me Henri, just take a moment to check a car," his curiosity replied. He closed the door and looked down over the railing. The driver's seat was empty. He strolled back to the stairs and descended to the ground level. He took the sidewalk beneath the upper level, and walked into the space between his Jeep and the car. It was a Ford sedan with a rental tag on the rear bumper. Just why it had a foreign tag—Germany, was a puzzle, but he assumed it could have been transported from a European franchisee.

Suddenly the front window of the second floor exploded, glass shattered and a shower of tiny dagger slivers fell to the ground. Bruce dashed to the stairs and took giant steps to Henri's apartment. The door was jammed. He thrust his muscled shoulder against the door and shoved it open with one mighty thrust. The room was filled with smoke, choking smoke with the pungent smell of gunpowder. Bruce pulled his shirttail over his nose and mouth, and pushed into the dismal thick smoke. He frantically searched for Henri, and his anxiety forced a yell, "Henri, where are you? He screeched. He heard a faint rap on a door; he surged to the bathroom, banging his fist on the door.

A faint voice, "Bruce, is that you?"

The door swung open and Henri grabbed Bruce by his shoulders.

Anxiety subsided, panic vanished. Bruce led Henri to the bed and he sat. Bruce opened the front door for the smoke's escape and walk back to the bedside. "What happened, Henri?" he asked impatiently.

"When you left, I heard a noise in the back bedroom. It sounded like a window open," he said through a slight cough. "Dr. Caruso had warned me not to investigate an intrusion, and I locked myself in the bathroom," he replied, brought his hands to his throat, and collapsed.

Bruce dropped to his knees placed his ear over Henri's mouth. He wasn't breathing. Quickly he bent over his face and immediately administered mouth-to-mouth respiration. Henri coughed, swallowed dryly and pushed to his elbow. "What happened?"

Bruce stood him upright. He gripped both shoulders with a relaxing smile on his face, "I asked you first. What did happen here?" he chuckled.

The apartment manager rushed into the room followed by a policeman. "What's going on here?" he screamed.

Again Bruce smiled. "Now everybody wants to know what happened—you tell me."

"We heard an explosion, my wife saw the smoke, and I called the police," he explained in rapid fashion.

Bruce suddenly ran through the open door and look down to the ground. The Ford sedan was gone. The

officer walked up beside him. Bruce turned and faced him. "There was a Ford sedan parked beside my Jeep—it's gone."

He nodded. "The right fender damaged your rear fender. I'll have the lab take a paint sample; maybe we can identify the car."

"Thanks, officer, here is my card. You can reach me at the White House."

Captain Woolsey notified the Admiral they had arrived at the South Pole and were beginning to dock just off the shore of the location of *Neuschwabenland.* Admiral McHenny placed the phone back on the hook having just received an overseas call from Bruce Allison. He leaned over to the intercom. "Dr. Caruso to the flagship cabin," squawked the speaker on the bridge.

Woolsey turn to Robby, "Something's up in Denmark."

"I expect you are correct," he said and left the bridge. He hurried down the aisle passed the galley and climbed the ladder through a hatch to the second level. A steward glued to the wall allowing him to pass as he rushed by. Finally he slowed his stride at the cabin door, gently rapped his knuckles on the mahogany surface.

"Enter," said the familiar voice of the Admiral.

Robby opened the door, closed it behind his entry. "You called, Admiral."

"Yes, there is news from stateside."

"More information from the White House," he assumed.

"Have a seat, Robby."

He sat by the chair facing the flagship desk, crossing his leg. The lines on the forehead of the Admiral expressed a personal story but was it the message he had called him for?

The Admiral folded his arms on the desk. "The message was from Bruce," he said and paused. The expression on Robby's face actually anticipated what he was about to report. "A bomb was placed in Henri's apartment."

Robby pushed to the edge of his seat, his mind had already calculated who had performed both these dastardly deeds. The Admiral stared into his eyes hoping to calm any wrong actions.

"Bruce saved Henri's life with mouth-to-mouth respiration."

Robby slumped in his chair, the air sucked out of him by anger. He knew Casey had struck again, and he wouldn't stop until Henri and the President were dead.

"Is Henri okay?" he whispered, refusing to allow anger to speak.

"I understand his lungs were somehow scorched by the fumes. He's in the hospital and Bruce is there with him, including the FBI." He saw something in the eyes

of Robby. "Do want to fly back to stateside—one of the F-15s is available?"

Robby stood. "That won't be necessary. Bruce will see that Henri is safe. We must complete our mission."

The Admiral nodded. Caruso may have been lacking in his social graces, but he had no shortage of patience. "Robby, I want to commend you for the wisdom of leaving Bruce stateside. At the time I thought it unwise, but you understood the situation." He paused gathering the courage to say what was on his mind. "I'm damn glad to have you on this mission. Now get back up to the bridge before I change my mind."

20

The azure blue sky was as bright as he'd ever seen it since they left Antarctica three months ago, thought Captain Coates standing in the conning tower of the submarine. Even in these turbulent Atlantic waters the waves were rippling on the shore feather soft. He snatched the microphone from is rack in the conning tower. "Kosaku to the conning tower," blared the ship speakers.

He replaced the mike and gazed out on the icepack. A few penguins were huddle together like bowling ninepins. He wondered if the land crew could find the entrance, then Marty stuck his head through the hatch, and stepped up beside the Captain.

"You called, Captain."

"Yes, Marty. As we discussed coming out I want you to pick a man of your choice and take the dinghy over to the icepack. I can only give you a guess where the entrance may be located. You will navigate the icepack north along the shore. Take a radio with you in case there is trouble."

"Aye aye Captain—will do." He stepped through the hatch and made his way to the rear of the sub.

Coates again took the mike from its bracket on the wall. "Dr. Caruso to the conning tower," he spoke, his voice echoing through the open hatch. He replaced the mike gazing at the icepack. He wanted better advice for his men when they reached the shore.

Caruso climbed the ladder into the conning tower. "What's the scuttlebutt, Captain?"

Coates removed the binoculars from his eyes. "Marty is preparing to take the dinghy over to the icepack. I couldn't give him much information on where or what to look for—what's you thought?"

"Henri said the returning flying saucers entered just north of the entrance to the city," he pointed.

Coates nodded. "That's about all I told Marty."

"He should know it when he sees it. It has to be a rather large opening for the 24-meter diameter machines," he replied. "I'm betting we have to take the submarine into the opening. No doubt there will be

another dam as well," he elucidated, yet he could be certain.

Coates adjusted the focus on his binoculars. Marty and his partner were exiting the rear hatch, donned in standard winter issue. The deflated dinghy punched through the hatch, and Marty pulled a level. Immediately the dinghy inflated in 20 seconds. It was the latest issue by the Navy with a rubberized floor more rigid than aluminum, a drop stitch air deck, and three individual chambers constructed of 1100 denier 0.9mm PVC. Marty tossed the inflated dinghy overboard holding onto the lanyard. The partner took the lanyard as Marty stepped to the rear seat. The partner stepped in the front, gripped one of the two paddles, placed it against the Sub hull and pushed away. He placed both oars in its oarlock and rowed toward the icepack. Marty noticed the submarine silently motoring ahead on battery power.

The twosome landed and pulled the dinghy onto the icepack. Marty shouldered the battery radio, and they marched off northward. They trudged along the arctic-white snow pack, penguins marching behind them like little ducklings. Suddenly two porpoises angled through the waters just offshore, poking their bottle noses out of the water, shaking their heads chattering as if they wanted the two men's attention. Marty focused his binoculars and sure enough they were being signaled.

He dropped the binoculars strapped around his neck. "Let's follow those two dolphins," he barked.

They hastened in stride, for the dolphins were racing up the coast. They passed the submarine.

Coates dropped his binoculars, shaking his head. "I don't believe it. Those dolphins are leading Marty," he chuckled. "All stop—Dr. Caruso to the conning tower."

Marty shaded his eyes and saw the two dolphins chattering noisily. "That must be the spot," he said, facing his partner. He sensed his mission, and the partner raced up ahead of Marty completely mystified by the action of the dolphins. Up ahead a rather large rise in the topography of the icepack, the snow a whale-bone white. Suddenly, a death-like silence draped the land. A flying machine zoomed from the rise and angled upward, passing over the submarine.

Coates grabbed the mike. "Call the Carrier, a flying saucer is heading directly toward the flagship," he screamed.

The radio operation on the Carrier punched a code on his light board. "Alert! Alert! We are imminent for attack."

Up on deck a squad of F-15's fired up their turbines. Two roared off the deck and soared upward. Two more flying saucers exited the tunnel. A third F-15 went airborne and banked northward on the trail of a flying saucer. The Saucer was much faster than the F-15, but the pilot compensated by judging the speed—like shooting birds back in Tennessee. As the UFO dove to a

lower level approach to the flagship, the F-15 launched two sidewinder missiles that leaped from its wings leading his aim just ahead of the UFO. The first missile missed, the second exploded ahead of the saucer. The shrapnel slammed against the pilot's windshield, the impact multiplied by the high speed. The UFO wobbled, and then turned south. Another F-15 pilot witnessed the tactics, and held his position directly in front of the damaged saucer, but his tactics were different. He was playing "chicken."

The distances were closing swiftly. The F-15 pilot held his position, arming his sidewinder missiles. Apparently the pilot of the saucer could not see directly ahead because of the windshield damages. Suddenly two sidewinders blasted from its racks and soared away at supersonic speed, and the F-15 veered away climbing for space. The pilot had no idea what fueled the UFO but there would be an explosion. The saucer erupted into a billowing cloud of smoke and debris, great pieces of jagged metal tumbled into the sea.

Down on the carrier decks the sailors were waving their caps shouting. The second saucer dove toward the carrier, a death ray beaming a shaft of ominous light. The foredeck exploded, a plume of black smoke rose into a dark cloud, fire flaming on the deck fed by the wind. Both the remaining flying saucer pilot had never engaged in a dogfight with F-15s before, and decided not

to risk it after losing one UFO. Both saucers plunged into the sea.

Captain Coates turned to Dr. Caruso standing in the control room. "Did you see that? Do you think there's a base under the sea?"

The both stood there in hushed silence. But Caruso remembered Henri's discussion of another base where the UFO's entered from the sea.

Admiral McHenny closed the file and put it down, and leaned forward as if he was about to spring from his chair but thought better of it. "If you're asking for my permission, Captain Woolsey, the answer is an unequivocal no!"

"You place me in an awkward position, Admiral." The words came from a man who sat facing the Admiral. He was tall and his shoulders broad as the chair. He wore the standard uniform of a naval Captain. Unconsciously, every so often, he ran his fingers through his wavy hair. He peered through brown eyes that never blinked under the Admiral's blazing eyes. "I had sincerely hoped we would have no disagreement. However, since that is not to be, I must inform you that I shall go with Dr. Caruso without permission."

Meanwhile, the Admiral called a conference. He sat in the boardroom with Captain Woolsey nibbling finger sandwiches and drinking coffee. He thought it necessary to clear the air. "Woolsey, I'm deeply sorrow for my

testy remarks. I only thought of your need on the flagship, but I completely forgot that Caruso needs you more without Tunney."

Woolsey stood and saluted the Admiral. "Sir, I have never lost respect for your command."

"I appreciate your confidence, Captain," he said embarrassingly. He stood, looked once more into Woolsey's face, forced a smile, and went to the radio room. He had the radio operator contact the submarine and ordered both Captain Coates and Dr. Caruso to attend the meeting. He made his way back down the aisle and saw Woolsey walking his way.

"Let me buy you another cup of coffee, Captain," he grinned.

A broad smile creased his face. He understood it was the Admiral's way of apology. "Thank you, Admiral. I could use another cup, if we go Dutch?"

"You're on. I've had a pot sent to my office."

They entered the flagship office and selected a seat. McHenny poured two cups of coffee from the pot, and sat down across from Woolsey.

"Captain Coates has an idea that the Germans may have a base under the sea," McHenny said, shaking his head resolutely.

"Possible, but that's the reason Dr. Caruso and I will be going over to that icepack," Woolsey replied.

"Then we shall wait for your assessment Captain."

Chatter in the aisles told the couple that Caruso and Coates had arrived, and the door swung open. Woolsey stood and extended his hand to Caruso. "It looks as though we have another mystery on our hands," he smiled.

Caruso nodded. "First, I need a cup of java," he replied pointing a finger at the pot.

The Admiral's face spread into a smile. "Give the man a cup. Caruso's mind can't function without caffeine," he said, suddenly laughing.

Coates poured two cups, pushing a cup over to Caruso. He wrapped his hands around the barrel, facing the Admiral. "I suppose you are wondering about those two flying saucers that dove into the drink."

"What's your thought on an undersea base?" McHenny asked.

Caruso exchanged knowing looks at Coates. "I thank Coates is right, Admiral. We can't answer your question without an expedition."

The Admiral stood. "You and Coates take the sub, and whatever you need. Just get the answer," he said, without reluctance. "And take Woolsey with you—he makes me nervous."

21

If Captain Coates had called on fairies, he wouldn't have gotten a calmer sea that the dreamy waters seen from the conning tower. The waves were crawling gently against the icepack, the sounds murmuring hypnotic. During breakfast Marty Kosaku had prepared two diving suits for Dr. Caruso and Captain Woolsey to make an exploratory dive seeking anything that looked like an underwater hangar for the flying saucers. During the previous excursion, no saucers were seen entering the designated opening to the under the ice city. Yet two saucers had been seen diving into the sea—there must be a hanger somewhere else.

The two adventurers had finished a breakfast that Caruso thought would have cost at least fifteen dollars in any of the better hotel on Bermuda, when Marty stepped into the galley. "Whenever you gentlemen are ready, the diving suits are prepared with dual tanks compressed with helium mixture."

Woolsey faced Caruso; they both grinned and followed Marty back to the rear of the sub. This would be the first time either had suited for diving together. Usually Caruso had Bruce as his right hand man. It was the first dive for Woolsey since his induction into the Navy. It occurred to him that he was in good company with Dr. Caruso, a veteran of undersea exploration. And it struck him that this interesting guy was so close to the President.

Marty assisted Woolsey in donning the diving suit. Caruso stood already dressed, inspecting the equipment in his backpack. When Woolsey was dressed he completed packing instruments in his backpack. Caruso strapped a knife to his right calf, and slipped his arm into the backpack snuggling it comfortably on his back. He remembered that Woolsey had contacted the Coast Guard yesterday.

"What did the Coast Guard say when you called?" Caruso asked.

He stuffed a lantern in his pack. "An iceberg is in the vicinity and warned the flagship—saying something about avoiding another Titanic," he grinned.

Caruso returned the grin. "If it is, then it has defied every drift pattern in the book."

"They marked it with a red dye, I'm told."

"Those dyes contain calcium chloride; a necessary ingredient for deep penetration—takes weeks, sometimes months for the stain to melt away."

Captain Coates took the Con as he gazed out over the rear deck. The hatch suddenly opened. Marty emerged from the hatch dragging a deflated raft through the hole onto the deck. He pulled a lever on the inside of the raft and it inflated in just a few seconds. He pushed the two-seat unit into the water next to a net ladder, holding the lanyard. Dr. Caruso exited the hatch, and took the lanyard.

"Thanks Marty."

Marty smiled holding a lantern. "Thought you might forget this—Woolsey has one, I'm a bit safety conscious." He opened Caruso's pack and stuffed the lantern inside. Caruso slapped him on the back.

"When we return help me remember to place a call to Bruce—you guys have a lot in common."

Marty nodded and took Woolsey's hand assisting him through the tiny hole as Caruso descended the net ladder.

Woolsey navigated the net and stepped into the raft. Caruso sat in the rear seat inserting the oars in the oarlocks. Marty turned and stepped into the hatch, took

one last look at Caruso paddling the raft toward the icepack. He partially descended the ladder, closed the hatch cover and sealed it shut by rotating the wheel, compressing the hatch gasket.

Marty heard the sub ballast blow as he made his way to the galley. When he pulled back the curtain, Captain Coates sat drinking a cup of coffee.

"Sit down, Marty, join me with a cup," said Coates, retrieving his extended legs into the tight space.

Marty sat, placing his cold hands around the warm barrel of the mug, steam rising into his face. "Captain, I'm worried about Woolsey. He hasn't had much undersea training."

"No need to worry, Caruso is a marvelous teacher," he replied removing his lips from the edge of the cup.

"Scuttlebutt says they are searching for an undersea hanger for those UFOs."

"If there is one, Caruso thinks it should be near the mouth of the runway tunnel."

"I noticed that Woolsey has a folding shovel in his pack."

"Yes, I understand that the President wants a bone sample of the man in the first grave," he said and stood. "Enjoy your coffee, Marty."

Bone sample, Marty thought, wondering who was buried under that ice. He swilled down the last swallow and went to the rear of the sub to prepare for the return of the two men.

Shafts of light poured on the sea, the sinking sun still a celestial fireball on the sharp horizon. Its hours of blazing beams had not melted the snow at the Antarctica yet had given the penguins a warm bath of sunlight. The moon was like a ghostly-silver disc in the fading blue of the sky. Soon the specter of night would send out its apparitions and dance on the deepening shadows.

The sea undulated and churned like a cannibal's cauldron. It heaved and bulged, pushing up giant waves from the fathomless gullet of its depths. The wind screamed like a banshee's wail and whipped at Caruso's metal helmet. He turned to Woolsey submerged to his neckline, and yelled through the 6-inch diameter Plexiglas window. "We had best sink beneath the—" Before he finished his sentence the waves eerily subsided as if some great hand had halted the ebb and flow. The sea was still as death! A terrible silence followed, and then Caruso completed his sentence. "Let's get below the surface before the devil himself steals the night."

Both divers dipped beneath the surface, dual tanks of helium-mixed air strapped to their backs. Down they dove, each beaming atomic lanterns that unveiled the tiniest fragment in pulsating light. They leveled at twenty fathoms registered on wrist depth gages. In the gory distance long tentacles of frozen mud streamed downward underneath the icecap. Caruso suddenly

stiffened, thrust out his hand for silence, listening intently. Fortunately sound was amplified underwater, and though faint, it was there. Through the density of seawater it came as a steady drone: the sound of a pump running at high rpm's.

The two divers swam toward the sound; the irresistible hum lured them like a tractor beam, ever pulling them into the dark doldrums beneath the icecap. They swam silently, effortlessly as if suspended by an invisible wire, the darkening colors, the blue green now transforming slowly to soft gray. They swam in no chosen direction drawn by the increasing sound of the hum. Hovering under the icecap, the dark tentacles seemed more spaced apart, open spaces emerged under the glow of their lanterns. Suddenly the image of a rectangular object appeared nothing ghostly, metal fabrication erected by skilled human hands. As they neared they grew larger, the appearance of a huge garage. Within six feat of the fabrication, it stretched fifty feet in width, twenty feet in height. On close inspection it seemed to open by remote control. If so, there must be an infrared receiving module, Caruso deduced and surveyed the front edges of the fabrication. On the right side at the ten-foot level he spotted a module. He instinctively snapped off the cover, and focused his eyes on the electrical connections. Finally, he gripped the handle of his sheathed knife strapped to his right leg. He gently laid the blade between to wires

and shorted the connection. Eureka! The door opened into a hanger the length of a football field. Two flying saucers sat moored! Against the entrance wall Caruso discovered a huge pump. Adjacent to the pump was a room accessed by a watertight door similar to a submarine. He rotated the 8-inch wheel, and the door opened into a 6 by 6-foot square room. They stepped into the room, and Woolsey closed the door and sealed it by rotating a familiar wheel. Woolsey stood beside Caruso pointing to another door that seemed to be an elevator! Caruso nodded and pressed a button mounted on the sidewall. The pump came to life and evacuated the water in the room within three minutes. The suction of the water glued their feet to the steel floor.

Caruso removed his helmet. “The pilots must come into this room and evacuated the water,” Caruso surmised.

“Then their flight suits must be watertight, just like those we wear,” replied Woolsey holding his helmet in his trembling hands. “You know it’s cold down here.”

“The utilities must be inoperative because of the blast,” Caruso deduced.

They both laid their helmets against the room wall, and Woolsey activated another button on the wall of the double doors. They opened into an elevator just like any hotel. Hanging on hooks against the sidewall Caruso feasted his eyes on two holstered German lugers. He tapped Woolsey on the shoulder pointing to the weapons. “We forgot those,” Caruso said.

“How foolish, yet who would dream we’d find this fabrication?”

Caruso nodded. “Those flying saucers don’t have alien pilots—they are German clones! Maybe we should have brought reinforcements,” he grinned, pushing the button that closed the elevator doors.

Woolsey smiled. “Now which button should be select?”

Caruso returned the smile. “That’s easy—this icon here,” he said pointing to the letters, “NEUS.”

The elevators opened!

Neuschwabenland was a wreck, building structures strewn here and there, debris a mass two-feet thick. Some places were navigable; others had rubble heaped twenty-feet high. Fortunately, the area to the left had the least wreckage and it was open for the alert like Woolsey, who had brought a shovel.

Caruso gazed at his friend, the surprise of sudden affection written on his countenance. “You are always prepared—give me that shovel,” he grinned.

He shook his head, eyebrows elevated. “How are we going to dig up a grave without a shovel,” he smiled. “And how will we take a bone sample without a drill,” he laughed rhetorically, removing a battery surgical drill from his pack.

"I'll be hog-swallowed," he replied. "You do think of everything—you wouldn't happen to have a hamburger I guess?"

"I promise you a steak dinner back in DC—if we get out of here."

"You're on—give me that shovel, you nut," he winked.

The pathway was finally open except for a few pieces they could step over. The two friends navigated the debris piles and looked over the wreckage hoping to identify the hill where the graveyard was located. On they walked and finally Caruso spotted the hill. They were in luck, the graveyard was beyond any construction, but he noticed it was also close to the airfield where the flying saucers originally landed before the fabrication of the undersea facility. Added to that dilemma, he also saw the building where the pilots resided, it too undamaged. He stood unmoving for nearly a minute, groping for words. He started to say something but thought better of it and instead simple nodded his head in silent understanding.

But Woolsey didn't understand his silence. "What is in that devious mind of yours?" he asked a frown on his face.

"Nothing—thought I saw something."

"Well, stop your lollygagging and let's get on to that graveyard."

Caruso through the shovel over his should and stepped out front, satisfied that his decision was correct; no need to worry the old salty Captain. He dropped his self-gratified contentment and marched onward up the sloping hill.

Finally they reached the peak, a few lava rocks scattered randomly but the graveyard was untouched by the explosion. He swung open the gate; he felt resistance as the hinges squeaked noisily, apparently expanded by the heat. Woolsey lit his lantern and illumined the first gravestone. Caruso dropped the shovel from his shoulder, placed his big foot on its metallic edge, and removed the first shovel of dirt, mostly pumice. After three-feet of digging, Woolsey insisted on taking over the burden of the next few feet. Caruso didn't argue, wiping the perspiration from his forehead.

A pile of dirt rose three-feet in height, sloped like a pyramid. Finally the blade of the shovel struck something. "It's a casket, metallic I think," Woolsey announced, and shoveled the remaining dirt from the top.

Caruso lowered to his knees on one end and Woolsey likewise on the opposite end. They scratched down to a handle and strained at the weight. Woolsey decided to remove some of the dirt around the casket.

Caruso stood. "Good idea, buddy."

Several scoops later, they got on their knees once more and strained at the reduced weight. Suddenly the casket broke free and they managed to bring it to the edge of the grave. They stood and gazed upon an emblazoned swastika on the lid. Without resting they inspected the lid. Time had sealed it stubbornly. Caruso gripped the knife from its sheath. He pried the blade around the lid in several positions, and they managed to unseal it. This time they stood resting a moment; each one wondering what they might see when removing the lid. Yet they realized from the smell that something was rotten.

Caruso looked at Woolsey. "Ready to pop the cork?"

"Why not?"

Each man kneeled and grabbed the lid with both hands at each end. Caruso counted off the lift: one, two—three! The lid was free. A stuffy and grotesque smell of death floated from the casket. They laid the lid on the ground, startled expressions distorting each face as they looked into the casket.

If it was Hitler, his hair was twelve inches long and his mustache had grown down to his chin. Where to take the sample; that was the question? Caruso suggested the leg because the clothing was rotten with easier access to the bone. Woolsey retrieved the drill from his pack. Caruso leaned over the smelly casket peeled back the rotted fabric. He pushed the slid switch

on the drill and placed the drill bit on the femur bone. Suddenly he shut off the drill, turned to Woolsey embarrassingly.

"What do we have to contain this sample?"

Woolsey shook his head. "And you a chemist," he replied and handed him a zip-lock plastic bag. "While you are at it take theses sterile plastic gloves, we don't want to contaminate the sample."

Caruso said nothing, and handed him his knife. "I suppose you have alcohol in that bag," he replied, derisively smiling while donning the plastic gloves. "And this plastic bag came off the shelf of a supermarket. It's not sterile," he said.

Woolsey's eyebrows elevated as he reached into his bag and gripped the plastic bottle of alcohol. "Of course it is. I sterilized it with this alcohol. Somebody had to be prepared," he replied, returning the smile. He drenched both sides of the blade, waving it in the air to dry. "Now perhaps I don't have to take the sample, too."

"If you do, then I shall disavow the results of the test," he grinned. He activated the drill, collected the fillings on the blade as they fell from the drill. He gently dropped the fillings in the bag, zipped it closed. "Here, take this drill and the sample," he said and stood, retrieved a camera from his pack.

Woolsey placed everything back into his backpack, facing Caruso. "Well, you did bring a camera I see—that something anyway."

Caruso only smiled adjusting the lens of his Nikon. He snapped several pictures and placed the cap on the lens.

Woolsey slapped him on the back. "Let's get this lid back on the casket."

As the lid lay snuggly on the casket, Caruso stepped from the grave. "I find it not necessary to bury this casket—let's get back to the sub."

Woolsey smiled. "For once we agree—let's roll."

Somehow they made it to the raft. Each took off their backpacks and tossed them into the raft. Woolsey took the lanyard as Caruso stepped to the read and took the oars. As Woolsey pushed off, Caruso placed the oars in the oarlocks. Caruso rotated the raft with his oars and began to row with all his might.

Suddenly Caruso swore aloud. "We forgot our helmets!"

Woolsey grinned. "That's not quite accurate," he said pointing to the deck of the raft. There lay the two helmets.

Caruso shook his head humiliatingly. "Maybe I should pay the check for those steak dinners," he said, suddenly laughing.

As they passed under the long tentacles, the light from the outside transformed them into dripping ice that apparently had frozen. Woolsey sat in front of the raft and thought he heard loud noises out where the sub

was when the left. It must have submerged, he thought. They rowed out a few meters from the shore. It was then that Woolsey realized what had caused the noise. The carrier was under attack by flying saucers—probably the two saucers they saw in the undersea hanger.

In a sudden blast of ballasts, the submarine surfaced. Caruso wildly rowed the raft and finally bumped the steel hull. He saw the hatch open and two sailors waiting to help them aboard.

One sailor took the lanyard, and Woolsey stepped on the deck with both helmets in his hands. Caruso grabbed his knife and punctured the raft in several places, and leaped on the deck with the two backpacks. As they ran to the hatch the raft slowly sank. The last sailor seized the rope and closed the hatch as the as the submarine dove beneath the surface.

One sailor assisted Woolsey to disrobe the diving suit. The other sailor assisted Caruso. Before they took off their backpacks, Captain Coates entered the rear area.

"That was a close one."

"How long has the Carrier been under attack?" Caruso asked anxiously.

"About twenty minutes. The Admiral ordered the F-15s into the air when the saucers first rose out of the ocean."

Captain Coates peered through the periscope. One saucer was just hit by a sidewinder missile, it wobbled and twisted, smoke whizzing by the swastika on its nonstandard stabilizer. Fire blazed over the underside and crashed into the sea. The other saucer had shot down two F-15s, both pilots safely parachuted. The remaining saucer terminated the attack with two F-15s on his tail and dove directly into the water.

Coates grabbed his mike. "This is the Captain. Arm the bow torpedoes. Helmsman, come to course four, six, one, steady as she goes . . . Fire one . . . Fire two."

Two torpedoes coursed toward the undersea hangar like watery arrows. The impact was sudden, the water exploded in a plume of water and mist, jagged pieces of debris fell from the sky, red embers of fiery chunks of wood blotted out the sun. A stench enveloped the area in an effluvium of death.

"Down Scope, take her to ten fathoms," Coates said.

22

Captain Woolsey stood on the open bridge of the carrier with Dr. Caruso at his side, his binoculars focused on the dawning sun eclipsed by the sharp horizon, a mist forming over the Southern continent of Antarctica. Penguins waddled on the icepack toward the shore dressed in their natural tuxedos for a morning dip into the cold Atlantic, gathering food. Woolsey dropped his binoculars on its strap, his eyes refocusing from the glare of the blue-white reflection. "I hope that bone sample is not contaminated," he mused, his eyes captivated by the golden half-circle of the dawning sun, spears of light

showered the lonely ice in a blur of dazzling illumination.

Caruso stared below on the deck at the few F-15s, his mind swept by incomprehension, straining to readjust his eyes to the light of dawning day. Yet the shadows of celestial light reminded him of the dogfight of Nazi UFOs. He dropped his gaze. "Perhaps we were lucky," he surmised.

"The President will be surprised that we were even able to acquire the bone sample," Woolsey said shivering, his body reacting to the vision of the moment of exhumation down under the ice. "I suppose now that Captain Coates has torpedoed *Neuschwabenland* the rash of UFOs will terminate," he guessed.

"Don't count on it, Nazism is alive and well in Argentina and America, and don't forget there are those who still believe Hitler's dream will live for a thousand years," Caruso postulated.

"You can't really believe Neo-Nazis' have UFO technology."

"If our scientists can retrofit German technology, so can they—the German archives are open to the public," Caruso rebutted, a frown suddenly seizing his face. "Listen, Woolsey, those archives may have a few of Hitler's personal effects."

"Personal effects," he mimicked, unsure of his meaning.

"Anything personal that will contain DNA."

"Your premise is good, the possibility almost nil—I need a cup of coffee, are you coming?"

"In a moment," he replied, as Woolsey descended from the bridge. Caruso gazed out upon the Atlantic thinking. Were the chances nil of finding comparison DNA? He must investigate. He filed a note in his brain. He would propose a trip to those archives when he met with President Darcy soon as they arrived. He terminated his gaze, a plan conceived, and found his way to the galley. On the way down the narrow aisle it struck him that the President was wounded!

The aircraft carrier finally raised Puerto Rico on the horizon, the easternmost island of the Greater Antilles, changing its course up the coast passed the Florida Keys. The evening shadows danced on the waves now more docile as the sun had dipped below the horizon, the winds subsided. The Admiral estimated docking by 7:00 tonight. A conference had been called down in the Admiral's flagship office, including the presence of the Carrier captain, the Sub captain and Dr. Caruso in attendance. A coffee pot and refreshments sat on the glass top of the mahogany conference table. All guests were present, and the Admiral sat with a folder he was reading lying on the table.

Admiral McHenny lowered his coffee cup. "Captain Coates, would you care to comment on your decision to torpedo *Neuschwabenland*?"

Coates leaned forward and placed his elbows on the table. "I made an executive decision to kill that last UFO pilot, Admiral. We have gotten all we need, so I destroyed the place."

He fingered his mandrake beard. "Be that as it may, it wasn't your damn decision to torpedo the evidence," he replied acidly, slamming his fist on the table.

"Begging your pardon, Admiral, in times of war it is the Captain's prerogative."

The Admiral dropped his acidic expression and said nothing more. Captain Coates was not as unassuming as Tunney had been. He was decisive in his commands, and he understood Coat's point. Coates was correct. As Admiral it was his duty to balance all the decisions. Swiftly, it was over. "Dr. Caruso, how did you and Woolsey perform?"

Caruso looked a Woolsey. You tell him, my friend."

The Captain winked. "We not only found Hitler's grave, but a totally different landing area under the ice with an elevator, and pumps that evacuated the water. And Admiral, I think Coates was correct to torpedo Neuschwabenland—there is no need to return to Antarctica," he replied. "We gave the bone sample to the FBI laboratory."

Caruso grinned. "I have an idea about a comparison sample for the DNA, Admiral."

"Yes, I had completely forgotten the analysis needs a comparison—what's your idea?"

"Hitler's personal effects."

His wrinkled face frowned. "Damn, Robby! Where in hell do you think you'll find that kind of evidence?" he replied stonily.

There was almost a full minute of angry silence before Caruso replied. "The German Federal Archives, Sir."

McHenny leaned back in his chair, an embarrassing countenance stealing the truth of his next statement. "I'm sorry, Robby. This case is responsible for my testy remarks." He paused, pouring a new cup of coffee and slid it over to Caruso. "When do you leave for Germany?"

The shock of McHenny's sudden display of apology slowly faded from Caruso's countenance. "Soon as we hit stateside sir, I've already made an appointment. It seems there is a lady who stocks the archive items."

23

Reagan Airport was surprisingly busy at the midnight hour. Caruso parked his car in the parking lot, took a small case from the front seat, and locked the door. He made a mental note of the aisle where he parked, and strolled at rapid pace toward the active entrance of the airport. As he reached the crosswalk the wheels of an international plane touched the airfield with a noticeable squeal, engines revving in reverse thrust. He waited for two cars to pass and crossed over to the curb, slowing for the other travelers, and ascended the three steps to the pavement. An attendant offered to take his case but Caruso pleasantly

refused, and the attendant gave his attention to a lady touching his shoulder.

Caruso took note of the Flight Screens and found his flight at Gate 2. He gripped his case and turned left in the corridor toward the even numbered gates. He stopped at a refreshment shop and bought a newspaper, shoved it under an arm and moved out into the line of milling passengers. As he pushed into the maze, he saw Gate 2 up ahead and eased his stride. He squirmed over and found himself behind a woman pulling a luggage cart and slackened his stride in a sudden tiptoe. Finally, he pealed out the stream of humanity, directly in front of the ticket stand. It was like leaving the womb, being born again. He breathed a sigh of new birth, fingered his crumpled boarding pass from his inside coat pocket and gave it to the ticket agent, who stood gazing at the frazzled man.

"Just a little cramped out there wouldn't you say?" she grinned

For the first time after entering that millstream he smiled. "You are surprisingly observant," he grinned.

"You ought to fly at the Christmas holiday," she replied, scanning her boarding list and look up. "Your flight is on time, Dr. Caruso, arriving in ten minutes," she said flashing a captivating smile of white teeth.

"Thank you," he replied. "You have restored my vanity," he chuckled and took his boarding pass.

"Aren't you cute," she said with raised eyebrow.

He dropped his gaze with a nod, and stepped into the waiting area facing four rows of padded chairs, all occupied it seemed. He spied an empty chair, and as he approached the backside of a passenger seated on the opposite row seemed somehow familiar. He'd seen those broad shoulders before. The passenger stood and walked around the row. He turned into the adjacent row, smiling.

"I didn't want you to leave the country alone," said Bruce Allison.

Caruso sat his case on the floor, and pulled Bruce into his arms in a manly hug. He couldn't have come at a better time. Extending him at arm's length, he smiled. "Gosh, I'm glad you came."

"It was Captain Woolsey's idea. He phoned, asking if I might take this flight."

He nodded. "Woolsey is a good man."

"He certainly thinks a great deal of you, Robby."

He cleared his throat. "Well, let's have a seat. We should be boarding soon. Did you get your boarding pass?"

"Yeah, I've been here about twenty minutes. And before I forget, both our wives are flying to Washington next week."

A tear nestled in the corner of Caruso's left eye. It was such tender news, seemed like a year since he had left Jenny Lynn waiting in the Bahamas. The private

thought was cancelled by the loud announcement that their flight was ready for boarding.

The Boeing 747 climbed to its assigned lane in the sky highway, moving out over the Atlantic climbing up to 36,000 feet. Bruce sat in the window seat gazing out at the boundless arc of celestial-blue fringed with sliver clouds. His mind wrestled in the shadows of a conversation he'd had with Jenny Lynn. She had had a premonition. She broke down in tears when she called last night. In her dream a man in black had attacked Robby. Suddenly the sound of rolling wheels invaded his reverie, the man in black faded in a cloud of indecision.

A flight attendant walked the aisle pushing a cart with refreshments.

Bruce rustled in his seat, as Robby requested a cup of coffee and a bag of potato chips. Bruce acquiesced and took a coke instead with chips. Robby pulled down the little shelf embedded in the back of the seat facing him, and sat his cup on it, steam rising into the AC.

"Tell me Bruce, what really prompted your joining me—was it actually Woolsey?"

Bruce swirled the ice in his cup of coke. "Yes and no."

"Can you be more specific?"

"Yes, Woolsey did call, and he did suggest I take this flight."

"And "no?"

"If you must know, Jenny Lynn called last night."

He rotated his head back into the steam of his coffee. "She's worried about me, I take it."

"She called your office off and on for three days, and then out of desperation she called me."

"Now I remember, you promised to take care of me," he replied, moisture flooding his eyes.

Bruce responded with trivia. "Throughout history all women have sat at home and waited for their man to come back from somewhere. What can they do but worry."

"Yes, what else can they do?" he agreed, suddenly pausing. "I don't remember you having a degree in psychology."

"You don't want me to tell you everything, Robby. Why don't you tell me what's so important in Berlin?" he advised, taking a sip of his soda.

"The German Archives," he said.

Bruce pulled out his cellphone and punched a few codes. "The archives are in Koblenz, Rhineland."

"We can have breakfast in the hotel café. I'll bring you up to speed then," Caruso replied, as he hit a lever beneath his seat and leaned back for a nap. His eyes closed, the hypnotic hum of the turbines lulled him to sleep.

Somehow his brain replayed the history of his destination. The Celts were believed to be the first inhabitants of Germany generating into tribes. The

Franks gained supremacy in Western Europe under Charlemagne, who was crowned Holy Roman Emperor. By the Treaty of Verdum, Charlemagne's lands east of the Rhine were ceded to the German Prince Louis. This grant gave Germany approximately the land it maintained in the Middle Ages. The Thirty Years War, between 1618 and 1648, devastated Berlin. One third of its houses were damaged or destroyed, and the city lost half of its population. Frederick William, known as the Great Elector, who had succeeded his father George William as ruler in 1640, initiated a policy of immigration and religious tolerance. The Edict of Potsdam of 1685 offered asylum to the French Huguenots. By 1700, approximately 30 percent of Berlin's residents were French because of the Huguenot immigration. Frederick the Great came to power and led Germany as one of Europe's enlighten monarchs until Napoleon Bonaparte marched into Berlin in 1806. In the early 20th century Berlin had become a fertile ground for the German Expressionist movement fresh from France. Berlin's history had left the city with a polycentric organization and a highly eclectic array of architecture and buildings. Her demise came in 1933 when Adolph Hitler and the Nazi Party seized the chancellorship. Today, following the reconstruction after World War II, Berlin is a particularly dense city-state.

24

A Boeing 747 entered the airspace of Berlin and set the controls for a proper heading to Schönefeld Airport located just outside the southeastern border of Berlin-Brandenburg Metropolitan Region. The 747 received a flight path for landing and dropped flaps, gliding down to the runway. The wheels touched the pavement, and the engines reversed thrust. The pilot followed the lights to the boarding location. Finally the aircraft pulled up to a Jetway. The accordion-shaped cab bumped against the door of the fuselage.

It took thirty minutes to get their luggage from the carousel. As they walked out to take a taxi, Robby

looked at the skyline, recalling a previous trip to Berlin two years ago. Berlin, a city of plateaus; town twinning began with its sister city of Los Angeles in 1967.

They took a taxi to the hotel and found the reserved rooms. Caruso decided to go down to the café and have dinner, and of course, Bruce agreed especially since Caruso approved paying the bill. They found the café modestly full but two tables were available and the waitress seated them at one by the window. Robby always desired to be far away with his back to the wall; it was a trick of his older days drinking beer New York bars. His work in those days was with the CIA and he had enemies in the Mohair. The waitress served them with a menu in English, which Caruso thanked her for being patient. Robby ordered his usual, a steak and baked potato. Bruce chose fish with a fries.

As they waited, Bruce gazed around the room. The restrooms were to the right, and he excused himself. Caruso drew parallel lines with his fork on a napkin. Suddenly he saw someone familiar in the corner of his eye walk into the door. He couldn't believe his eyes. It was Sean Casey! Had he followed them to Germany or was he here on a job? Bruce walked up to the table, and Casey cast his eyes up and saw his worst enemy. He bolted out the door. Caruso pushed back his chair and ran to the door and out into the street.

He saw no one, nothing at all, and walked to the edge of the hotel, nothing there neither. Caruso's eyes

were drawn to parallel skid marks. The tire prints were telltale, but the knife lying on the pavement where the driver jumped into the car seat was tangible evidence of Sean Casey, he thought. He stooped and picked up the sheathed knife; he'd seen it several times before, it was Casey's all right. Somehow his car must have been parked here in front of the hotel. One more look around the bushes and he was satisfied Casey was not here.

They ate dinner, but Caruso's mind was fixed on Casey and his knife tucked away in his briefcase. He must have had another job here in Germany; it made no sense that he had followed them across the Atlantic. He drank his last cup of coffee and they went up to their rooms. Bruce opened Robby's door and gave him his key.

"Put Casey out of your mind for tonight. Tomorrow is a big day," he advised. "I'll awaken you at 6:00 in the morning."

A grasping hand slapped the left thigh, the other hand gripping the steering wheel of an Audi sedan soaring along the docks down near the Havel River. Sean Casey slammed on the breaks, angrily swung open the door and stepped out on the road, his motor idling. Honking cars swerved recklessly, but his mind was not on the traffic; indeed, he wasn't aware that he was standing in rushing traffic. The Velcro strap on his thigh was torn, his knife missing!

A screaming voice broke his trance. "Hey buddy, get out of the road!

He turned, stepped into the seat and carefully pulled to the side of the road. He stumbled out to the bluff, fell to his knees and cursed aloud, his cry echoing over the black waters. The outburst was totally out of character for this suave debonair, but that bowie knife was an inheritance from a deceased uncle, who had fought in the Texas Revolution against Mexican forces of Santa Anna. The many stories harbored in his youthful mind of how the knife was a gift from Jim Bowie's brother, Rezin. It was said to be a prototype of the bowie knife left in the ashes of the ALAMO. As a small child this uncle had taught him how to kill with a knife. He related that more fatalities were by knife than gun; it was silent and effective.

The Celtic moon lit the crest of the tranquil river reminding him that he must change his plans tonight; the knife was more valuable than even the first payment of $30,000. He would register in another hotel; it was a mistake to rent a room in the same hotel as the elusive Dr. Caruso. He drove the Audi the three blocks to another hotel facing the lake. His thoughts centered on freshening up and taking in a concert. The thought calmed the angry issues coursing through his mind, and Casey gazed out over the lake. In the distance, the moonlight glistened on the northeastern Oberbaum Bridge spanning the historic Spree River which empted

into the river Havel. He returned the Audi at the rental agency beside the hotel and entered the side doors to the hotel proper. Following the overhead signs to the lobby he finally registered and took a room on the second floor.

Just washing his face and brushing the dust from his tuxedo restored his vanity. He took the elevator to the ground floor and stepped out to the curb. Presently a cab pulled up and stopped. Casey folded his tall body in the backseat.

"Potsdamer Platz," he told the cab driver.

The taxi pulled into the street, the driver gazing at the debonair-dressed man in the rearview mirror.

"The Philharmonie Orchestra features Beethoven tonight," he ventured.

There was no response and the driver dropped his gaze concentrating on the traffic driving over the Oberbaum Bridge. He coursed through the lanes of traffic, patrons probably going to the same destination eager to get to the concert on time. Finally he pulled up to the street named for the orchestra's longest serving conductor, Herbert von Karajan.

Casey stepped out and paid the taxi driver, leaning his head in the window. "Beethoven is not my favorite composer, but I thank you for the information," he said, and tipped him handsomely.

His eyes focused on the billing lights coursing across the overhead. The taxi driver was accurate; the orchestra was indeed performing one of Beethoven's ten symphonies. It was appropriate for the city of Berlin, although Beethoven lived in Vienna, he thought.

He took his seat in the huge auditorium. Gratefully he absorbed the calming music. Funny, he thought how a few cleverly placed notes could be so restful. It may have been that he slept through the Allegretto of the Seventh Symphony, but the booming notes of the Fifth awakened him.

As he left the concert his cellphone buzzed. He walked over to a corner. "Yes."

The voice was recognizable: Hans Grübber. "You failed your mission. There will be no pay until the President and Henri are dead."

There was a click and the dial tone buzzed.

Casey closed the phone staring into space. He would not leave Germany until he found his missing knife; then it struck him, it was a strong possibility that Caruso had the knife. He had been his adversary for years and constantly hounded him from city to city. Yes, he thought, this must be done—find that knife.

Casey rented a car and drove directly to Caruso's hotel. Since he had been registered there himself, he was pleased that he entered the lobby unnoticed. He took the elevator and stepped out looking both ways down the hall. Caruso's room was left and he briskly strode to the door. He placed his ear on the door.

Satisfied that the room was vacant, he removed a set of skeleton keys from his pocket. The fourth key fit and he swung open the door. He went directly to the bedroom closet and pulled out a suitcase, placed it on the bed. He opened it and pulled out the laundry: Nothing. He stuffed the laundry back in the case and sat it back in the closet. Turning hurriedly his eyes surveying the room, he spotted a briefcase sitting by the dresser. Quickly he opened the case—there on top of papers lay his knife!

Casey's heart thumped wildly, realizing the odds of finding the knife so quickly. In one motion he shoved the knife into the inside pocket of his coat and closed the briefcase.

A knock at the door: "Maid service."

He heard a key being inserted in the lock. Swiftly he glued his body against the wall of the bedroom. The maid entered the bathroom, flushed the toilet and began cleaning the sink. He stealthily moved to the entrance door, gently rotated the knob and stepped into the hall, gently closing the door behind his exit.

In 1946, the German Central Archive was founded in Potsdam. At that time it was in the Soviet occupation zone and later in East Germany. By the end of the 1950s records that had originally been seized by the government of the Soviet Union in the aftermath of the World War II had been returned to the archive. While in

West Germany, the Cabinet of Germany created a new Federal Archive in Koblenz in 1950, a project that was not complete until 1952. The United States and the United Kingdom had also seized records from Germany following that war. In 1955, a military Achieve Division was established as part of the Federal Achieves designed as a place to receive the returned records. The collection of the German federal Archives today include older document from Germany's imperial past, Nazi Germany. All of the records that were never public have been merged into the Federal Archives by a bill amending the Federal Archives Act of 1988 in which the Federal Archives came into force on 13 March 1992. These were the records that would interest Dr. Caruso.

Dr. Robert Caruso ascended the steps leading to the front entrance of the German Federal Achieves in Koblenz. Bruce pointed to the delicate frieze carved along the concrete wall of the entrance. It was a massive building designed in two wings merged by twin towers of stairs and elevators. They walked into a large open lobby and approached the front desk. A receptionist who spoke English fluently smiled.

"May I assist you?" she said, her blonde hair bundle on her oval shaped head, an impressive broach securing the chignon.

"Yes, my name is Dr. Caruso, this is Bruce Allison. We are on a mission of President Winston Darcy of the United States.

Her blue eyes widened.

"I have been in contact with Heidi Strassenberg. Is she available?"

The woman glanced down at a pad lying on her desk. "Ms. Strassenberg is due back from lunch in about ten minutes. May I get you some refreshments?" she smiled.

"Thank you, but that won't be necessary," Robby replied his eyes suddenly focused on a handsome woman walking from a side door. She carried herself languidly and stood tall. Her shape was pencil thin. Her hair was salt and pepper and gracefully styled, wearing a blue smock.

The receptionist stood. "Ms. Strassenberg, this is Dr. Caruso and Bruce Allison from America."

She scanned her visitor whom she had talked with on the telephone. Caruso's face was tanned, his shoulders broad. He was a handsome man in his mid forties, hazel eyes that melted a woman's resistance. "How nice to see you at last, Dr. Caruso," she said extending her small hand.

"The pleasure is mine, Heidi," Caruso replied, kissing her hand.

"Won't you and Bruce follow me to my office," she beamed.

Heidi walked beside Caruso, admiring such a handsome man standing three inches above her tall frame, as she thought not many men this good-looking

came into the Archives. Bruce lagged behind the two and realized her intentions were obvious even if Robby didn't. He smiled.

Finally they reached a room near the central elevators and she inserted a key in the lock. The door swung open and she invited them inside, reaching for the light switch by the door. "Please have a seat while I put on a pot of coffee—I understand Dr. Caruso that you like coffee almost as much as me. Do you take it black?"

"You've read my mind, Heidi."

She chuckled. "I also know you are married."

Bruce heard the comment and it confirmed his diagnosis of her intentions. He took a seat in a chair facing a sofa. Robby rested his aching back on the sofa. Bruce leaned forward, cupping his hand beside his mouth. "Heidi is hot on you, ole buddy," he whispered with a grin.

Caruso did not reply, crossing his leg relieving the pressure on his back.

Heidi returned from the kitchen with a pot of coffee and some finger sandwiches. She sat them on the table before the sofa and sat down beside Robby. She poured three cups and Bruce stood for his cup. She placed a second cup on the table for Caruso and brought the third cup to her ruby red lips. "You mentioned Hitler articles for a DNA test," she said directly to the point.

Robby sat his cup on the table. "Yes, we have a bone sample—

"So I understand, but where did you acquire it," she interrupted abruptly.

Robby realized it was a sensitive subject. "How much do you know about Neuschwabenland?"

"I have a file on New Swabia a mile high, but no indication that Hitler was there."

Caruso uncrossed his leg, looking directly in the cornea of her blue eyes. "Trust me, he was there. We exhumed his grave."

She cocked her oval-shaped head. "Correction; you exhumed *a* grave," she insisted.

"You can put it that way, that's why we need a comparison sample," he rebutted.

"That might not be so easy," she added.

"Come now Heidi, you know this facility like the back of your hand—you are the last hope we have."

She didn't respond immediately, and looked into his hazel eyes. "Why must you open this painful scar again," she pleaded.

He sensed her discomfort relative the Holocaust. "My dear Heidi, truth is important to all the families of that horrible war. The cover-up of Hitler's death is a festering sore on the conscious of the entire world."

She accepted his answer without reply. Her only joy was the fantasy of holding him in her arms. The fantasy faded but was not forgotten.

Bruce realized then that he would just be in the way. He touched Robby's shoulder. "I'm going back to the lobby, you don't need me here. Take your time."

Robby nodded.

Heidi unlocked a drawer in a cabinet behind her, and laid a pad on the table. She read a few columns. "I can take you to the basement of the archives," she replied, deciding to investigate a box that had not been disseminated. "There are some old boxes stored there received from Russia."

"These are the records seized by the Soviet Union in the aftermath of World War II?" Caruso guessed.

"Yes," she said, not surprised at the accuracy of his remark. "Just a few boxes we haven't assimilated into the new files as yet," she replied.

They left the office, Robby lagged behind admiring her feminine strut. They passed the corner to the elevators, and Heidi suddenly pushed Robby against the wall.

She kissed him.

"Does that bother you?" she said placing his arms around his waist. She kissed him again. "It doesn't bother me—I like it," she smiled seductively.

Robby suddenly reversed positions and kissed her. "Doesn't bother me either, but my wife has a 38 Smith and Wesson."

She smiled and kissed him again. "You only live once," she winked.

The elevator reached the basement, and Heidi stepped out with her handbag shouldered. She led him down the main aisle, and they passed row after row of large boxes on shelves. They reached a door at the very back wall and Heidi produced a flashlight from her handbag. She selected a key from a ring of keys and inserted one in the lock. The rusting tumblers made it difficult to rotate the lock. She jiggled the key and finally the tumblers aligned with the serrations of her key. The door swung open with a creaking sound. A pungent smell floated from the dark room.

Heidi activated the flashlight. "Wait here," she said and slowly moved with caution to the back wall following the light beam. She opened the metal door of an electrical service box, and inspected all the circuits. Finally she placed her thumb on a switch and toggled it over to the 'on' position. The dark room flooded with incandescent light.

"Over here," she waved, and led him to a row at the very back. Down the row about ten meters, she pointed to a box on a dusty shelf above her head. "Can you reach that box, Dr. Caruso?"

He stepped forward. "Sure." He stuck three fingers in an opening which vaguely resembled a handhold, tugged gently, and then twice more. The box unstuck from years of drying moisture that had transformed into substantial glue. He slowly pulled it out and supported the bottom of the box with his other hand as it cleared the shelf. He sat it on the floor.

Heidi knelt, and laid back the four lids of the file box. She pointed her flashlight into a dusty cloud of multiple colors dazzling her eyes. "What in the hell is that," she moaned, embarrassed by her sudden vulgarity.

Caruso chuckled. "It's called the Tyndall Effect. Your light beam reflects the dust particles in rainbow colors, an atmospheric effect."

She shook her head, "Whatever," pointing to a small metal container in the corner of the box. "Would you remove that container, please?"

"Of course," he replied, reaching down into the dusty contents visible only by the flashlight beam. He fingered the box and gently lifted it out of the dark void. He closed the lids of the box and sat the container on top. "Would you do the honor of opening this container?" he said.

She dryly swallowed, taking the tiny box in one hand and prying the top off with the other. Her eyes beamed. "I don't believe it. You must be psychic, Dr. Caruso."

He said nothing gazing at the surprise in her face, and then focusing on a comb and brush, suddenly narrowing his eyes. "Look, Heidi there's a note on the bottom," he said somewhat gleefully, if not astoundingly.

"Don't touch it," she warned, donning a pair of sterile plastic gloves taken from her smock pocket. She gripped the corner of the paper note and gently pulled it from under the comb. Again, she swallowed, opening the folds of the note. It was a handwritten note in classic German language!

Caruso's mind surged alert. "Can you translate it," he asked, only skilled at a few German nouns and verbs?

She laid the note open on the box and beamed the flashlight on the black letters. "I quote: *I certify that this is the personal brush and comb of Adolph Hitler.*"

Heidi raised her startled face. "It's signed, Otto Günsche," she gasped.

"And who is Otto Günsche?"

She gently folded the note, placed it in the container and closed it. "Günsche was Hitler's SS adjutant," she replied, peeling off the gloves. She grasped the metal lid and placed it on the box, suddenly retrieving her hand.

"You cut your finger," he gasped.

"It's nothing."

Caruso instinctively stuck her finger in his mouth and sucked. 'Nothing' he thought, his mind racing back to his history courses. He stood in the very city of great scientists in chemistry and medicine: Max Planck, who held the Nobel Prize for his founding work in the quantum theory, the Planck constant in his radiation law and many quantum physic laws of energy, Rudolf

Virchow founder of cellular pathology, and Robert Koch the great bacteriologist who developed vaccines for anthrax, cholera, and tuberculosis.

Suddenly something struck him, sharply twisting in his gut. The scientist of most interest to the death ray was Nikola Tesla. He slowly removed Heidi's finger from his mouth, gazing studiously into the dusty file box his eyes fixed on a folder.

"What is it?" she asked, retrieving her finger.

He didn't respond, his eyes glued on a legal-size binder—not so much the modern plastic as the scribbled note on its spine. His hand instinctively thrust into the box and seized the binder. Pages spilled from the rusty binding rings. Both hands quickly gathered the papers. Heidi grasped the binder. Caruso's eyes focused on electrical drawings and sketches. He couldn't believe what his eyes feasted upon, but the information in his mind confirmed his thoughts. These were the missing pages from Tesla's notebook—the death ray equations!

Heidi's face screwed confusingly. "Is this what I think it is?" she murmured.

"Is there somewhere we can examine these pages?" he said without answering her question.

"Put that box back on the shelf, and follow me," she said directly.

They entered the elevator, Heidi's heart racing with the significance of their discovery, Caruso clutching the dusty binder tucked tightly against his thigh. Upward the elevator rose and suddenly stopped on the third floor. Heidi stepped out first and led Caruso to an area overlooking a balcony. Shelf after shelf of books, aisle and aisle of tiled floor occupied the first section. They crossed a hallway and a row of reading rooms appeared against a wall, beginning with a line of personal computers.

"In here," Heidi said twisting a doorknob.

Her injured finger flipped the toggle switch activating a row of fluorescent lamps in the ceiling. She grimaced, stuck the finger in her mouth. "Take a table while I find a band-aid," she said sucking her finger.

Caruso smiled, as he pulled up a chair and sat. He laid the binder on the desk, carefully opened the pages. The binding edges of the pages were obviously ripped from another notebook. This situation fit the reports. When Tesla died several crates of his notes and files were at his home. Yet the original notebook from which these papers were ripped had never been found. Then it occurred to him that Tesla had appeared in the newspapers hoping to sell the notebook to acquire funds for his research. Caruso suddenly stood, and stepped out the door.

Heidi returned from a kitchenette attached to the reading room, and found Caruso missing, the door open. She stepped out and discovered him sitting at one of the computers giddy as a kid reading his first Agatha

Christie novel. "Will you stop for a moment and let's converse a while," she blurted.

He clicked out of the document, and turned from the black screen. "Sorry, of course, you are correct," he said standing.

They walked back into the room. Heidi closed the door turned and faced the handsome man. She kissed him on his tanned cheek. "Can I get you a cup of coffee," she said with a wink, but decided it best that she comply with her own request.

"That would be nice," he replied, a sheepish expression on his face.

She strolled into the kitchenette. Caruso sat before the open files on a table, leafing one sheet over another, electrical diagrams and notes, a number of equations. His eyes fixed on a sketch. It was a circular column three feet in diameter, twenty feet tall, wrapped with a continuous row of copper wire—a giant coil! Perched on the top was a circular wire cage. Affixed electrically to the apex of the coil, was a ceramic "nozzle" extending three feet from the cage. The entire edifice sat on a twelve by twelve feet stand rising four feet from the concrete base. Beneath the base were three massive generators of direct current.

Tesla was a Croatian-American electrician and inventor who made practical the use of alternating current. He emigrated to the U.S.A. in 1884 and worked briefly with Thomas Edison. His demonstration in 1886

of how a magnetic field could be made to rotate by supplying two coils at right angles with alternating current of different phases led to his patenting of the alternating-current motor, and its sale to George Westinghouse, who made it the basis for the Westinghouse power system. Tesla did noteworthy research on high-voltage electricity, transformers, telephone and telegraph systems, radio, and plants for wireless power transmission.

Heidi returned with two cups of coffee. She sat the cups on the table and heaved a chair to the table. “What have you found?” she inquired.

He leaned back in his chair, stuck his finger in the ceramic ring of the cup and sipped slowly. “You make a good cup of coffee,” he said, avoiding her question.

“Never mind the accolades—what do those pages say to your curious mind?” she said and sipped her cup.

“It says that I have to board a plane to the United States as soon as possible.”

Her eyebrow arched. “Suppose I say you cannot take those files unless you tell me what they contain,” she said officially.

He shuffled his feet enjoying her tightfisted standpoint. “These are the missing pages from Tesla’s notebook,” he said bluntly.

“The death ray drawings,” she conjectured.

“I suspect so,” he nodded.

"Okay, you can take them on one stipulation," she said.

"And that is?"

"Come here you devil," she said and kissed him. She took his hand and led him to a back room and locked the door.

History reveals that the cost of progress has many facets; that cost is variable, sometimes requires the ultimate payment. In Dr. Caruso's case both the facet and cost is in a woman's hands; one who loves, the other who lusts for him.

25

The mounting stress of the day fell upon him like the glistening moonlight on the waters of the River Spree. Only the metal box in his right-hand pocket gave him any satisfaction. But Tesla's notebook in his briefcase was worth a million dollars. Tesla's notes, he thought. Suddenly it hit him. When he placed the notebook in his briefcase, Casey's knife was missing!

He was tired, and suddenly realized Casey was closer than he'd realized. Night had fallen over Berlin. Because of what Heidi had told him about the nightlife in this old city, he thought he might call Bruce and have him meet him at the airport. Tonight was the annual

International Film Festival with around 500,000 in attention. It was the largest public attendance in the world. There would be fireworks galore. Caruso punched a code in his cellphone; two rings and the circuit clicked. "Hello, Bruce . . . yeah I've got it, and I think we might have dinner in the airport before we leave . . . okay, I'll meet you there in an hour."

Caruso drove his rental car just outside Berlin on the autobahn to Brandenburg, heading to the Schönefeld Airport. The streetlights gave the moonlight a murky glow, the shadows shifting like dancing fairies. Up ahead his headlights illumed the tall stacks of the Heizkraftwerk power plant. It was fortunate that the power lines were underground or he would not have had this magnificent view. He taxed his tired mind to review all that had happened on this eventful day. The President would be pleased that he had the evidence, the reason for this trip. That fulfillment was satisfying enough, and he was ready to get back to the Washington.

The airport finally appeared and he steered the car in the off-ramp. The sign for the airport was brightly lit with a row of lights. He chose the four-lane road for boarding passengers. Flights departing from Berlin served 163 destinations around the globe, and there were two flights departing for Washington, DC tonight.

Sodium light illumed the parking lot fashioned on tall lampposts. Bruce saw the sign for rental cars and drove over the lot for return cars. He parked and

noticed this lot was not as nearly lit as the larger lot. He removed the key, placing it in his trouser pocket, and locked the door. On the pavement he momentarily glimpsed a man's shadow. Suddenly he felt something poke him in the back and the sound of a familiar voice. "Raise your hands, Caruso," said Sean Casey.

Caruso's eyes squinted, chiding thoughts for not being alert. Knowing he had no time, he spun with the finesse of a cat. The elbow knocked the Beretta to the ground. They struggled. Arms gyrated, hands cupped in karate fashion, bodies twisting and swaying. Casey was no fool and had expected this man to make his move. He gripped the handle of his knife from its sheath strapped to his calf. Caruso seized the knife hand, swung Casey's arm into his armpit, twisting the wrist until he heard the elbow snap. Casey screamed and thrust his knee toward Caruso's crotch, yet he shifted his torso, reaching down for the Beretta. Casey grabbed his knife with his good hand during the instant Caruso was bent down. He raised the knife, a devious grin on his face. The hand thrust downward the blade shimmering in the moonlight. Yet Casey's empty hand hit Caruso's back!

Suddenly his arms were gripped by strong hands that wrenched them behind his back. Again, Casey screamed; the nerves in his elbow sending pains of agony to his brain. Bruce Allison tied the arms with his belt. "Sorry Casey. Your career ends here," he said, waving the knife in his tormented face.

Caruso stood. "I owe you one, Bruce."

"You can by my lunch, Robby," he replied picking up the Beretta.

Alert bystanders had alerted the police and two guards from Airport Security ran over. One guard perused the situation. "What's going on here?" he asked in a thick-tongue accent.

Caruso straightened his back, a sudden attack of sciatica frowned his face. "Officer, my name is Dr. Caruso. We are from America on a mission of President Darcy. This man is Sean Casey who attacked the President," he said opening his wallet, handing him a business card:

He handed the card to his partner. "We shall have this man extradited to Washington Police, if that is satisfactory," he said.

Caruso received the card from the other man, stuck it in his wallet. "That will indeed be satisfactory. Thank you officer," he replied. "We were about to have breakfast—would you gentlemen care to direct us to the cafeteria?"

"It's on our way, Dr. Caruso," an officer replied, applying handcuffs to his prisoner. "Does this belt belong to someone?"

"Thank you, officer. The belt is mine."

A curiously group of men, two Security officers, two hungry men, and a mad assassin walked toward the Airport.

"Have you instructed Admiral McHenny and the others that we are flying back tonight?" Bruce asked, the twosome sitting in the Airport cafeteria, sipping coffee. He, like Caruso, had decided to eat breakfast; they had had enough German food for this trip.

"As a matter of fact, I haven't—intended too, but Casey intervened," he replied, and searched his coat for his cellphone, thinking he might have lost it in the struggle. But he found it, and punched a code looking into Bruce's direction.

"Thought you'd lost the phone, huh?" Bruce grinned.

He smiled. "Admiral, this is Caruso . . . yes, thought we'd fly out tonight . . . got it right here in my pocket . . . sure! We'll meet you in Washington on the weekend."

He closed the phone and stuck the plastic nuisance back in his pocket.

A male waitress approached with two platters of sausage and eggs. As they sat eating, the unexpected peaceful moment a blessing, Bruce leaned back with his glass of iced tea clenched in his hand. "You haven't said much about your archive search today?"

Caruso wiped his mouth with the cloth napkin. "A very successful search; Heidi was quite helpful."

Bruce smiled. "Your secret is safe with me, Robby."

"What secret?"

"Heidi, the woman had a crush on you."

"Nothing happened."

"Then wipe that lipstick off your cheek," he said, suddenly laughing.

He wiped the cloth napkin across his cheek, a red smear resulted, and it was not blood, unless Jenny Lynn thought otherwise.

They reached the airport with an hour wait for their flight back to the U.S.A. Somehow they decided to wait in the food court, Bruce was already hungry again. Robby carried his briefcase on his person, the contents too valuable to become baggage. As they sat the PA called Dr. Caruso's name, and he went to central circle where the call originated. The lady standing behind the counter realized that the man approaching may be her party.

"Dr. Caruso," she implied.

"That's right—you called?"

"Yes sir. You have a telephone call," she said pointing to the phone. "Punch 9."

Caruso lifted the receiver and punched code 9. "This is Dr Caruso."

"Detective Reichstag, Dr. Caruso. I have some embarrassing news. Your prisoner Sean Casey has escaped," he said.

Caruso's face frowned. "When?"

"We discovered the empty cell ten minutes ago. The last cell check was about an hour."

"How long would take a taxi to drive to Schönefeld Airport?'

"In this traffic I'd say two hours, no less."

"Thank you for calling detective."

"For what it's worth, we issued an APB."

"Thanks again, detective," he replied and hung the phone. He strolled back to the food court his mind replaying the scenario he calculated that Casey would exercise in this situation. This crowded airport would suit him just fine.

He finally reached the food court and found Bruce eating a hamburger with fries.

He stared up, swallowing. "Who was it?"

"That detective who took custody of Casey."

"And?"

"And Casey has escaped."

Bruce choked on a bite of hamburger. "What?" he coughed.

Caruso sat, stretched out his long legs. "He doesn't have a weapon, but that won't stop him. If Berlin is like America, he can purchase whatever he needs," he said thinking aloud.

"I gather you expect Casey to make his move in this airport."

"It's tailor made," Robby said, and turned to Bruce. "It is best if we draw him out."

"You'll need bait to catch a rat."

Caruso smiled at his best friend. "I'm the biggest bait," he said, and I think the restroom is a good place to set the bait."

"Wait Robby, don't look. Casey just entered the west side door."

Caruso raised his cellphone, and punched the code for Security Police. He had entered that code the last time he had met the guards here at the airport. The phone answered. "Security Police."

"This is Dr. Caruso—

"We meet again, Dr. Caruso," a voice injected.

"May I speak with Detective Heinz Hoffman, please?"

"This is Hoffman, Dr. Caruso. I suspect you are calling about Sean Casey—

"How is it you know Casey?" Caruso probed.

"Afraid I'm flying under false colors, Dr. Caruso. You see the Berlin police called and told us you were here in the airport. Sean Casey is the target I assume."

"That's correct. Be careful detective, this man is a killer," Caruso said. "I'll be in the food court—you will be careful I assume," he said and closed his cellphone facing Bruce. "Where is Casey now?"

"He entered that restroom near the west door," Bruce replied.

A man walked down the aisle heading to the food court dressed in street clothes. He drew near, and Caruso recognized him as detective Hoffman. He nodded at Caruso, and leaned against the corner smoking a cigarette.

Caruso pointed to the rest room. Again Hoffman nodded, speaking into a radio. Suddenly Casey exited the restroom door, surveying the floor of the airport. For some unknown reason his eyes focused directly on Hoffman. Immediately he headed toward the front door in the midst of the crowd. Hoffman dropped his cigarette and almost ran in his eagerly haste not to lose Casey in the crowd.

Suddenly Casey stopped and turned, aiming a revolver and fired.

Hoffman dropped to a knee. His arm hit in the femur, but he shook off the pain, and raised his revolver, but had no clear shoot. He spoke rapidly into his radio. Three officers stood spaced across the front door. A special team of officers came through the side door armed with assault rifles. Casey grabbed a woman using her as a hostage, moving toward the door. She screamed; the crowd bolted away from the sound. At that moment Casey repositioned.

Hoffman had a clear shot.

Disregarding the pain in his arm, he rested the revolver on his knee, blood dripping on the floor. He took aim and fired. His aim was on target! The bullet hit Casey just above the ear.

Casey dropped dead in his tracks.

The officers quickly roped off the area as a crime scene. Ambulance sirens pierced the night. Two paramedics raced into the lobby following a police

escort. Dr. Caruso knelt beside Hoffman and tied his handkerchief around his bleeding arm just above the beneath the shoulder as a tourniquet.

Hoffman's eyes fluttered open. "You warned me that he was a killer," he gasped.

"You were magnificent, my friend! You can be on my team anywhere, anytime," Caruso said, gently patting his hand.

"A tear nestled in Hoffman's left eye."

The two paramedics gingerly laid Hoffman on the stretcher-trolley. One paramedic released the tourniquet; the other placed an oxygen mask over the patient's mouth. Finally they covered him with a blanket, and wheeled him toward the ambulance.

The Security police placed the body of Casey on a stretcher. "Dr. Caruso, I assume this man was a U.S. citizen. I will place him on your flight, if that is satisfactory," said a Lieutenant.

"You are too kind. That is quite satisfactory. Thank you, Lieutenant—and take good care of Hoffman."

He smiled. "He has been taking care of us for many years, Dr. Caruso."

Robby followed Bruce down the aisle to the gate of their flight. On his mind was the final solution of Sean Casey and in the back of his mind was the condition of Hoffman. If that bullet shattered the bone, he would be a long time healing. He consoled his thoughts by

focusing on the comb and brush evidence certified to have belonged to Hitler. The sign over the next gate was their flight, and Robby walked up to the desk and requested their boarding passes.

The attendant ran her finger down a list. “Dr. Caruso, we also have your boarding pass for the coffin brought in this afternoon,” she said handing him three boarding passes.

“Thank you, shouldn’t I pay for the flight of the coffin?” he asked, a raised eyebrow wrinkling his forehead.

“Let me see,” she said glancing down at her notebook. “The fight has already been paid,” she smiled.

The eyebrow returned to is proper location replaced by a deep frown. “Who might I ask paid for it?”

Again she consulted her notebook. “Detective Heinz Hoffman of the Berlin Police Department,” she replied.

Bruce smiled. “Wherever you go, Robby you always make friends.”

Robby did not react. They went to the waiting area until the time for boarding. Before he sat, Robby went to the newspaper stand located across from the gate. As he approached the stand, the shadows flickering in aisle suddenly brightened in the lights of newsstand. The side door opened from the parking lot, and a wheelchair rolled in being pushed by a woman. As the chair approached in the light, Robby recognized it was

Hoffman seated in the wheelchair! He couldn't believe his eyes.

"Hoffman, I'm so pleased you're arm is stabilized," he said, as the wheelchair rolled out of the shadows. He said, noticing the arm was in a sling.

"Thanks to the tourniquet," he said, handing him a neatly folded handkerchief.

Robby took the handkerchief. "Are you sure this is mine?" he replied, noticing its cleanliness.

"Ursula washed and dried it at the hospital," he smiled, raising his head over the sling on his arm. "Ursula this is Robert Caruso—the nicest guy you will ever meet." Robby this is my wife, Ursula."

She stood tall and thin in a pair of slacks and knit top, brown hair neatly combed. Her eyes were dark brown, with a smile that could slay the unaware. She extended her slender arm. "Thank you Robert Caruso for taking such good care of my husband."

Robby received her hand and kissed it. "You have a find husband, Ursula," he replied, and then a notion spoke. "May I invite you both to Washington, DC?"

Ursula smiled, giving her face a seductive appearance. "I would so like you to meet your wife, Dr. Caruso."

Hoffman responded, rubbing his arm beneath the sling. "That may be possible. My commissioner suggests that I take this time of convalescing to attend

an exchange program on terrorism strategy in Rockville, Maryland next month."

"Great! Here's my card—look me up when you arrive."

Ursula gently kissed Caruso on his cheek, and smiled. "Be kind to your wife," she whispered, and winked.

Bruce and Robby sat at the gate waiting for their flight departure. Bruce stood, stretching his arms as he wandered over to the windows extending the entire length of the loading area. The snow had stopped and the runway was cleared by snowplows. Down on the tarmac he glimpsed a motorized cargo cart moving to a 747. The cargo was a coffin. And he realized it contained Casey's body. He turned and faced his friend.

"Casey's coffin is being loaded," he said strolling back to this seat.

Robby only nodded his mind in deep thought. Would the comb and brush in his briefcase actually prove to the world that Hitler did not commit suicide in the *Führerbunker*? And would they believe he escaped to *Neuschwabenland*? Or could they be convinced that a neo-Nazi organization was staffed with German clones who had been the pilots of the rash of UFOs since the days of Roswell?

Bruce understood Robby better than even his wife. They had been friends since high school. They were

both getting old, too old for these covert operations. Jenny Lynn really wanted him to retire, but she would never suggest it. And Consuela was entirely different. She had no difficulty with him being away even for weeks. When he first saw her he knew she was an independent woman. Her father was killed and her mother died, and she had to deal for herself for years. That was why he loved her; she never tried to change him. She accepted him just as he was and he reciprocated in like manner.

The aircraft soared up from the runway as the sun was setting on the horizon; sunset over the Atlantic, what a nice thought Bruce said to himself. The wheels locked in its wells, as the 747 turned over the ocean before it ascended to its assigned corridor. Bruce sat in a window seat looking out at the sun sinking below the horizon. The unlimited veil of stratosphere-blue was stitched with tuft clouds. Suddenly he glimpsed a flock of petrels far out at sea in search of creatures swimming near the surface. These were webfooted nocturnal birds dressed in dark plumage. They were strong swimmers and sleek flyers, the webfooted eagles of the north. Sleek flyers, Bruce thought. This sleek Boeing invention could fly itself in most any kind of weather. Bruce felt the change in thrust as the aircraft leveled off at forty thousand feet high above the clouds now laced with angel wings.

Robby placed his briefcase under his seat, not willing to assign it to baggage; too valuable to risk losing it. A cart caught his attention rolling down the aisle. It was a meal flight over the ocean, he remembered. As it reached his seat, Robby ordered the standard packaged meal and coffee. Bruce leaned over. "Make that two, if you please."

"Wonder if the girls will meet us at the airport," Robby mused.

"That was the idea," Bruce replied. "I asked Kawasaki to call Consuela and give her our flight number."

Caruso nodded. "Let's hope he remembers."

"If you like, I'll called Consuela when we reach U.S. airspace?"

"That won't be necessary," Robby replied and depressed the level releasing the back of his seat. He leaned back for a nap before the meals arrived. But he couldn't sleep, wondering if the DNA would be conclusive, if he and Woolsey had been careless possibly contaminating the sample. And then his mind change synapses and gave him a vision of Henri. The world owed the brave clone their admiration. Without his testimony the story of the Third Reich's plan to form a new Germany under the ice of the Antarctica would never have been revealed. But would historians comply with the new evidence; why not, they often rewrote history inserting their one opinion.

26

The deep blue color of the Gulf of Mexico came into view in the distance, and the Boeing 747 contacted the Reagan Airport for its flight path. She was just now turning to its new course along the seacoast. As they descended beneath the clouds, seagulls floating over Key West were languishing in the waters of the Florida Keys.

A flight attendant took a microphone off the front wall: "Ladies and gentlemen we will be landing at the Reagan National Airport in a few minutes. The area was originally known as Gravelly Point, it's where Captain John Alexander built a home called "Abington" in 1746. A descendant, Philip Alexander, donated most of the land on which the City of Alexandria was built, and it

was so named in his honor. Abington was purchased in 1778 by John Parke Custis, the adopted stepson of President George Washington, and was the birthplace of Washington's beloved granddaughter Eleanor "Nelly" Parke Custis. Abingdon was destroyed by fire in1930 and the ruins stabilized. In 1998, the metropolitan Washington Airports Authority preserved the site and created an exhibit of artifacts now located in Terminal A. It will be worth your while to see this exhibit before you exit the airport. Have a wonderful day in the capitol of USA. "

Up the coast the aluminum bird flew, her broad wings supporting the fuselage with massive airlift of ocean air. The left flap dropped forty-five degrees, and she tilled inland, coursing for eight minutes then leveling in its approach to Washington, D.C. The pilot saw the runway of Reagan National Airport looking like a postage stamp on an airmail letter. Flaps dropped to maximum, the nose dipped gracefully, the magnificent bird descended 1,000 feet and leveled, coursing for another guarded time. Again flaps dropped and the aircraft nosed down to 500 feet, the airport in the near distance. Airspeed was cut to landing speed, the stalling flaps engaged in a descending idle. The wheels unlocked and descended from its wells beneath the wings. Suddenly the wheels touched the pavement, the squeal momentarily cloaked by the noise of engine rear-thrust. The metallic bird powered down the runway toward the

tarmac, and finally reached the Jetway debarking systems.

Bruce watched the long contraption rollup to the exit door of the aircraft, remembering the days he and Robby had to walk out in the rain to board a DC-3 climbing up a set of mobile steps. The cab of the unit was accordion-like canopy which allowed Jetbridge to dock with the aircraft. The Jetbridge was invented by Frank Der Yuen. Yet, it wasn't until 1954 that United Airlines tested an early prototype "Air Dock." There still are small airports around the world that use mobile stairs, or ramp stairs; particularly those airports that support low cost carriers. Bruce smiled. With the high cost air travel it might be wise to return to the mobile stairs, he thought chuckling.

"What's so funny," Robby asked.

"You don't want to know," he replied.

They both felt the Jetway cab bump against the airframe and stood. Robby gripped his briefcase. They stepped into the aisle in the First Class section and were the first passengers to enter the Jetway. The passengers filed out rather rapidly and Robby walked over to Terminal-A Soda Shoppe and ordered a cup of coffee. Bruce came to the table with a milkshake. As he sat, Robby grinned.

"That will make you fat," he predicted.

"Fat or not, it got fairly stuffy on the flight."

"Let's drink up quickly; the wives should be here somewhere."

The two air travelers purposefully walked past the historical artifacts of this historical airport. Robby, a history buff always made it a point to exit this way. Finally they stepped through double glass doors leading to the parking lot. A large sedan parked by the curb twenty feet from the door honked its horn. A tall blonde stepped out and ran toward her husband. Jenny Lynn jumped into Robby's arms and kissed him twice; one on the cheek and on his lips. "Your flight was on time—what took you so long," she smiled.

Robby smiled. "Bruce needed a milkshake," he smile.

She grinned. "Don't tell me you didn't need coffee," she said, suddenly laughing.

Bruce opened the passenger side of the sedan and took Consuela's hand. "Come here, my princess."

Her dark eyes squinted. "Take me home, you slave," she beamed her arms wrapped his waist.

Bruce sat in the backseat with Consuela. Robby was selected to drive, Jenny Lynn in the passenger's seat. He touched the light switch and halogen headlights beamed down a wet road. Robby passed under the exit sign at fifty miles per hour, and took the four-lane road to downtown.

Reporters from around the world were jammed into the press room of the White House. Andrew Evans was astonished at the full capacity crowd and the doors rolled up on each side for other reporters still cramming inside. Technicians were busy bring in chairs. TV cameras from the U.S. networks and from foreign countries were lined across the back. The click of laptop keys was audible even above the chatter because of the number of reporters typing their introductions, each expecting a Pulitzer Prize for this historical announcement.

Dr. Robert Caruso stood in the area directly behind the doors to the dais. In his nervous hands he held the laboratory report from the DNA analysis of the bone sample compared with the brush and comb. He pulled a white handkerchief from his hip pocket, and dabbed at the sweat rolling down his temples, smiling from his memory of Wilhelm's wife laundering this very same handkerchief. Evans closed the door after completion of his estimate of the attendance to this press conference called by the President and advertized relentless by the media. They waited for the President's appearance.

Evans' cellphone rang. As he listened, his eyes ballooned, and he released the nuisance from an ear, gazing somberly at Caruso. "Robby the President requests that you begin the conference, he has been called to the Pentagon."

Caruso dabbed the recurring sweat on his temple. "I won't ask the reason for the Presidents absence, but these reporters will—what may I tell them?"

"You report the DNA analysis and I will handle the President's absence," he replied, more tense than Caruso had seen his reactions, even when the President was injured by the bomb blast.

Robby opened his cellphone and called his office. He closed the unit, his face white as snow. A neo-Nazi group had attacked the Pentagon where Henri Weismann was visiting and he was captured, another group broke into the laboratory that analyzed the DNA sample and stole the brush and comb.

"Let's get this conference offer before this news breaks," he blurted.

"Yeah!" Evans said and opened the door behind the dais.

The crowd stood, expecting the President. Evans moved to the lectern tested the microphone. Evans' eyes swept over the crowd with a look of concern. "I must report that the President is unavailable. Dr. Robert Caruso, assistant to the director of Homeland Security with direct this conference," he said to a numb crowd and turned to Caruso standing by the dais. "Dr. Caruso."

Caruso stepped to the lectern with a small air of contemplation, the DNA report clutched in his hand. Did he have the answers to their questions? He laid the

document on the lectern, gripped both edges and stared over the crowd. "I must apologize for standing in for the President—you could do better."

The noise of laughing chatter rose from the crowd in release of tension, but Caruso felt more relieved than they. A report from ABC stood on the left side. "I am not at all sure that you aren't the proper person, Dr. Caruso. I can't tell you how often I have stood in for my boss."

"Don't be too sure—you haven't heard the report yet," Caruso smiled.

A roar of laughter soared over the room. Evans grinned. The President would be pleased, he thought.

Caruso looked down at the report. "You all have reported on Henri Weismann and the destruction of Neuschwabenland. President Darcy sent the task force back to the South Pole when Henri described another entrance to that city beneath the ice. He took us to a graveyard in the dark and the first tombstone was etched with the name, Adolph Hitler."

A bellow of chatter was acidic. "What proof do you have," screamed a CBS reporter, with a howl of question-approval from the crowd.

"Here in my hands is the DNA report," he said. The sound quieted. He stepped to the edge of the dais. "The President requested we exhume the grave and take a bone sample, the German Achieves supplied a certified

comb and brush belonging to Hitler—this is your proof," he declared waving the report.

Three reporters stood. The more dominant voice prevailed. "What certification?"

Caruso propped his hands on his hips. "Hitler's personal SS adjutant— Otto Günsche."

The crowd buzzed with questions, reporters fitfully talking with their adjacent reporters. As Evans moved to the lectern, the reporters slowly acquiesced. His familiar appearance silenced the room.

"You will find a full report on tables in the lobby as you leave." He stood firm his feet slightly spaced beneath his slim statue. "President Darcy wishes you to accept his apologies for not being here today—his absence was unavoidable." Again he stood firm, glancing at Caruso. "I must report that Henri Weismann has been shot and is gravely ill. The President is at his side," he said in measured statements.

Robby bolted out the back. The entire crowd stood and advance haphazardly to the exits. Evans raised his cellphone. The medley of humanity took nearly thirty minutes to clear the conference room under the unsuccessful direction of White House guards.

Evans went to his office.

27

Walter Reed Hospital was brightly lit. The parking lot, usually filled to capacity, now jammed more tightly as another car roared up to the curb directly at the front door. The driver jumped out of the car, the door left wide open and raced to the entrance. A guard who apparently knew him only gestured as he smiled and ran through a set of automatic doors.

Dr. Caruso hustled to the front desk and inquired of a patient. The gracious lady typed a few keys at her computer, and informed that the patient was in intensive care. She advised that he would have to wait in the ICU on the third floor. Caruso thanked her,

apologizing for his testy remarks, and stepped to the elevators watching the light above the doors. The doors opened with a dinging sound and he stepped inside not really cognizant of his surroundings. A man stepped inside, reached over, and punched an icon. Robby's mind was somewhere else but he instinctively pushed the ICU icon.

When the elevator doors opened on his floor, Robby stepped out, but the man went up to another floor as the doors closed. For some reason his ever searching eyes noticed muddy footprints made at the entrance of the elevator but thought nothing of it. When he finally reached the ICU, he recognized Bruce and the two wives sitting in the waiting chairs.

Jenny Lynn rose and met Robby, her eyes swelled from crying. "The physician told us Henri was treated for a gunshot in the upper chest. But he has been taken back up to surgery. Seems they discovered a murmur in his heart. The diagnosis is a birth defect in the pyloric valve," she quoted from her experience as an ER nurse.

Robby said nothing. He stood numb, Jenny Lynn's head on his shoulder. His mind was recounting the rudimental cloning procedure. It was his personal diagnosis that this birth defect was the result of the human cloning technique.

"I know what you are thinking Robby," she said, her blue eyes gazing into his tormented face. "The Germans were in the experimental stages of human cloning."

The numbness vanished. Reality stared him in the face. This woman had the nagging ability of reading his mind. “Yes, you are perfectly right,” he admitted. “Henri will need close supervisor by professionals if he survives this operation.”

She saw his anguish. “Heart surgery is no longer experimental, Robby. Henri has a good chance of surviving.”

Bruce and Consuela approached the couple. “Consuela suggests we go down to the cafeteria. The nurse says we will be notified over the PA system,” said Bruce.

Robby took Consuela’s dainty hand, weary of worrying. “Thank you for that apropos suggestion—I’m bushed, dry as the wind,” he said, his lips pulled into a tense grin.

Chitchat and wordplay consumed an undetermined moment until Jenny Lynn diplomatically guided them to the elevators.

As they sat in the cafeteria, not completely crowded, they took a table near a window. Bruce and Robby were each in the line armed with the requests of their respective wives; neither had a substitute should the items not be on the menu. They finally exited the line and stepped to the cashier. Bruce paid both tickets. They left the line and strolled to the table. As they sat eating, a medical technician approached their table.

She was dressed neatly in a blue smock with a badge that identified her as "Clara Pritchard, ER Nurse." She wore white sneakers and white hosiery, a nurse's cap. "Pardon me. I have been assigned to the case of Henri Weismann. He is not due out of surgery for another hour or more."

Jenny Lynn extended her hand. "Won't you join us, Clara?"

She seemed a bit fidgety. "For just a minute," she said and Bruce pulled up a chair. She sat, more fidgety.

"Can I get you something from the cafeteria," Robby asked?

"No thank you." She began to relate a story that captured their attention. "I was in the emergency room when Henri was brought in. I thought a man who came in with the stretcher was a relative. But he stood in the background obviously checking on something, and don't think it was the welfare of the patient," she reported.

Robby sat his cup on the table. "Would you recognize the man if you saw him again?"

"That's just the point. I have seen him again here in the hospital," she blurted. "That's the reason I sought you out."

"What's your perception of this man," Bruce asked.

"Only that he is tall, blonde and has deep penetrating blue eyes. His face was unshaven, his shoes muddy."

Robby's head snapped back, muddy footprints, he thought. "That's quite a lineup description," he added, extending his business card. "We will be up at ICU for a spell. If you see this man, page us. If in the future you have something or just wanted to discuss it, call me at that number."

She gazed down at the card, her left eyebrow rising. "You are the gentleman who brought Henri Weismann to that press conference a few weeks back," she recognized.

"Yes, and this is my wife, Jenny Lynn, former ER nurse. This is Bruce and Consuela, his wife."

They talked briefly, mostly questions from Clara. Jenny Lynn walked Clara off down the hall for a spell. They stood in the distance, only the walls heard their voices, the memories of mutual ER nurses echoed in the ears of fairies. Not many knew that fairies always attended nurses.

The rains transformed into a mist as Caruso reset a lever on the steering wheel for random motion. The wipers seized movement for three seconds and the moved and repeated the cycle. He stopped at the stoplight on Constitution Avenue, the pavement wet from the melting snow. Several cars motored through the green light, headlights glistening on the pools of water. Caruso sat pondering, his turn-signal blinking rhythmic cadence, thinking of those muddy footprints. The green arrow lit. He turned toward the White House.

He steered the rental sedan to the rear, his mind meditating on Henri's murmuring heart. There could be more serious problems, it suddenly struck him. The continual use of one set of genes could produce a bleeder, a hemophiliac. His thoughts vanished as he pulled up to his private entrance. Parking the car, he noticed the familiar face of the guard who always stood at his post when he entered his office.

"Good evening, Willey. How is the wife?"

He stared at Caruso his broad lips pulled tightly into a toothy grin. "Just a little bit cranky in our old age, Dr. Caruso."

He smiled. "Keep the faith, Willey."

"Yes sir, I will—have to in this world."

Caruso entered the glass door, lights on ecological dim. He stopped at his office before venturing to the Oval Office. He had earlier phoned Evans for an appointment with the President, and there was something he might need at the meeting. He inserted his key and unlocked his office door, flipping on the light. He walked directly to his desk and sat, pulling open a side drawer. He retrieved his copy of Henri's document, one of the copies the President had given him. He locked his desk and shut off the lights as he relocked his office. He tucked the document under his arm and navigated to the Oval Office. The late hour

revealed the missing secretary as he approached. Andrew Evans stepped from his office and met Caruso.

"Good evening Robby, the President should arrive from the hospital in a few minutes. Can I get you some refreshments?"

"Thanks, Andrew; I'll let the President make that choice."

"That's fine. We can wait in his office, he said retrieving a ring of keys from a metallic key-holder attached to his belt, nodding at a guard who returned his nod. He chose a key and inserted it in the door of the Oval Office.

As they sat, Evans ventured an opening statement realizing Robby had much on his mind. "I understand Henri Weismann is undergoing another surgery."

"Yes—this is the third attack," he said and bowed his head.

Evan's suddenly realized the admiration Robby had for Henri, and changed subject. "The President is anxious for your report."

A knocking sound emanated from the door. A guard cracked it open and stuck in his head. "Dr. Caruso, there is a lady here who says she was told to meet you."

He stood. "Yes, send her in," he said walking to the door. A petite slender young lady dressed in beige slacks and knit pullover, a ponytail swishing lazily entered the Oval Office. "Dr. Caruso, I'm so glad to

inform you that Henri Weisman is out of danger. The operation was a complete success," she smiled brightly.

"Thank you Carla that is good news. Won't you sit? We are waiting for the President. This is Andrew Evans, the President's chief of staff. Andrew this is Carla Pritchard, ER nurse attending Henri."

She extended her slim hand. Andrew took her hand, glancing at Robby. "Perhaps I should order refreshments," he said, raising his cellphone.

A noise stirred in the open hallway, and the President entered the Oval Office, leaving two Secret Service agents stationed outside. His eyes focused on the petite young lady. "You are the nurse at hospital—Carla, isn't it," he said gazing on the pleasant face."

She nervously nodded. "I voted for the other guy," she blurted, unable to fine other words.

A chorus of mutual voices broke the dismal atmosphere.

The President rounded his desk and sat in his favorite leather chair. "Well Robby, what's this news you bring?" he asked directly as the door opened.

A woman followed by a guard, entered with a tray of finger sandwiches, a pot of coffee and several cans of orange juice. She sat the tray on a table. Evans returned her nod, and followed her out.

"Perhaps we should break for refreshments," the President advised fingering a cheese sandwich. "Good news from Germany."

Robby sat a cup of coffee on the side table. "I think we may have a picture of Henri's attacker."

The President always enjoyed the reports from his favorite investigator. "That would be a blessing," he predicted.

"It is possible that Carla has seen this man."

The President's face beamed with a wide smile. "Well, pretty lady. What can you tell us?"

She swallowed wryly. "Ah, Mr. President it's like I told Dr. Caruso. He was tall, blonde with blue eyes and he had muddy feet."

The President stood, shoved his hands into his pockets and studied her words. "That description is any worthy of any detective on the police force, Carla," he replied, and then turned to Caruso. "Robby can we locate this man with the FBI's assistance?"

"Professional assistance would be helpful, sir," he replied and opened the document he had brought with him.

The President noticed the document. "That's Henri's document—the copy I had printed," he said.

"Correct, sir. There is a biography of photos in the appendix, and I thought Carla might identify one if our man is in the file."

"Good thought," he replied.

Carla took the open book from Dr. Caruso, her face flushed from the idea of seeing a photo of that man. She

laid the book open on her lap, staring intently on the first page of photos.

"Take your time, Carla."

The President leaned back in his chair, his palms pressed together at each matching finger. Finally, he unclasped his hands and leaned over to the phone. He punched a code, looking at Carla turn another page. "Andrew, contact the FBI and have them send an agent over to my office."

Carla's pristine face suddenly blossomed, turning to Dr. Caruso. "This is the man—I'm sure it's him," she barked! He took the book, but there was no name beneath this particular photo.

The President placed his elbows on the desk leaning forward. "Well, how is he?"

Robby laid the book open on the desk, his finger on the photo, "No name here, sir."

Robby poured a glass of orange juice and gave it to Carla. "You did well, Carla. I don't know how to thank you."

The President closed the document. "Perhaps the FBI can give us a name," he said, disbelievingly, and then stood and poured another cup of coffee, took another sandwich.

A light wrap on the door, and Andrew Evans stepped inside followed by an agent from the FBI. The President opened the document to the second page of photos. He

drummed his finger on a photo. "Can you identify this man?"

He studied the picture for a moment. "I will run the photo through our files," she said and took the document.

"I shall expect your report within the hour," the President said.

Evans led him out the office and closed the door behind them.

Robby drove Carla back to the hospital. Along the way she sat still as a mouse staring at the lines in the road disappear beneath the hood. Robby thought he understood her quietness.

"Carla, honey you did your part. You identified a photo. It's up to the FBI to find this guy. Now cheer up," he said as a demand, not a request.

She closed her eyes and turned. "I can't be sure if this man did anything—it's only my suspicion," she pleaded, her eyes clouded with tears.

"Listen to me, Carla. A man stepped out my elevator at the hospital leaving muddy footprints. I think this is the man you saw and he may just be the villain that attacked Henri."

She scooted over and snuggled beside Caruso. "I do hope you are right," she whispered.

Robby sat with Jenny Lynn in the hospital cafeteria. Neither enjoyed their meals, picking at the salad with forks. "How is Henri," Robby asked.

"He can have visitors tomorrow," she replied.

Before he could respond to her reply, his cellphone buzzed. "Excuse me, Jenny Lynn—better answer it; expecting a call from the FBI." He placed the tiny speaker against his ear. "This is Dr. Caruso." He stared into Jenny Lynn's expectant face as his mind recorded the message. "Thank you."

Jenny Lynn could not tolerate the silence as she waited for Robby's explanation, void of patience. "Well?"

He closed his cellphone. "Wilhelm Kastler."

"That's the man in the photo?"

He nodded. "He reports to a Neo-Nazi leader in Baltimore."

"Nazism doesn't sound good," she reasoned aloud.

"If Henri is the product of a plan to establish a Fourth Reich your point is well taken."

"Did the President elaborate?" she probed, the usual way she dug information from Robby who rarely volunteered.

"The FBI has an open file on the organization . . . in fact, I have a file on the leader," he added with sudden realization.

"Does he have a name?" she probed further.

"Hans Grübber," he said standing. "Let's get back to our hotel. It's getting late."

She smiled and placed his arm around her waist. "I know its dinner time and you're hungry—it's always about your stomach!"

As they left the table, Robby fingering for his credit card, she noticed the telltale smile on his face. "Okay, what is it this time?"

"Sean Casey was associated with Kastler."

"So?"

"Kastler is associated with Grübber."

"Bingo!"

28

The Potomac was lonely tonight. There was no moon to reflect her elegant flowing stream from the Alleghany Mountains to the Chesapeake Bay forming the Maryland-Virginia borders. Her estuary was navigable by large vessels to Washington, D.C. Her cold waters ran through bone-white mountains and towering walls of snow rumbling down the sloops. The gleeful stream trickled through valleys, where the deer clattered across her meadows and eagles guided her way for a distance of two hundred eighty seven miles. She had witnessed the early French Indian Wars marching on

her shores, the founding days of Washington and Madison, Jefferson and Franklin.

Robert Caruso and Jenny Lynn sat in a quaint little restaurant in Rockville, Maryland, a stone's throw to the Potomac. Caruso had just received a telephone call from Heinz Hoffman; seems his terrorism conference was this weekend and he and Ursula were registered in a local hotel.

"Hoffman and his wife should arrive soon," Robby said his mind on measuring the significance of Hoffman's presence. He had killed Casey, and now Kastler stepped in the picture.

"I'm anxious to meet Ursula," Jenny Lynn replied, thumping her nails on the table.

Robby reasoned her mind was at the hospital. She and Carla Pritchard had become instant friends. A pot of coffee sat on the table by the window overlooking a waterfall. He poured a cup and peered out the window searching his mind for answers. But his focus was drawn to the waters pouring into a pond. Its colors were Mediterranean-blue and magical, accented by multicolor lights. It originated from an unnatural rock face swishing over the professionally placed rocks joyfully, quietly splashing down into the pool in a magnificent spout. Carp swam in the final pond dug just outside the window.

Caruso's cellphone buzzed. He pressed the speaker to an ear. Hoffman and Ursula were driving into the

parking lot. He closed the phone and stood. "I'll meet them in the lobby and escort them here," he said and kissed Jenny Lynn on her powdered cheek. She watched the man she married leave the table, and as usual her mind replayed the day they met. He was brought to her hospital by ambulance, a covert attempt to kill him, and she nursed him back to health. She could still hear his words that had forever endeared him in her heart: "When in hell can I get out of here, and can I have a date?"

Caruso met the couple in the lobby. Ursula was arrayed in a stunning party dress that revealed all her female accolades, her face a light tan, with earrings hanging from pierced ears, standing on six-inch high heels. Hoffman stood proudly beside her, only an inch above her head, the woman he married who gave him two kids now in university, both boys. He stretched out his hand, no sign of a sling, healed completely from the gunshot wound in the arm.

"How nice to see you again, Robert," he announced, looking proudly at the man who had become his chief disciple.

Caruso took his hand and drew him into his arms in a manly hug. "I thought of you just recently when the FBI identified a photo of an associate of Sean Casey."

"Really," he mused.

"Let's drop the shop talk—are you two hungry," he smiled.

He led them passed the bar to the window table where Jenny Lynn sat dying to meet Ursula. Was she all that Robby had remembered? As she waltzed beside Hoffman he saw that she was—every description correct from a man's memory.

Robby pulled out a chair for Ursula, and pushed her near the table's edge. Hoffman sat beside her, just now sniffing her perfume. Jenny Lynn reached out and placed her hand over Ursula's lovely hand. "So pleased to meet you, Ursula."

She smiled gracefully. "Robert has told us so much about you, Jenny Lynn."

A waitress approached the table, her order pad in hand. She stood in an unbuttoned blue sweater, a flowered apron, pencil stuck in her bundled hair just above the ear. She placed menus around the table. "Would you care to order drinks," she smacked on gum.

Robby waited for Heinz, who looked over his menu. "Give us two martinis; hold the olive on one only."

She jotted down a few codes, looked up at Caruso.

"Two martinis, as well, with the olive on both."

"Thank you she said, sticking the pencil in her hair, and waltzed off.

Hoffman poured a cup of coffee. "Tell me, Robert who is this associate of Casey?"

His name is Wilhelm Kastler, grandson of a German immigrant family of Baltimore."

Ursula cocked her head. “That’s right here in this state,” she added.

Hoffman touched her hand. “That was eighty years ago, honey. I doubt Kastler’s parents are living.”

Caruso came to Ursula’s aid. “I think she means that he—Holy Toledo!” Robby gasped, the wheels of his mind churning. “Thank you Ursula. Kastler just might be hanging around the old household,” he replied raising his cellphone, smiling at Ursula. “Andrew, Robby here, would you ask the FBI to see if they have an address for a Kastler family living in Baltimore,” he said pausing for a reply. “Yes, thank you.”

The martinis came and they ordered. As the waitress left the table, Caruso’s cellphone buzzed. He stood, excused himself and walked over to the window. He finished his call and went back to the table. Jenny Lynn was in a conversation with Ursula. Hoffman wiped his mouth with a cloth napkin. “Any word on Kastler’s family home?”

He sat and stretched his arm gripping his martini glass at his place. “Expecting a call from the FBI soon.”

The hour grew late at Walter Reed hospital. Carla had drawn the late shift and had just finished her duties in the ER. The emergency nurses had clocked in, and she was in the restroom preparing to leave. She thought at the last moment to check on Henri Weismann now in a room. She took the elevator to the third floor and

walked the hall to Henri's room, 327. Though not surprised, she was impressed that the President had left two guards to protect Henri. Someday, she thought she would discuss Henri with Dr. Caruso. She presented her badge and the guards allowed her to crack open the door. The patient was asleep. She thanked the guards and took the elevator down to the basement where her car was parked.

As she approached her car in the dimly lit basement, she heard an unfamiliar sound. She stopped in her tracks, surveying the garage. She opened her purse, and retrieved a handgun she had license to carry. Walking to her car, a man suddenly stepped from behind a van forty feet away. She squinted. It was Kastler—that awful photo emblazon on her mind! What to do, she thought raising the seven-shot automatic instinctively. The shadow kept its pace moving toward her. She waited until he was in range, following her training at the shooting range.

"Stop!" she screamed. "I know how to use this thing."

Kastler broke into a run.

She fired, once then twice.

Kastler stumbled and slumped, holding his knee. Clara jumped into her car, and wildly drove out of the parking garage into the street. Only a block down the road, she reached a service station on the right, and pulled into the parking lot. She dropped her head on the

steering wheel, sobbing. Finally she sniffed, reached for her cellphone.

They had just finished their meals and were drinking wine. A cellphone buzzed and Caruso suddenly realized it was his nuisance, and he flipped it out. "This is Caruso . . . what? Stay there. I'm leaving now.

He hurriedly punched another code. The phone rang in Security Office of Walter Reed. A guard answered. "Listen closely: This is Dr. Caruso of Homeland Security. A fugitive of FBI has been seen in your garage. He may be wounded, and he is armed. I'll check back within the hour."

Hoffman's eyes squinted nearly shut, his forehead a mass of wrinkles. "What's up?"

Wilhelm Kastler is on the prowl," he said. "He attempted to grab Carla and she shot him in the basement of Walter Reed. She is waiting for me at a service station about five miles from here. Want to come along Hoffman," he said, and faced Jenny Lynn. "Would you go back to Hoffman's hotel with Ursula and lock your doors?"

She nodded. "You guys be careful."

He pulled out his credit card and stretched it out to her. Jenny Lynn shook her head. "I've got money—you guys get going. Carla may be in danger."

A mist reappeared from a passing cloud. A cold front was pushing in over Rockville, Maryland. Robby jammed the accelerator of his Rover heading over the Potomac, the wipers swiping the windshield at maximum speed. Hoffman sat in the passenger's seat tightening his seatbelt. Suddenly, swirling red lights seemed to set the rear window aflame as sirens pulsated behind the Rover. Robby pulled off the road, realizing he was speeding without grasping the consequence; not the speeding ticket, but the life of Carla. A patrolman walked up to the driver's door flashing his light on the wet pavement. Robby rolled down the side glass and presented his business card. The patrolman took one glance. "Where is the fire, Dr. Caruso?"

"The service station on Wilson and Grant," he replied.

"Follow me," he said, and raced back to the patrol car. He pulled from the curb in front of the Rover, tires squealed as the 440 cc engine revved to maximum torque, leaving black tracks on the pavement.

Hoffman faced Robby. "Pays to have friends."

Robby said nothing as he pulled back on the road, again jamming his foot on the accelerator. He finally caught up with the patrolman. "Sorry, Hoffman," he whispered. If Kastler returns and harms Carla, I won't have any friends." Then it occurred to him once again: Evans' suggestion: would he use Walter Nichols in this case, could he be useful?"

The patrol car pulled up to a traffic light, the swirling lights flashing, and sirens screaming. He pulled under the light and blocked the traffic. The Rover pulled into the service station parking lot on the far corner. The sleek Ford sedan followed the Rover and parked beside it. Robby stepped out of the Rover, his eyes surveying the area. One car was pulling off from the pumps, another was pumping gasoline, and a third car was parked on the side. It could have been the operator's car, but Robby made it his business to be sure. Hoffman didn't see him leave and followed the patrolman into the service station.

Carla jumped from a seat at the far end. "Dr. Caruso—thanks for coming," she gasped.

He took her hand, they said a few words, and Robby dashed outside.

Hoffman spun around and saw Robby outside wrestling with a man. He tapped the patrolman's shoulder and pointed. They both ran outside. The man hit Robby on the head with the butt of his automatic, and dashed into the one of the mechanic stalls. Robby momentarily shook off the cobwebs and ran in ahead of the others. A car was elevated on a hoist, a man below in the well changing an oil filter. The patrolman walked through the back door shining his flashlight on a ditch.

Suddenly, a shot rang out!

Robby ran through the door and found the patrolman on the ground, obviously wounded. Yet, his revolver was drawn aiming at a ridge of the ditch. A second shot zinged past Robby's head and shattered the window glass. The patrolman's revolver fired three shots.

All quiet.

Hoffman had drawn his automatic, searching the area from where the shots were fired. He circled to the right and up to the ditch surveying as he walked. Several empty casings were on the ground. There was very little water in the ditch and he could barely see footprints leading out of the ditch toward a building in the rear of the station. He crouched low and made his way toward the building. It was a steel building bolted to a concrete slab, probably for storing parts. He noticed a broken glass pane in the single window by the door. Brief inspection did not convince Hoffman it was where the assailant had entered the building. He tried to open the door. It was locked as suspected. He cautiously sneaked to the edge of the building. He heard a noise but it came from his backside. He turned. It was Caruso.

"Did you check the building," he whispered.

"It's locked," he answered. "I think our assailant is in the woods back here."

"Leave it at that, Hoffman. Let's get back to the wounded patrolman. I've called for an ambulance."

"Right," he agreed. "It's your show."

The service station attendant had the patrolman propped up against a crate. Carla had removed his jacket and located the wound. The bullet was lodged in his shoulder. Just as Caruso and Hoffman arrived they heard the ambulance drive up. Two paramedics jumped out, one to the patient, the other removing the stretcher-trolley, which automatically locked as it rolled out on wheels. One paramedic checked his blood pressure and placed an oxygen mask on his nose and mouth. The other inspected the wound.

He raised the microphone of his radio. "Rampart we have a gunshot in the shoulder, bleeding has stopped. Patient is conscious and strapped to a backboard. Over."

"Roger, A-2. Apply cervical collar and transport immediately. Over and out.

The two medics moved in practiced professional fashion. Each gripped an end to the backboard and placed the patient on the stretcher. One paramedic grabbed the satchel and radio, and the other rolled the patient to the ambulance. The end of the trolley inserted into the wheel channels, the base retracted, and the stretcher rolled into the ambulance and locked. One medic stayed with the patient checking his vital signs. The other drove the ambulance. The vehicle raced away with sirens shrieking.

Over in the woody forest Wilhelm Kastler sat on a log, nursing his wounded knee. He decided to make his way to a walk-in clinic and see the physician assigned by Hans Grübber. Then he would rent a room in a small motel, giving him the time to plan an attack on Carla Pritchard. But Kastler knew nothing of destiny. It was never capricious.

The evening sun was beginning to filter through the branches of the dark forest. Every child in the village had laughed at the folklore passed down by woodcutters. Now that the villagers were gone, swept away by an invisible hand, the forest animals were being trespassed upon by modern squatters and the folklores remained true. The forest was primordial. Centuries-old trees with sprawling limbs guarded the darkness. The decaying air and stifling atmosphere provided the perfect abode for poisonous plants and venomous snakes. In the dense shadows, spiders clutched their snare-strings. Their webs shimmered like meshed steel dipped in silver. Eyes aflame were hungry, hoping to dine on bloated bodies and slurp on hot blood. Mounds of old gnawed bone, a midden heap of gleaming ribs and grinning skulls laid waiting in their destiny. The timber rattlesnake, native to Virginia, often migrated into the dark forests of Maryland searching for food. One particular venomous snake had a meeting with destiny.

Wilhelm Kastler's leg began to throb so badly he hobbled, and then unable to walk. He stumbled to a log by a stream. Somehow the sound of the moving stream calmed him briefly. Streams were the liquid soul of the forest. But Kastler was not to enjoy its murmuring kindness. A timber rattlesnake felt his foot step on its tail; it coiled and struck, stabbing its fangs in his wounded leg. Kastler grabbed his leg. The venom raced into his bloodstream. He began to vomit. His heart's muscular rhythmical contractions forcing the circulation of life-giving blood through left and right auricles and ventricles suddenly stopped. Lack of oxygen starved the brain. His body permanently terminated.

Kastler lay dead on the ground, birds pecking his eyes. Destiny had arrived.

Baltimore, just 40 miles northeast of Washington, D.C., the greatest city in America, the motto says, get in to it! Founded in 1729, now the second largest seaport in the Mid-Atlantic. The city's Inner Harbor was one the second leading port of entry for immigrants to the United States and a major manufacturing center until recent years. With hundreds of neighborhoods, Baltimore was the resident of writer Edgar Allan Poe including a list of musicians, singers, actors, filmmakers, and the baseball player Babe Ruth. It was from this harbor that Francis Scott Key wrote the national anthem.

Robby drove his Rover downtown, closing his cellphone. The FBI had identified the family of one Wilhelm Kastler. His family came to America in the 1920s. After being accepted at Ellis Island, they settled in Baltimore and were the proprietors of a little Meat

Market Shoppe down near the Inner Harbor. The shop closed in 1948, and Wilhelm went to Harvard, financed by the sales money. He was influenced by German students from the old country and introduced to a Neo-Nazi group.

Robby found the street where Kastler had lived located down on the Inner Harbor, the Emerson Bromo-Seltzer tower visible in the background. He turned down the narrow street, and in the distance a number of cars were parked along the curb on both sides of a house. He parked a block away and walked up to the house, the address numerals attached to the gable of the wraparound porch; it was Kastler's old home place. Two or three couples stood out in the yard conversing as Robby mounted the recently painted wooden steps. A man met him at the door, inquiring of his ancestry. He concocted a quick story of only being a friend of the family. The man apparently understood, and led him into the great room at the rear of the house.

The family of three generations sat randomly in the large room, many standing around the walls. A gray-haired woman seated in a wheelchair with a blanket over her lap was apparently the center of attention. Yet Robby was drawn by the open casket under a row of high windows; his information said nothing of Kastler's death! He respectfully approached the casket and stood beside a lone man. He was tall and slender dressed in a black suit, his head bowed reverently.

"Did you know Wilhelm?" the slender man asked staring straight ahead.

"Only casually," Robby whispered.

"He was my distant cousin," the man said, and turned to the stranger standing beside him. His eyes suddenly popped wide open. "Why Dr. Caruso—why . . . how is it you . . . he bowed his head and sobbed.

Robby stood amazed. "Walter Nichols. You are a cousin of Kastler," he remarked in measure phrases.

He raised his head, brushed away a few tears with the back of his hand. "Yes, our families came over from Germany in the 1920s. Wilhelm and I played together, went to the same school. When he went off to Harvard, I joined the police department, finally recommended to the lower ranks of the CIA where I met Winston Darcy and Andrew Evans."

"Will you have lunch with me?"

"Yes, first let me pay my respects to Wilhelm's grandmother."

29

The restaurant Caruso had selected sat on a corner, two blocks from the National Aquarium. The morning sun shone brightly reflecting off the large glass windows encased in granite walls. Caruso and Nichols walked side-by-side following a waitress to a table. He ordered coffee; Walter had hot tea for starters. Nichols leaned back in his chair, squirmed in his seat.

"I suppose you wonder how Wilhelm died," he said just as openers.

Clearly expecting he died from an infected wound in the knee, he replied, "It was on my mind."

"The autopsy report said he was bitten by a venomous snake."

Robby cocked his head, his mouth stretched open. "That is odd," he replied.

Local hunters found him in the forest behind a service station on Wilson and Grant."

Robby shut his eyes, shaking his head. It's a small world he thought. "Andrew tells me you have some information on a Neo-Nazi group."

"Yes," he confirmed, his mind reaching deep into the synaptic caches containing his childhood years and his growing-up days. He took a deep breath, leaned back in his chair. "When I was a policeman," he began. "Wilhelm and I had a long conversation about his involvement with this Nazi group. I advised him to get out of the organization and we quarreled over the issue for weeks. Finally I rarely saw him, until his grandmother called me this week."

"Can you locate the whereabouts of that group?"

He nodded. "I have a file at home that I built while with the CIA," he replied.

"Would you meet me at the White House on Monday with that file?"

"Say about nine in the morning?" he replied, sipping his tea.

Robby nodded. "That's fine," he replied, lowering his coffee cup.

Late Sunday afternoon was oddly serene in Georgetown, D.C., when children were normally playing in the streets, a number of street preachers standing on the corners giving out hopeful words in a neighborhood of parentless children. Gangs were the teachers, the police their "fathers." The shops were all closed but the game rooms busy with children spending the money they had gained from selling drugs.

Monday would roll around sooner than Nichols had suspected, standing outside the home of Hans Grübber. The more he thought of meeting with Dr. Caruso, the more he wondered how Andrew Evans would receive the startling story that he was kin to Wilhelm Kastler. Therefore, he had decided to follow his leads himself before confronting Caruso, not too smart he realized but a way to leave an apology to Evans and the President. He had decided he should resign.

He was a patriotic American citizen and had always stayed clear of his cousin while working with the CIA. Family ties were stronger than many members suspected, but he was not one of them. He would arrest Grubber, before meeting with Dr. Caruso. This was his plan. But foolish plans more often than not usually went awry.

The light in the front room suddenly lit and Nichols decided it was time to make his move. He checked the Beretta shouldered behind his jacket. Satisfied that he could handle an old man in a wheelchair, he stepped to the window beside the fireplace. He found the telephone wires following the lines from the pole on the street

stretching the line to the house. He thrust his hand into his pocket and opened his knife, cut the wires. His ears were drawn to the window, and he heard the television reporting the evening news. He saw the shadow of the wheelchair on the floor reflecting from a lamp on the opposite side of the room. Nichols stooped below the window and waddled around the corner. Standing erect, he stepped up on the front porch and inspected the lock. From his inside pocket he took out a set of skeleton keys. He selected a key designed for the front door lock and inserted it in the keyhole. The tumblers clicked, and the doorknob turned. Quietly he pushed open the door and shut it behind his entrance. The front atrium was dimly lit only from the streetlights shining through a stain-glass window. He moved stealthy through the arched entrance into the parlor, a door to the kitchen on the left, a room on the left with a shaft of light casting the shadow of the wheelchair on the floor. Slowly he unsheathed the Beretta and tip-toed to the front room arch. He stood without movement using his sense of sound for identification of the situation in the room.

Suddenly he heard the grinding sound of a flint-roll of a lighter, the puffing of a cigarette, and then a voice that terrified his innermost being.

"Come in Mr. Nichols," said a raspy voice, smoke rising to the ceiling where it vanished in a puff,

flickering light from a fireplace, flames dancing like little fairies.

The kitchen door opened and two men walked out, each pointing 45-automatics. The two thugs waved their ominous weapons, gesturing to enter the front room. Seated in his wheelchair sat the old national boss of the Neo-Nazi movement with a grin on his unshaven round face. "Have a set by the fireplace, Mr. Nichols," he said, and nodded at the nearest man. "Get our guest some warm cider."

Nichols sat as directed, convinced by the 45-automatics. Hans Grübber wheeled his chair over near Nichols, and locked the wheels. "I hear that you have lost your cousin, Wilhelm Kastler."

The statement stunned Nichols. "How is it you know my family," he shot back.

"I know a great deal about your family," he said and paused for the mugs of cider to be passed around. He swilled a long swallow, and swiped his hand across his parched lips. "Your mother, Mr. Nichols, was my sister!"

Nichols choked on the cider. He stared uncomprehendingly through glazed eyes. Surely Grübber jested, but his stern demeanor said otherwise. Everything Nichols stood for, strived for, even fought for suddenly evaporated. How would he ever explain to Andrew Evans and Dr. Caruso that Hans Grübber is his uncle? He gulped and took a deep breath. "Then who really is Kastler?"

He leaned back in his chair. "Wilhelm Kastler was my son," he barked. "His mother was killed in an automobile accident that left me paralyzed. Your supervisor, Andrew Evans pulled out in front of my car and pushed us into a 14-wheel tractor and trailer."

Nichols sat stoic. He couldn't move; the gravity of the words left his mind hanging on the thin edge of reality. He was a nebulous shadow of who he thought he was. His cognizance was occupied with his thoughts, and he didn't realize that the two thugs had grasped his arms.

Grübber leaned forward in his wheelchair. "Take him to the basement," he growled. "You know what to do," he said, and rolled back his head with devilish laughter that echoed through the room. Nichols was dragged to the door by the two thugs. The door opened exposing a long stairway down into a dismal dark place, Grübber's cackle reverberating down the steps. They pulled him down the steps by each arm until he stood on a concrete floor, large rats racing into their hiding places. He was thrust into a chair and his arms tied behind his back. One sleeve was rolled up and a hypodermic needle glimmered from a shaft of ghostly silver moonlight shining through high windows. Nichols eyes squinted shut as the needle stabbed his arm. The ampoule from which the hypo was filled was labeled 'scopolamine'—the SS's favorite truth serum.

Nichols' heart thumped wildly as his mind digressed into a hazy mist.

Nichols sat tortured; his face a map of bruises, his heart erratically pumping. He was not sure if he was alive or dead. He coughed, felt a sting in his foot. He managed to look toward the floor. A rat was feasting on a toe, having gnawed through his shoe. The pain seemed to disappear, camouflaged by stomping feet upstairs. Several shots rang out, the stairway door opened. Feet stumbled down the stairs. Standing before him had to be a dream. Surely the thugs had come to finish him. His burred eyes strained to focus.

Dr. Caruso stood before him. "Hold tight, Nichols," he whispered, untying his hands. A policeman came down the stairs as Caruso assisted Nichols to his feet. But he was too weak to stand. Caruso cradled him in his arms. The policeman found an ampoule and hypodermic syringe, and followed them up the stairs.

Several policemen had handcuffed the two thugs. But Nichols was surprised there was no sign of a wheelchair. He tugged at Caruso's arm. "Hans Grübber was here—where is he?"

Caruso scanned the room. "Look in the other rooms for a man in a wheelchair," he shouted to the policemen.

Four policemen scurried off, two upstairs, two into the kitchen and bedrooms. A nurse entered the room and checked Nichols' blood pressure. She checked his

eyes and temperature. He was extremely dehydrated, and she reached into her bag and took out a syringe. She rolled up his sleeve and injected a hydrate. Nichols' face winched, not from the injection, but the memory of the drug the thugs had used. The policeman had the same premonition, and presented the hypodermic from downstairs. Written on the label was 'scopolamine'.

Caruso took the syringe, admiringly gazing into Nichols' battered face. He said nothing, but Nichols' managed to speak. "Grübber wanted the date of the President's trip to Camp David," he weakly whispered.

Nichols slumped. The nurse advised no more questions. Two paramedics placed Nichols on a stretcher and rolled him out to the ambulance.

Andrew Evans sat in his office listening to an unbelievable story from the lips of Dr. Caruso. "Do you think Nichols compromised the President's visit to Camp David?"

"I think we should ask Nichols," he said. "The man has suffered and needs his rest. I think we should concentrate on Hans Grübber. According to Nichols that was Grübber's personal residence we raided."

Evans nodded. "Fortunate that an alert neighbor phoned the police," he pondered. "If the scopolamine worked and Grubber knows the date maybe we can set a trap."

“Not a bad approach, but I still think we should speak to Nichols.”

30

Montana, the land of shining mountains, northern extension of the Rocky Mountains, sparsely populated with glaciers and plains of the western prairie terrain and badlands located on the eastern half of the state. She is a big lady, two-hundred and fifty-five miles long and six-hundred and thirty wide, featuring some of the coldest winters of the 50 states and some of the most beautify territory in the winter and summer that ever graced the nation. Sitting on the Canadian border, her elevations soar to 12,807 feet at Granite Peak and plunge to 3,400 feet at Kootenai River on the Idaho border. The upper region of Yellowstone reaches into her borders creating hot springs, marketed

for an annual six million tourists. Before the creation of Montana Territory (1864-1889), various parts of Montana were part of four other territories: Oregon, Washington, Idaho, and Dakota.

An entourage of vans traveled west on U.S. Highway 94 past Billings and turned on State Road 59 north to a new building going up on a fifty acre site. A twelve foot electric fence was being installed around the property as the vans pull up and stopped. Professor Dietrich Shuster was on hand supervising the construction of a seventy-five by eighty-four foot two-story building going up. It would serve as the teaching center on the second floor, restrooms at each end and a cafeteria floor with a large office space for the director, Professor Shuster.

The foundation was laid and the framework completed. A dirt road had been cut in from the S.R. 59 to the property with a courtyard between the building site and a trailer where Professor Shuster temporarily lived during the construction. Off to the side of the building site a small tent city was prepared to receive the 3,000 cloned men from Neuschwabenland. Professor Shuster directed the vans to the road leading to the tents. He had hired two of his students to supervise the tent city. They had stocked refrigerators and pantries with food. The main power had been brought into the site by Spring City Utilities including water and sewage.

Shuster sat in his trailer, his feet propped on a stool, speaking to Hans Grübber on the phone. "The students have just arrived and are being introduced to their quarters in the tent city. The main building will be completed in a month. A crew is laying the foundation for the dormitory next week."

"What is your goal for completion of the dormitory," Grübber asked?

"Two months. I have arranged for an inauguration holiday and we want you to speak to the students. I'll arrange for you to reside at one of the hot spring facilities in Billings."

He grunted approvingly. "I plan to come in next weekend and I'd like you to rent a room for me at one of those facilities, and Dietrich, you are doing a good job, I'm grateful."

Grübber closed his cellphone, sitting in his home located in Georgetown. His thoughts shifted from Montana to Camp David.

Camp David, a country retreat for the President of the United States had its location in the wooded hills of Catoctin Mountain Park near Thurmont, Maryland, also near Emmitsburg, Maryland about 62 miles northwest of Washington, D. C. Officially known as the Naval Support Facility Thurmond, it is technically the military installation and staffing provided by the United States Navy and the United States Marines.

A king-cab truck followed by an ambulatory van rode into Emmitsburg, Maryland, and parked in the woods adjourning the Catoctin Mountain Park. As calculated, the sun slowly dropped behind the mountains when they arrived. Professor Dietrich Shuster ordered his four students to prepare to scale the mountain in the sketch he had prepared. These were selected Neo-Nazi clone students with expert mountaineer training, and were cognizant that it was a suicide mission. They each had climbing gear, boots, gloves and protective hats, with backpacks containing C-4 explosives. They each had a German luger with silencer strapped to the right calf, and night goggles for the nocturnal climb.

The first student, an expert mountaineer, led the group. He climbed up about twenty-five feet, drove a stake, and cinched the rope for the next man. He continued his climb up the 600 feet elevation to a ledge just 400 feet above the Catoctin Mountain Park. From this location, though precarious and heavily guarded, the climbers expected to reach the vicinity of Aspen Lodge before daybreak.

Daybreak was about two hours before the sun exploded in the valley. Scanning through night goggles, the leader had located the Secret Service and military guard points. Their mission was to assassinate the President, and Hans Grübber couldn't have chosen a more protected place than Camp David. Still these men were trained to commit suicide before or during

captivity. In fact, the mission could probably be more easily completed from a capture position.

Four men lowered on ropes down behind the rocks at the foot of the mountain without being seen. The leader decided they would sleep until the time was right to complete their mission. They removed sleeping bags from their backpacks and hunkered down until the leader gave the signal. Those who could not sleep used their time checking the equipment.

Early in the wee hours of the predawn morrow, the leader sat up in his sleeping bag. He touched the arm of the man near him and four men finally stood. They donned backpacks and checked their German lugers. The leader laid out a diagram of the mission: Aspen Lodge, the President's cabin sat on top of a hill with a beautiful view of the surrounding Maryland countryside. It had upper and lower terraces, several bedrooms with fireplace and bath, a small office, several fireplaces, a kitchen, and a large outdoor flagstone patio. Out behind the lodge were a heated swimming pool, hot tub, and a single golf hole with multiple tees. The plan was to reach the back window of the President's bedroom after locating the guards in their positions. Three men navigated the rocks and positioned themselves to eliminate the guards. The leader proceeded to the back window. He mounted a C-4 packet designed to be shot from the barrel of the luger. The packet contained a

squib stuck in the C-4 that fired ten seconds after impact. He fired the luger through the window and raced toward the rocks. An undiscovered SS guard had tracked his movements and fired two rounds into his chest.

The bedroom exploded.

Naval personal burst from every direction. Rapid fire took out the remaining three intruders. Three naval persons were killed. Four intruders were dead.

The presidential bedroom was empty

The Maryland hospital was quiet in the late hours of the evening. Nichols lay in bed his wounds cleaned and dressed. An IV was fixed to a cannula on his wrist for continually feeding hydrates from a bag hung by a tripod. The television in his room ran stories for the last thirty minutes about a failed attack on Camp David. Nichols rose in his bed and scanned the room for his clothes, and then remembered the nurse had hung them in the closet. He snatched the needle from the cannula, threw back the covers and stepped from the bed. His first step toward the closet warned him that he was a bit dizzy. He opened the door and carefully and quietly took his clothes off the hangers. He peeled off the embarrassing hospital gown and threw it on the closet floor. Somehow he managed to dress himself and put on his shoes. The harder issue was sneaking out of the hospital and locating a taxi.

Somehow he managed to sneak out the door. Finding a taxi was easier because the cabbies came to hospitals expecting fares. He spotted a cab parked by the curb just beyond the front door. Fortunately he had his credit card, but no bills and not much change. He stepped into the backseat and tried to think. Suddenly he remembered. "Catoctin Mountain Park—quickly, please."

All the way to the park, Nichols thought of all that had happened and all that would happen if he couldn't somehow contact Dr. Caruso. He'd lost his cellphone and suddenly realized he must stop somewhere. He gazed out the window and saw the turnoff to the park.

"Would you let me out at that service station on the corner?" he barked above the road noise, if not the buzzing in his head, pointing his finger.

The taxi pulled off the road in front of the service station. Nichols gave him his credit card. The taxi slid the card through a device on the dash, and handed him a receipt to sign and a pencil. After signing the receipt, he handed Nichols his receipt.

"Shall I wait," he asked.

"If you don't mind. I have to make a phone call."

His eyebrow elevated. "Hell, use my cellphone, I'm in no hurry," he said reaching into his shirt pocket.

"That's very kind, sir," he replied fingering the metal case. He punched a code and the tiny speaker buzzed the number. It buzzed four times.

"Dr. Caruso here."

"Listen very carefully, Dr. Caruso. This is Walter Nichols. Hans Grübber is responsible for attacking Camp David. He has a camp in Montana where he trains 3,000 Neo-Nazi clones. I don't know the exact location. But you must destroy that camp. I know where Grübber is and I will take care of him," he said, and closed the circuit.

Guarded silence.

Without an introduction, the muscular cabby with arms and legs like railroad ties and flaming red hair looked at this important man with eyes that could burn through steel. "Mr. Nichols, just show me the way."

Nichols smiled. "Straight down the road," he pointed.

He wheeled the cab around and shoved it in gear and roared up the mountain, spray gravel beneath the tires.

The Catoctin Mountain Park did not indicate the location of Camp David on park maps due to privacy and security concerns, although it could be seen though the use of publicly accessible satellite images. Nichols believed Grübber's men would have accessed Aspen Lodge from this mountain, and the old man would not miss the action. If his guess was accurate, he would find the old goat up on this mountain somewhere.

As the taxi pulled up to a magnificent view from South Bob's Hill, Nichols recognized the special van

prepared for Grübber's wheelchair parked near the bluff, its cab facing the view.

"Pull over here," he said to the cabby. They stopped, shielded behind a large outcropping of rocks. "If we are going to be partners you might tell me your name."

His tanned face tightened with a smile. "Jeremy O'Sullivan."

Suddenly a shot rang out, and hit the windshield of the cab. Jeremy instantly opened the glove compartment, and gripped his automatic with a 15-shell clip."

Nichols grinned. "Do you have a license to carry that thing?"

"Of course, the places I pick up clients in the District—one would be crazy not to have a gun."

A second shot hit a rock and zinged out into space. Nichols saw the flash from the driver's seat of the van. One of Grübber's goons, no doubt he thought. Jeremy, a captain in the National Guard opened the door and slid out behind the rocks. Nichols also got our and stood behind a tree. Jeremy fired a shot at the van and hit the windshield. The door opened and the drive stepped with his hand over one eye. Apparently the glass had injured his eye.

Nichols seized the chance. "Jeremy, cover me," he shouted, and ran to the van. The half-blind goon raised his automatic. Jeremy fired. The goon dropped.

Nichols waved thanks, and jumped into the driver seat. Through the rearview mirror, he saw Grübber in his wheelchair. He cranked the van and backed it toward the bluff. Grubber stirred in the chair moving back toward the cab. Nichols slid the back glass open.

"Your days are over, Grübber. The world will be better without you."

Grübber's face exploded. "I will kill you Nichols," he screamed.

Nichols jammed the accelerator wide-open, shoved it in first gear, released the clutch, and leaped out of the cab in one dangerous motion. The van roared over the bluff and fell 500 feet, crashing on rocks below.

31

The camp in Montana lay quiet in wintery cold of twilight. Six inches of snow glimmered zombie-white. Winter's lacerating hurricanes and whining winds had come and gone, leaving a terrible calmness. The skies above were an unholy mixture of shale-grey clouds and pasty streaks. Callous winter was stifling the Montana plains with its icy breath. The few clones left in the camp stamped their frozen feet and thumped their chilly bodies to warm up. Their ears caught fire and turned an icy-blue where their knit scarves couldn't reach. Nose-icicles dripped from their frozen faces. Their wheezy, wind-filled lungs were belching out steam as they itched and scratched at their raw skin. They slipped and slithered on the polished ice. Their teeth were chattering when they crawled back into their dormitory rooms, the windows sealed in white.

Professor Dietrich Shuster had closed the camp, the teachers had been dismissed owing to the inclement weather, and he had decided to drive into Billings for dinner tonight. The news from Grübber's Camp David event was not as palatable as a good steak. He took the 4-wheel drive truck and left just at dusk blanketed the camp. As he drove along some ten miles yet from Billings he thought he heard distant gunfire. He gave it no mind, and pulled into the restaurant he had visited frequently during the weeks of building the camp. He took a seat at a window. As he gazed out the window he could see the shimming light in the direction of the camp.

A rupture of moonstone-yellow appeared in the carnal black sky. The Montana camp was aflame. Cobra helicopters were blasting the buildings with rockets and rapid gunfire. Berry-red blood squirted from wounds, the young men wasted by the lust of world rule. They were battered and beaten by modern weapons they had rarely seen back in Neuschwabenland. A storm of arrows was buzzing and fizzing from the wings of the ominous helicopters. They had no chance from the beginning.

Dr. Robert Caruso had ordered the attack on the Montana camp after receiving the message from Walter Nichols. This young man he had taken under his wing at the request of Andrew Evans had performed masterfully.

He would recommend that Nichols receive presidential recognition for his performance in the treasonable attempt to form a Fourth Reich on the soil of America.

Washington was sealed a sleety snow. Traffic had nearly ground to a halt as the snow plows pushed and scraped the icy roads. Despite the inconvenience, the pressroom in the White House was filled to capacity. The world waited for news from America.

The President of the United States stood behind his presidential seal in the pressroom of the White House. Seated on the dais behind him were Dr. Robert Caruso, Andrew Evans, Henri Weisman, and Walter Nichols. The President scanned the crowd. The cameras of the world were focused on this meeting, that would explain the attack on Camp David and the defeat of a Neo-Nazi group staged to takeover America with a Third Reich based in Montana, and staffed by clones from Neuschwabenland.

The President gripped both ends of the lectern. "Ladies and gentlemen of the press, and my fellow Americans. It is my distinct pleasure to report that a diabolical plot to takeover America has been defeated. Before I entertain questions, let me as Dr. Robert Caruso to bring us up to speed on the events of the last two weeks. Dr. Caruso."

An applause rose from the crowd. As Caruso approached the lectern, the applause dwindled. He paused briefly gazing out over the crowd. "You all know

the events at Camp David from the news reports. What you don't know is one man saved the President. Before I introduce that man, let me mention the events that led to the attack yesterday. Hans Grübber, the leader of a Neo-Nazi organization established here in America for the sole purpose of establishing a Fourth Reich in this nation orchestrated the Camp David fiasco. You will remember Henri Weismann, the fact that he was cloned in Neuschwabenland. It was Grubber's mission to amass a regiment of clones trained at a camp in Montano as the nucleus of the Fourth Reich. Walter Nichols singlehandedly terminated Hans Grübber in his bid to kill the President at Camp David. In addition he warned my office of the intended attack on Aspen Lodge and the existence of the training camp in Montano. What Nichols will not tell you is this: he had inadvertently overhead the discussion between me and Andrew Evans concerning the date of the Camp David visit of the President. Before he approached Grübber, he had had himself hypnotized to reveal the wrong date of the President's visit under the influence of scopolamine. This is the reason our President stands before you today."

Dead Silence gripped in awe.

The President stepped to the lectern. "Thank you Dr. Caruso. Would Walter Nichols come to the lectern?"

A roar of applause exploded in the pressroom. TV Cameras zoomed in, laptop keys were fingered busily. Cameras flashed pictures.

The President held up his hands and finally the crowd stilled. Andrew Evans stepped up and handed the President a small case. He sat the case on the lectern.

"Walter Nichols, for bravery beyond the call of duty in the face of an enemy of the nation, it gives me immense pleasure to award you the Presidential Medal of Freedom," he said.

Again the crowd erupted!

Andrew Evans leaned over and whispered in Caruso's ear. "Good show, Robby. Good show, indeed."

Bermuda was ablaze with sun, a glowing medallion in the sky. A Boeing 747 lazily lowered its flaps above the airport. She reduced speed and squared her wings in the center of the runway. The wheels lowered from its wells in the fuselage and locked. As her wheels touched the concrete runway with an audible screech, the turbine engines reversed thrust. She reached an intersection and taxied to the tarmac directed by a waving baton to the assigned Jetway. The engines shutoff, and the accordion-type Jetway bumped against the door of the fuselage.

Four people left the first-class seats, and led the line of passages through the Jetway. They marched to the carousel. They waited for the luggage to move into the

airports. Suddenly the carousel came alive with luggage riding around on a moving belt.

Dr. Robert Caruso grabbed the handle of a suitcase. Bruce Allison did the same, and the two couples left the carousel. At the insistence of Dr. Caruso, he led them to the cafeteria. As they walked along, Consuela beside Bruce, and Jenny Lynn beside Robby, Jenny Lynn asked her proverbial question.

"How long will you be home before the next caper?"

There were not many moments of home life, or time of being together but this was a moment in time she would remember. It was a good time to be thankful.

Made in the USA
Columbia, SC
27 August 2022